Second Workshop on Fact Extraction and VERification 2019

Hong Kong, China
3 November 2019

ISBN: 978-1-7138-0081-1

EMNLP 2019

FEVER

Fact Extraction and VERification

Proceedings of the Second Workshop

November 3, 2019
Hong Kong

We thank our sponsor Amazon for their generous support.

Order copies of this and other ACL proceedings from:

Association for Computational Linguistics (ACL)
209 N. Eighth Street
Stroudsburg, PA 18360
USA
Tel: +1-570-476-8006
Fax: +1-570-476-0860
acl@aclweb.org

ISBN 978-1-950737-73-4

Introduction

With billions of individual pages on the web providing information on almost every conceivable topic, we should have the ability to collect facts that answer almost every conceivable question. However, only a small fraction of this information is contained in structured sources (Wikidata, Freebase, etc.) – we are therefore limited by our ability to transform free-form text to structured knowledge. There is, however, another problem that has become the focus of a lot of recent research and media coverage: false information coming from unreliable sources.

In an effort to jointly address both problems, herein we proposed this workshop to promote research in joint Fact Extraction and VERification (FEVER). We aim for FEVER to be a long-term venue for work in verifiable knowledge extraction.

The Second Workshop on Fact Extraction and VERification is held at EMNLP 2019. It received 25 submissions of which five were system descriptions from teams participating in an adversarial attacks shared task. 18 papers and talks were accepted. A further 59 teams have participated in the ongoing FEVER shared task: the updated leaderboard will be presented at the second workshop.

Organizers:

James Thorne (University of Cambridge)
Andreas Vlachos (University of Cambridge)
Oana Cocarascu (Imperial College London)
Christos Christodoulopoulos (Amazon)
Arpit Mittal (Amazon)

Invited Speakers:

David Corney (Full Fact)
Hoifung Poon (Microsoft Research)
Sameer Singh (University of California, Irvine)
William Wang (University of California, Santa Barbara)
Emine Yilmaz (University College London)

Program Committee:

Nikolaos Aletras (University of Sheffield) Isabelle Augenstein (University of Copenhagen) Matko
Bošnjak (University College London) Tuhin Chakrabarty (Columbia University) Weiwei Cheng
(Amazon) Fréderic Godin (ELIS - IDLab, Ghent University) Ivan Habernal (UKP Lab, Technische Universität Darmstadt) Andreas Hanselowski (UKP lab, Technische Universität Darmstadt)
Christopher Hidey (Columbia University) Alexandre Klementiev (Amazon) Jan Kowollik (University of Duisburg-Essen) Anjishnu Kumar (Amazon) Pranava Swaroop Madhyastha (Univer-
sity of Sheffield) Christopher Malon (NEC Laboratories America) Stephen Mayhew (University
of Pennsylvania) Paul Mithun (University Of Arizona) Marie-Francine Moens (KU Leuven) Jason Naradowsky (Preferred Networks) Yixin Nie (UNC) Farhad Nooralahzadeh (University of
Oslo) Wolfgang Otto (GESIS – Leibniz-Institute for the Social Sciences in Cologne) Ankur Padia
(University of Maryland, Baltimore County) Tamara Polajnar (University of Cambridge) Hoifung
Poon (Microsoft Research) Preethi Raghavan (IBM Research TJ Watson) Marek Rei (University
of Cambridge) Laura Rimell (DeepMind) Jodi Schneider (UIUC) Diarmuid Ó Séaghdha (Apple)
Sameer Singh (University of California, Irvine) Kevin Small (Amazon) Christian Stab (UKP Lab,
Technische Universität Darmstadt) Motoki Taniguchi (Fuji Xerox) Paolo Torroni (Alma Mater -
Università di Bologna) Serena Villata (Université Côte d'Azur, CNRS, Inria, I3S) Zeerak Waseem
(University of Sheffield) Noah Weber (Stony Brook University) Johannes Welbl (University Col-
lege London) Menglin Xia (Amazon)

Table of Contents

Conference Program

3rd November

1200–1230   **FEVER2.0 Shared Task Talks**

1200–1210   *The FEVER2.0 Shared Task*
James Thorne, Andreas Vlachos, Oana Cocarascu, Christos Christodoulopoulos and Arpit Mittal

1210–1220   *GEM: Generative Enhanced Model for adversarial attacks*
Piotr Niewinski, Maria Pszona and Maria Janicka

1220–1230   *Cure My FEVER : Building, Breaking and Fixing Models for Fact-Checking*
Christopher Hidey, Tuhin Chakrabarty, Tariq Alhindi, Siddharth Varia, Kriste Krstovski, Mona Diab and Smaranda Muresan

1230–1400   ***Lunch Break***

1400–1445   *Invited Talk*
William Wang

1445–1530   *Invited Talk*
David Corney

1530–1630   **Research Poster Session + Coffee**

Aligning Multilingual Word Embeddings for Cross-Modal Retrieval Task
Alireza Mohammadshahi, Rémi Lebret and Karl Aberer

Unsupervised Natural Question Answering with a Small Model
Martin Andrews and Sam Witteveen

Scalable Knowledge Graph Construction from Text Collections
Ryan Clancy, Ihab F. Ilyas and Jimmy Lin

Relation Extraction among Multiple Entities Using a Dual Pointer Network with a Multi-Head Attention Mechanism
Seong Sik Park and Harksoo Kim

Question Answering for Fact-Checking
Mayank Jobanputra

The Second Fact Extraction and VERification (FEVER2.0) Shared Task

James Thorne
University of Cambridge
jt719@cam.ac.uk

Andreas Vlachos
University of Cambridge
av308@cam.ac.uk

Oana Cocarascu
Imperial College London
oana.cocarascu11@imperial.ac.uk

Christos Christodoulopoulos
Amazon
chrchrs@amazon.co.uk

Arpit Mittal
Amazon
mitarpit@amazon.co.uk

Abstract

We present the results of the second Fact Extraction and VERification (FEVER2.0) Shared Task. The task challenged participants to both build systems to verify factoid claims using evidence retrieved from Wikipedia and to generate adversarial attacks against other participant's systems. The shared task had three phases: *building, breaking and fixing*. There were 8 systems in the builder's round, three of which were new qualifying submissions for this shared task, and 5 adversaries generated instances designed to induce classification errors and one builder submitted a fixed system which had higher FEVER score and resilience than their first submission. All but one newly submitted systems attained FEVER scores higher than the best performing system from the first shared task and under adversarial evaluation, all systems exhibited losses in FEVER score. There was a great variety in adversarial attack types as well as the techniques used to generate the attacks, In this paper, we present the results of the shared task and a summary of the systems, highlighting commonalities and innovations among participating systems.

1 Introduction

Significant progress for a large number of natural language processing tasks has been made through the development of new deep neural models. Higher scores for shared tasks such as Natural Language Inference (Bowman et al., 2015) and Question Answering (Rajpurkar et al., 2016) have been achieved through models which are becoming increasingly complex. This complexity raises new challenges: as models become more complex, it becomes difficult to fully understand and characterize their behaviour. From an NLP perspective, there has been an ongoing discussion as to what extent these models understand language (Jia and Liang, 2017) or to what extent they are exploiting unintentional biases and cues that are present in the datasets they are trained on (Poliak et al., 2018; Gururangan et al., 2018). When a model is evaluated on data outside of the distribution defined (implicitly) by its training dataset, its behaviour is likely to be unpredictable; such "blind spots" can be exposed through *adversarial evaluation* (Szegedy et al., 2014).

The first Fact Extraction and VERification (FEVER) shared task (Thorne et al., 2018b) focused on building systems that predict whether a textual claim is SUPPORTED or REFUTED given evidence (see (Thorne et al., 2018a) for a task description), or NOTENOUGHINFORMATION in case Wikipedia does not have appropriate evidence to verify it. As automated systems for fact checking have potentially sensitive applications it is important to study the vulnerabilities of these systems, as well as the deficiencies of the datasets they are trained on. Such vulnerabilities were also the motivation behind Ettinger et al. (2017)'s NLP shared task that was inspired by the Build It, Break It, Fix It competition[1].

The second Fact Extraction and VERification (FEVER2.0) shared task is building on the dataset of the first FEVER shared task, but adopted the setup of build-it, break-it, fix-it where *builders* submitted systems based on the original FEVER dataset and task definition; *breakers* generated adversarial examples targeting the systems built in the first stage; and finally, *fixers* implemented solutions to remedy the attacks from the second

---

[1] https://builditbreakit.org

Proceedings of the Second Workshop on Fact Extraction and VERification (FEVER), pages 1–6
Hong Kong, November 3, 2019. ©2019 Association for Computational Linguistics

stage.

In this paper, we present a short description of the task and dataset, present a summary of the submissions and the leader board, and highlight future research directions.

2 Task Description

2.1 Task Phases

In what follows we describe the three phases of FEVER2.0 in more detail:

Build-It In the first phase of the shared task, "builders" constructed fact verification systems that were trained using the FEVER dataset released in Thorne et al. (2018a). Participants were required to submit docker images of systems which implemented a common web API that would facilitate interactive development of attacks through a sandbox which was hosted for the duration of the shared task.

The top 4 submission from the first shared task were submitted as baseline systems for this shared task: UNC (Nie et al., 2019), UCLMR (Yoneda et al., 2018), Athene (Hanselowski et al., 2018) and Papelo (Malon, 2018).

Break-It In the second phase, "breakers", were tasked with generating adversarial examples that induce classification errors for the existing systems. Breakers submitted a dataset of up to 1000 instances with equal number of instances for each of the three classes (SUPPORT, REFUTE and NOTENOUGHIN-FORMATION); half of which were released to fixers and half of which were retained as a blind test set. We considered only novel claims (i.e. not contained in the original FEVER dataset) as valid entries to the shared task. All of the claims in this submission were annotated were annotated by the shared task organizers for quality assurance and to measure correctness.

To aid with preparing their submission of 1000 instances, the organizers hosted a web-based sandbox. Breakers had access to 8 systems (4 top systems from the first FEVER shared task (Thorne et al., 2018b), the baseline from (Thorne et al., 2018a) and 3 new qualifying submissions from the 'Build-It'

phase) that were hosted by the shared task organisers. Participants could experiment with attacks by submitting small samples of 50 instances for scoring twice a day via a shared task portal which returned FEVER scores of all the hosted systems.

Fix-It Using the adversarial examples, the original builders or teams of dedicated "fixers" incorporate the data generated from the "break-it" phase to improve the system classification performance and resilience to adversarial attack.

2.2 Scoring Method

The submissions were scored using 'potency' and 'resilience' (Thorne et al., 2019) that compute a weighted average of FEVER scores: accounting for the correctness of adversarial instances.

Potency Intuitively, better adversarial instances induce more classification errors, resulting in a lower FEVER score of the systems they are evaluated on. We measure the effectiveness of breakers' adversarial instances (a) on a builder's system (s) through the average reduction in FEVER score (from a perfect system) on the set of predictions made by the system $\hat{Y}_{s,a}$. The score is weighted by the correctness rate c_a of the adversarial instances. Instances are correct if they are grammatical, appropriately labeled and meet the annotation guidelines requirements described by Thorne et al. (2018a).

$$\text{Potency}(a) \stackrel{\text{def}}{=} c_a \frac{1}{|S|} \sum_{s \in S} \left(1 - f(\hat{Y}_{s,a}, Y_a) \right)$$

Resilience A system that is resilient will have fewer errors induced by the adversarial instances, reflected in higher scores at evaluation. We wish to penalize systems for making mistakes on instances from adversaries with higher correctness rate. We define *resilience* of a system s as the weighted average FEVER score, weighted by the correctness rate for each adversary, $a \in A$:

$$\text{Resilience}(s) \stackrel{\text{def}}{=} \frac{\sum_{a \in A} c_a \times f(\hat{Y}_{s,a}, Y_a)}{\sum_{a \in A} c_a}$$

For the 'build-it' phase, we report both FEVER score of the system over the FEVER shared task test set (Thorne et al., 2018a) and the resilience of the system over the FEVER2.0 test set that comprises adversarial instances submitted by the breakers. For the 'break-it' phase, we report the potency of attack over all systems and the correctness rate. For the 'fix-it' phase, we report the score delta compared to the system submitted in the 'build-it' phase.

3 Participants and Results

System	Resilience (%)	FEVER Score (%)
Papelo	37.31	57.36
UCLMR	35.83	62.52
DOMLIN	35.82	68.46
CUNLP	32.92	67.08
UNC	30.47	64.21
Athene	25.35	61.58
GPLSI	19.63	58.07
Baseline	11.06	27.45

Table 1: Results from the FEVER2.0 Builder phase. Italicised systems are from the original FEVER shared task – submitted as reference systems for FEVER2.0.

System	Correct Rate (%)	Potency (%)
TMLab	84.81	66.83
CUNLP	81.44	55.79
NbAuzDrLqg	64.71	51.54
Rule-based Baseline	82.33	49.68
Papelo*	91.00	64.79

Table 2: Results from the FEVER2.0 Breaker phase. *Papelo's submission contained only NOTENOUGH-INFO claims which did not qualify for the shared task. Its potency is reported, but is not included in the calculations for resilience of the systems.

System	FEVER Score (%)	Resilience (%)
CUNLP	68.80 (+1.72)	36.61 (+3.69)

Table 3: Results from the FEVER2.0 Fixer phase.

3.1 Builders Phase

Team DOMLIN (Stammbach and Neumann, 2019) used the document retrieval module of Hanselowski et al. (2018) and a BERT model for two-staged sentence selection based on the work by (Nie et al., 2019). They also use a BERT-based model for the NLI stage.

The CUNLP team (Hidey et al.) used a combination of Google search and TF-IDF for document retrieval and a pointer network using features from BERT and trained with reinforcement learning.

Finally, team GPLSI (Alonso-Reina et al., 2019) kept Hanselowski et al. (2018)'s document retrieval and NLI modules. For the sentence selection they converted both the claims and candidate evidence sentence into OpenIE-style triples using the extractor from Estevez-Velarde et al. (2018) and compared their semantic similarity.

3.2 Breakers Phase

The TMLab (Niewinski et al., 2019) adversarial claims were generated with Generative Enhanced Model (GEM). GEM is a modified and fine-tuned GPT-2 language model fed with text sampled from two hyperlinked Wikipedia pages and additional keyword input. Claims were labeled by annotators and the evidence sentences were manually added. In addition, the team manually generated claims with SUPPORTS labels to ensure class balance in their submission.

One of the shortcomings of the original FEVER dataset was the lack of complex claims that would require multi-hop inference or temporal reasoning and the CUNLP team designed their adversarial attacks along these principles (Hidey et al.). They produce multi-hop reasoning claims by augmenting existing claims with conjunctions or relative clauses sourced from linked Wikipedia articles. For temporal reasoning adversarial examples they use hand-written rules to manipulate claims containing dates, for example changing "in 2001" to "4 years before 2005" or "between 1999 and 2003". Finally, they create noisy versions of existing claims by using entities that have a disambiguation page in Wikipedia and by using the lexical substitution method of Alzantot et al. (2018).

Team NbAuzDrLqg (Kim and Allan, 2019) submitted mostly manually created adversarial claims targeting the retrieval as well as the NLI components of FEVER systems. For the retrieval attacks, the team created claims that didn't contain enti-

Breaker	Attack	FEVER Score (%)	Label Accuracy (%)	n
CUNLP	Multi-Hop Reasoning	31.54 ± 13.19	51.64 ± 7.18	130
	Multi-Hop Temporal Reasoning	8.33 ± 2.08	24.48 ± 16.98	24
	Date Manipulation	27.53 ± 6.07	34.18 ± 4.50	94
	Word Replacement	28.87 ± 6.79	29.08 ± 9.28	71
	Conjunction	38.25 ± 18.01	42.50 ± 15.93	50
	Phrasal Additions	55.63 ± 13.16	55.63 ± 20.22	20
NbAuzDrLqg	NotEnoughInfo	76.39 ± 34.33	76.39 ± 34.33	18
	SubsetNum	0.00 ± 0.00	16.12 ± 17.08	38
TMLab	AI Generated	38.07 ± 13.29	40.63 ± 11.04	44
	Paraphrase	0.00 ± 0.0	43.06 ± 19.59	9

Table 4: Breakdown of attack type for each breaker and average FEVER scores and Label accuracy for the 8 systems used in the shared task. n = total number of instances of this class

ties that could be used as query terms for evidence documents/sentences. To target the NLI component, the team created attacks based on arithmetic operations, logical inconsistencies, and vague or hedged statement. Some of these attack types failed to meet the guidelines of the shared task and were not marked as correct instances by annotators: these have been excluded from the analysis in Section 4, Table 4.

Finally, team Papelo submitted only NOTE-NOUGHINFO claims and therefore did not meet the requirements of submitting a balanced dataset. While the potency results for this method are reported, it does not qualify for the shared task and this attack is not used in computation of system resilience.

The rule-based baseline system is a version of the adversary described in Thorne et al. (2019) where string transformations are applied to claims to generate new instances. The rules were manually constructed regular expression patterns that match common patterns of claims in the dataset and perform both label-altering and label-preserving changes.

3.3 Fixers Phase

The only submission to this phase was from the CUNLP team (Hidey et al.). Based on their own attacks during the Breakers phase they sought to make improvements in multi-hop retrieval and temporal reasoning. To improve multi-hop retrieval, they introduce an additional document pointer network trained with the top 4 layers of a fine-tuned BERT Wikipedia title-to-document classifier as input features. They also improve sentence selection by modeling the sequence of relations at each time step through training a network to predict a sequence pointers to sentences in the evidence. For temporal reasoning they employ a set of arithmetic rules on top of predicate arguments extracted with an OpenIE system. As seen in Table 3 they improve their system's FEVER score, but more importantly they increase its resilience by 3.69%.

4 Analysis

In the 'break-it' phase of the competition, breakers submitted adversarial instances that were designed to induce classification errors in fact verification systems. The shared task solicited metadata with each instance that described how the attack was generated. In Table 4 we report the FEVER score and accuracy of the systems for each of the breaker's attack types. We report only instances that were annotated as 'correct' and attack types with more than 5 instances.

There were two attack types which had a FEVER score of 0: the Paraphrase attack from TMLab and the SubsetNum attack from NbAuz-DrLqg. While some systems returned the correct label, no system had the combination of the correct label and evidence. The Multi-Hop and Multi-Hop Temporal Reasoning attacks from CUNLP also induced a high number of errors in the systems.

The SubsetNum attack from NbAuzDrLqg was a template-based attack which required transitive reasoning with respect to the area and size of geographic regions. The Multi-Hop claims from CUNLP were manually generated to require inference that combines evidence from multiple entities. Both these types of attacks highlight limitations of systems when performing inductive reasoning and composition of knowledge.

The TMLab paraphrase attack strategy was to re-write sentences from Wikipedia articles in terms borrowed from different texts (not included in evidence set) to mislead the systems. This highlighted a limitation of all systems as while correct labels were being applied, correct evidence was not identified in any of these cases. This attack had a higher potency than TMLab's other automated submission, 'AI Generated', which generated claim text from the Generative Enhanced Model (GEM). Similar to CUNLP, correctly classifying these claims requires compositional knowledge and reasoning with information from multiple Wikipedia pages.

5 Conclusions

The second Fact Extraction and VERification shared task received three qualifying submissions for the builder round and three qualifying submissions for the breaker round and one fixer submission. All of the breakers submitted adversarial instances that were more potent than the rule-based baseline presented in Thorne et al. (2019). In this paper we summarized the approaches, identifying commonalities and features that could be further explored.

Future work will continue to address limitations in human-annotated evidence and explore other ways in which systems can be made more robust in predicting the veracity of information extracted from real-world untrusted sources.

Acknowledgements

The authors with to thank the participants of the first FEVER shared task for making their code and models available and for being responsive to queries. The authors with to thank Tim Baldwin and Trevor Cohn for their advice.

References

Aimée Alonso-Reina, Robiert Sepúlveda-Torres, Estela Saquete, and Manuel Palomar. 2019. Team GPLSI. approach for automated fact checking. In *Proceedings of the Second Workshop on Fact Extraction and VERification (FEVER)*. Association for Computational Linguistics.

Moustafa Alzantot, Yash Sharma, Ahmed Elgohary, Bo-Jhang Ho, Mani Srivastava, and Kai-Wei Chang. 2018. Generating natural language adversarial examples. In *Proceedings of the 2018 Conference on Empirical Methods in Natural Language Processing*, pages 2890–2896, Brussels, Belgium. Association for Computational Linguistics.

Samuel R. Bowman, Gabor Angeli, Christopher Potts, and Christopher D. Manning. 2015. A large annotated corpus for learning natural language inference.

S Estevez-Velarde, Y Gutierrez, A Montoyo, A Piad-Morffis, R Munoz, and Y Almeida-Cruz. 2018. Gathering object interactions as semantic knowledge. In *Proceedings on the International Conference on Artificial Intelligence (ICAI)*, pages 363–369.

Allyson Ettinger, Sudha Rao, Hal Daumé III, and Emily M Bender. 2017. Towards linguistically generalizable NLP systems: A workshop and shared task. In *Proceedings of the First Workshop on Building Linguistically Generalizable NLP Systems*, pages 1–10.

Suchin Gururangan, Swabha Swayamdipta, Omer Levy, Roy Schwartz, Samuel R Bowman, and Noah A Smith. 2018. Annotation Artifacts in Natural Language Inference Data.

Andreas Hanselowski, Hao Zhang, Zile Li, Daniil Sorokin, Benjamin Schiller, Claudia Schulz, and Iryna Gurevych. 2018. Multi sentence textual entailment for claim verification. In *Proceedings of the First Workshop on Fact Extraction and VERification (FEVER)*, pages 103–108, Brussels, Belgium. Association for Computational Linguistics.

Tuhin Hidey, Christopherand Chakrabarty, Tariq Alhindi, Siddharth Varia, Kriste Krstovski, Mona Diab, and Smaranda Muresan. Non archival shared task submission.

Robin Jia and Percy Liang. 2017. Adversarial Examples for Evaluating Reading Comprehension Systems.

Youngwoo Kim and James Allan. 2019. FEVER breaker's run of team NbAuzDrLqg. In *Proceedings of the Second Workshop on Fact Extraction and VERification (FEVER)*. Association for Computational Linguistics.

Christopher Malon. 2018. Team Papelo: Transformer networks at FEVER. In *Proceedings of the First Workshop on Fact Extraction and VERification (FEVER)*, pages 109–113, Brussels, Belgium. Association for Computational Linguistics.

Yixin Nie, Haonan Chen, and Mohit Bansal. 2019. Combining fact extraction and verification with neural semantic matching networks. In *Association for the Advancement of Artificial Intelligence (AAAI)*.

Piotr Niewinski, Maria Pszona, and Maria Janicka. 2019. GEM: Generative enhanced model for adversarial attacks. In *Proceedings of the Second Workshop on Fact Extraction and VERification (FEVER)*. Association for Computational Linguistics.

Adam Poliak, Jason Naradowsky, Aparajita Haldar, Rachel Rudinger, and Benjamin Van Durme. 2018. Hypothesis Only Baselines in Natural Language Inference. (1):180–191.

Pranav Rajpurkar, Jian Zhang, Konstantin Lopyrev, and Percy Liang. 2016. SQuAD: 100,000+ Questions for Machine Comprehension of Text. pages 2383–2392.

Dominik Stammbach and Guenter Neumann. 2019. Team DOMLIN: Exploiting evidence enhancement for the fever shared task. In *Proceedings of the Second Workshop on Fact Extraction and VERification (FEVER)*. Association for Computational Linguistics.

Christian Szegedy, Wojciech Zaremba, Ilya Sutskever, Joan Bruna, Dumitru Erhan, Ian Goodfellow, and Rob Fergus. 2014. Intriguing properties of neural networks. In *International Conference on Learning Representations*.

James Thorne, Andreas Vlachos, Christos Christodoulopoulos, and Arpit Mittal. 2018a. FEVER: a large-scale dataset for fact extraction and verification. In *NAACL-HLT*.

James Thorne, Andreas Vlachos, Christos Christodoulopoulos, and Arpit Mittal. 2019. Evaluating adversarial attacks against multiple fact verification systems. In *EMNLP-IJCNLP*.

James Thorne, Andreas Vlachos, Oana Cocarascu, Christos Christodoulopoulos, and Arpit Mittal. 2018b. The Fact Extraction and VERification (FEVER) Shared Task. In *Proceedings of the First Workshop on Fact Extraction and VERification (FEVER)*, pages 1–9, Brussels, Belgium. Association for Computational Linguistics.

Takuma Yoneda, Jeff Mitchell, Johannes Welbl, Pontus Stenetorp, and Sebastian Riedel. 2018. Ucl machine reading group: Four factor framework for fact finding (HexaF). In *Proceedings of the First Workshop on Fact Extraction and VERification (FEVER)*, pages 97–102, Brussels, Belgium. Association for Computational Linguistics.

Fact Checking or Psycholinguistics: How to Distinguish Fake and True Claims?

Aleksander Wawer, Grzegorz Wojdyga
Institute of Computer Science
Polish Academy of Sciences
ul. Jana Kazimierza 5
01-248 Warszawa, Poland
`{axw,g.wojdyga}@ipipan.waw.pl`

Justyna Sarzyńska-Wawer
Institute of Psychology
Polish Academy of Sciences
ul. Jaracza 1
00-378 Warszawa, Poland
`jsarzynska@psych.pan.pl`

Abstract

The goal of our paper is to compare psycholinguistic text features with fact checking approaches to distinguish lies from true statements. We examine both methods using data from a large ongoing study on deception and deception detection covering a mixture of factual and opinionated topics that polarize public opinion. We conclude that fact checking approaches based on Wikipedia are too limited for this task, as only a few percent of sentences from our study has enough evidence to become supported or refuted. Psycholinguistic features turn out to outperform both fact checking and human baselines, but the accuracy is not high. Overall, it appears that deception detection applicable to less-than-obvious topics is a difficult task and a problem to be solved.

1 Introduction

Is deception detection more about writing style than verification of veracity against a database of credible information? Our paper attempts to answer this question by comparing approaches based on psycholinguistics with state-of-the-art fact checking systems.

In the case of the first method, the information is based on measuring psycholinguistic dimensions of language such as sentiment and emotional vocabulary, abstract or concrete character of utterances, analytical thinking, cognitive processes and so on. Using this type of features may lead to possibly more universal character of deception detection. According to Newman (Newman et al., 2003), the language of deception is linked to several psycholinguistic characteristics such as higher levels of abstraction. Psycholinguistic features were successful in the detection of falsified reviews (Ott et al., 2011) or prisoners lies (Bond and Lee, 2005). This method is universal and simple as no additional resources or references are necessary.

The second type of methods, namely fact checking systems, verify information using evidence from some credible source such as Wikipedia. Given a factual claim involving one or more entities (resolvable to Wikipedia pages), the system of this type must extract textual evidence (sets of sentences from Wikipedia pages) that support or refute the claim. Using this evidence, label the claim as supported, refuted (given the evidence) or not enough info if there isn't sufficient evidence. A number of systems of this type participated in Fever shared task (Thorne et al., 2018a).

2 Dataset

We analyzed 408 statements from 204 subjects who participated in a study of deception and deception detection conducted in the Institute of Psychology, Polish Academy of Sciences. Each subject was first asked to complete a short questionnaire. Based on its results we determined which two out of 12 debatable topics (eg. the right to abortion, attitudes towards immigrants, the best polish footballer, vegetarianism) the respondent has a clearly defined position on. Next they were asked to generate four statements. Two of them (which focus on one topic) were expressed in face-to-face communication and recorded while the other two were written on a web form (computer mediated communication). One statement on particular topic always represents the subject's real position while the other presents an opposing viewpoint. Subjects were also asked several standardized questions while giving statements so that each one contains the same elements: their stance, arguments for that position, and the subject's personal experience. The type of the statement (TRUE or LIE) as well as its form (writ-

Proceedings of the Second Workshop on Fact Extraction and VERification (FEVER), pages 7–12
Hong Kong, November 3, 2019. ©2019 Association for Computational Linguistics

ten or oral) were counterbalanced. In this paper only written statements were analyzed. The statements were first translated into English using Google Translate. After that we checked the quality of translations and manually corrected a few of them.

3 Psycholinguistic Analysis

In order to obtain psycholingusitic descriptions of each utterance we applied the General Inquirer (Stone et al., 1966) – a tool for text content analysis which provides a wide range of categories. It helps to characterize text by defining words in terms of sentiment, intensity, varying social and cognitive contexts. Word categories were collected from four different sources: the Harvard IV-4 dictionary and the Lasswell value dictionary (Lasswell and Namenwirth, 1969), several categories were constructed based on work of Semin and Fiedler on social cognition and language (Semin and Fiedler, 1988), finally, marker categories were adapted from Kelly and Stone work on word sense disambiguation (Kelly and Stone, 1975). The full list of categories along with their descriptions can be found on the General Inquirer's home page[1].

4 Fact Checking

For fact checking we used two selected top performing systems from the Fever competition (Thorne et al., 2018b). The idea of Fever is to verify a claim based on the content of Wikipedia. In consists of three subtasks – firstly, given a claim, system should choose Wikipedia articles that might be useful in verifying. Next, the system has to pick up to 5 sentences that are crucial for verification. Finally, the system must decide whether the selected sentences support the claim, refute it or don't provide enough information. Labels are same as in SNLI (Bowman et al., 2015) and MNLI corpora (Williams et al., 2017).

4.1 Augmenting Article Database

We have verified that all the topics (such as abortion, immigrants, football players) were present in the English Wikipedia available in the Wikipedia resources for Fever (Thorne et al., 2018a) except of two that were specific for Polish common discourse – the famous Polish fitness trainer and the most famous Polish pseudo doctor. Therefore, we have translated their web pages from Polish Wikipedia [2][3] into English and added them to the resources that Fever systems are searching in. All the links that were present on their pages were redirected to their corresponding webpages in English Wikipedia.

4.2 Domlin

The Domlin system was introduced for Fever 2019 competition [4]. To our knowledge, the official article hasn't been published yet, but this model is similar to the previously introduced system for fact checking by the same authors (Stammbach et al., 2019). For retrieval task it uses the module, that was introduced by team athene (Hanselowski et al., 2018) for Fever 2018. It uses Wikipedia library [5] that wraps the Wikipedia API [6] which finds articles which title overlaps with the noun phrases within the claim. For sentence retrieval Domlin system is using the hierarchical retrieval approach, which finds the first sentence that is an evidence to support or refute the claim, and next, using all outgoing links it finds second sentence that might be part of evidence. For recognizing textual entailment Domlin system fine-tunes BERT language representation model (Devlin et al., 2019).

claim	Since prehistoric times man has hunted and ate meat, which allowed him to survive in those conditions.
label	SUPPORTS
evidence	Humans have hunted and killed animals for meat since prehistoric times.
	Meat is animal flesh that is eaten as food.

Table 1: Example of a correct fact verification by the Domlin system.

---

[1] http://www.wjh.harvard.edu/~inquirer/homecat.htm

[2] https://pl.wikipedia.org/wiki/Ewa_Chodakowska

[3] https://pl.wikipedia.org/wiki/Jerzy_Zi%C4%99ba

[4] https://github.com/dominiksinsaarland/domlin_fever

[5] https://github.com/goldsmith/Wikipedia

[6] https://www.mediawiki.org/wiki/API:Main_page

4.2.1 Analysis of results

More than 95% of results was labelled as "Not enough info". With "Supports" and "Refutes" results we have noticed that system was behaving correctly only sometimes. It found proper evidences and correctly labelled many claims, e.g. supported "Vaccines are the best method to prevent serious infectious diseases." or "Meat has nutritional values, primarily protein." and refutes to "In addition, knowledge about vaccines is largely unverified". The example of properly supported claim by the Domlin system is in table 1. Sometimes it made mistakes (like refutes "Burning coal is dangerous to health and the environment." where evidences did not indicate any of this). But very often it tried to prove claims that were impossible to verify such as: "I will give an example.", "Why?" or "I have this thesis in support.". Example of such an example is in Table 2.

claim	I will give an example.
label	SUPPORTS
evidence	The name example is reserved by the Internet Engineering Task Force (IETF) in RFC 2606 [...] as a domain name that may not be installed as a top-level domain in the Domain of the Internet.
	Elliot John Gleave [...] better known by his stage name Example is an English rapper singer songwriter and record producer signed to Epic Records and Sony Music.

Table 2: Fact-checking of an unverifiable statement by the Domlin system.

4.3 UNC

The UNC system was the winner of FEVER 2018 task (Nie et al., 2019). In this system authors introduced Neural Semantic Matching Network (NSMN) which is modified version of ESIM (Chen et al., 2016). The NSMN is the architecture of neural network that is used in all three subtasks (document retrieval, sentence selection and claim verification). The three homogeneous neural networks conduct these tasks using some other features such as Pageview frequency and WordNet.

claim	Robert Lewandowski is a great Polish player
label	SUPPORTS
evidence	Robert Lewandowski [..] is Polish professional footballer who plays as a striker for [...] Bayern Munich.
	[...] he moved to top-flight Lech Poznan, and was the top scorer in the league as they won the 2009

Table 3: Example of a correct fact verification by the UNC system.

4.3.1 Analysis of results

More than 90% of results was labelled as "Not enough info". We have noticed behaviour similar to Domlin system – there were some correctly labelled statements (like "Vaccinations protect against diseases by the stimulation of the man's immune system", another example in table 3), some mistakes and many tries of unverifiable claims (such as "This is not good", "I will not agree to this", "Amen"). Interesting example is in Table 4 – one could argue whether the evidence supports the claim, but our insight is that this claim is not verifiable in the first place.

claim	Everyone should have a choice.
label	REFUTES
evidence	Most people regard having choices as a good thing , though a severely limited or artificially restricted choice can lead to discomfort with choosing and possibly an unsatisfactory outcome.

Table 4: Fact-checking of an unverifiable statement by the UNC system.

4.4 Verifiability

Our examination of fact checking systems revealed that systems try to find evidences to support or refute claims, that cannot be verified. Sentences like:"I will give an example.", "This is not good.", "These values that should be important to every citizen" are general opinions and cannot be verified. They are, however, processed because systems can find there noun phrases that are present in the Wikipedia (e.g. "Example" as English rapper, "This is not" – the fifth track from their Machine, "Every" – title in the Baronetage of England). It is not a flaw – they had specific trainset, so it is natural that they "overfit" and they don't deal perfectly with new data.

It might, however, point an interesting direction in evolution of fact-checking systems and tasks. If a final goal is a real-life application, hence verifying statements or information that appear in a public discourse, it is crucial to face a problem that was just presented. Our idea is to include verifiability to the system. There are already important scientific works on verifiability e.g. (Newell et al., 2017) and factuality e.g. (Lioma et al., 2016). Based on these works it is worth to consider a binary falsifiability criterion – to determine whether it is possible to prove that given claim is wrong, hence whether it is possible to verify this claim in the first place. The term "falsifiability" is inspired by Karl Popper's scientific epistemology [7]. We believe that sentence can be consider falsifiable if and only if it describes facts about real objects. It is also worth to notice that task on distinction between opinions and facts was the topic of SemEval 2019, Task 8A [8]. Adding data with unverifiable statements and adding recognition of falsifiability as pre-processing might significantly help fact-checking systems to work in real-life applications.

5   Results: Psycholinguistics

For each utterance, we used the General Inquirer in order to compute frequency vectors corresponding to each of 182 categories in the General Inquirer dictionary. The vectors were then used as an input to supervised classification algorithms: Logistic Regression, Support Vector Machines with radial basis kernel (rbf), and XGBoost (Chen and Guestrin, 2016). We tested two variants of the feature space: with scaling (frequency as a percentage of a given category of words in all words) and raw word category frequencies. Table 5 contains

---

[7]"I shall require that [the] logical form [of the theory] shall be such that it can be singled out, by means of empirical tests, in a negative sense: it must be possible for an empirical scientific system to be refuted by experience." *The Logic of Scientific Discovery*

[8]`https://competitions.codalab.org/competitions/20022`

mean accuracy of 20-fold cross-validation using each feature space variant. It reveals that the best performing classifier is XG Boost on scaled feature space, reaching 0.63 accuracy.

	scaled	raw
Logistic Regression	0.58	0.61
SVM (rbf)	0.57	0.60
XG Boost	0.63	0.59

Table 5: Mean accuracies of predicting deception in 20-fold cross-validation from the General Inquirer feature vectors.

6   Results: Fact Checking

In our experiments, we used each sentence of every utterance in our dataset as a claim to check with both Wikipedia-based fact checking engines (Fever shared task participants). We divided utterances to sentences using spaCy library [9]. Typically, most utterances contain between 5 and 15 sentences. Table 6 illustrates frequencies of labels generated by both tested systems represented as percentages.

	domlin	unc
NOT ENOUGH INFO	97.01%	93.84%
SUPPORTS	1.95%	4.21%
REFUTES	1.04%	1.95%

Table 6: Label percentages for both tested fact checking systems.

As it has been demonstrated, vast majority of sentences could not be fact-checked. However, for those that could, one may wonder how supported or refuted sentences predict honest (TRUE) or deceptive (LIE) utterances. We answer that question in Table 7 which shows the quality of such predictions on our data set as counts of each class as well as an overall accuracy.

7   Discussion

None of the tested methods achieved high accuracy. However, the problem is a very difficult one even for humans: it is well known and documented that most people perform poorly in lie detection experiments (Weinberger, 2010). Meta-analysis found that average accuracy in deception detection experiments is only 0.54, where 0.50 could

---

[9]`https://spacy.io/`

	domlin	**unc**
SUPPORTS-LIE	22	63
REFUTES-LIE	14	26
SUPPORTS-TRUE	26	58
REFUTES-TRUE	10	30
ACCURACY	0.55	0.47

Table 7: Label percentages for both tested fact checking systems.

be obtained by chance. This finding is extremely stable, with 90% of published studies reporting results within 0.1 of the across-study mean(Bond Jr and DePaulo, 2006). Studies show also that there is very little variance attributable to individual differences in judge ability (Bond Jr and DePaulo, 2008) or judge professional experience ((Aamodt and Custer, 2006), (Bond Jr and DePaulo, 2006)).

In the context of such baselines, one should not consider the results obtained using pschycholinguistic text features as entirely discouraging. The best of tested methods (XG Boost classifier) achieved mean accuracy of 0.63.

Using Wikipedia information to verify the veracity of utterances is not particularly useful when applied to a dataset of opinionated, often polarizing topics such as vegetarianism and abortion. This may be due to several factors. First, Wikipedia, as a community-edited resource, may simply not contain controversial or debatable claims. Second, lying seems to be a broad phenomenon, referring to the experiences, feelings and opinions of a given person and related to both cognitive and emotional load, which may end up in not referring to verifiable facts.

8   Conclusion and Future Work

In this paper we have compared two approaches to deception detection: fact checking and psycholinguistic features. We used data from a large ongoing study on deception detection in Polish. We concluded that psycholinguistic approach has an advantage, but the results may be related to often opinionated and controversial topics covered in the study, not easy for fact checking systems based on Wikipedia. The problem not only in very low recall (majority of sentences labelled as not enough info) but also in low precision when predicting deceptive utterances. In order to make our findings more broad, we plan to apply the same approach to other data types such as fake news.

9   Acknowledgements

Research funded by the National Science Centre Poland grant UMO-2017/26/D/HS6/00212

References

Michael G Aamodt and Heather Custer. 2006. Who can best catch a liar? *Forensic Examiner*, 15(1).

Gary D Bond and Adrienne Y Lee. 2005. Language of lies in prison: Linguistic classification of prisoners' truthful and deceptive natural language. *Applied Cognitive Psychology*, 19(3):313–329.

Charles F Bond Jr and Bella M DePaulo. 2006. Accuracy of deception judgments. *Personality and social psychology Review*, 10(3):214–234.

Charles F Bond Jr and Bella M DePaulo. 2008. Individual differences in judging deception: Accuracy and bias. *Psychological bulletin*, 134(4):477.

Samuel R Bowman, Gabor Angeli, Christopher Potts, and Christopher D Manning. 2015. A large annotated corpus for learning natural language inference. *arXiv preprint arXiv:1508.05326*.

Qian Chen, Xiaodan Zhu, Zhenhua Ling, Si Wei, Hui Jiang, and Diana Inkpen. 2016. Enhanced lstm for natural language inference. *arXiv preprint arXiv:1609.06038*.

Tianqi Chen and Carlos Guestrin. 2016. Xgboost: A scalable tree boosting system. In *Proceedings of the 22Nd ACM SIGKDD International Conference on Knowledge Discovery and Data Mining*, KDD '16, pages 785–794, New York, NY, USA. ACM.

Jacob Devlin, Ming-Wei Chang, Kenton Lee, and Kristina Toutanova. 2019. Bert: Pre-training of deep bidirectional transformers for language understanding. In *Proceedings of the 2019 Conference of the North American Chapter of the Association for Computational Linguistics: Human Language Technologies, Volume 1 (Long and Short Papers)*, pages 4171–4186.

Andreas Hanselowski, Hao Zhang, Zile Li, Daniil Sorokin, Benjamin Schiller, Claudia Schulz, and Iryna Gurevych. 2018. Ukp-athene: Multi-sentence textual entailment for claim verification. *arXiv preprint arXiv:1809.01479*.

Edward F Kelly and Philip J Stone. 1975. *Computer recognition of English word senses*, volume 13. North-Holland.

Harold D Lasswell and J Zvi Namenwirth. 1969. The lasswell value dictionary. *New Haven*.

Christina Lioma, Birger Larsen, Wei Lu, and Yong Huang. 2016. A study of factuality, objectivity and relevance: three desiderata in large-scale information retrieval? In *Proceedings of the 3rd IEEE/ACM International Conference on Big Data Computing, Applications and Technologies*, pages 107–117. ACM.

Edward Newell, Ariane Schang, Drew Margolin, and Derek Ruths. 2017. Assessing the verifiability of attributions in news text. In *Proceedings of the Eighth International Joint Conference on Natural Language Processing (Volume 1: Long Papers)*, pages 754–763.

Matthew L. Newman, James W. Pennebaker, Diane S. Berry, and Jane M. Richards. 2003. Lying words: Predicting deception from linguistic styles. *Personality and Social Psychology Bulletin*, 29(5):665–675.

Yixin Nie, Haonan Chen, and Mohit Bansal. 2019. Combining fact extraction and verification with neural semantic matching networks. In *Association for the Advancement of Artificial Intelligence (AAAI)*.

Myle Ott, Yejin Choi, Claire Cardie, and Jeffrey T Hancock. 2011. Finding deceptive opinion spam by any stretch of the imagination. In *Proceedings of the 49th Annual Meeting of the Association for Computational Linguistics: Human Language Technologies-Volume 1*, pages 309–319. Association for Computational Linguistics.

Gün R Semin and Klaus Fiedler. 1988. The cognitive functions of linguistic categories in describing persons: Social cognition and language. *Journal of personality and Social Psychology*, 54(4):558.

Dominik Stammbach, Stalin Varanasi, and Günter Neumann. 2019. Domlin at semeval-2019 task 8: Automated fact checking exploiting ratings in community question answering forums. In *Proceedings of the 13th International Workshop on Semantic Evaluation*, pages 1149–1154.

Philip J Stone, Dexter C Dunphy, and Marshall S Smith. 1966. The general inquirer: A computer approach to content analysis.

James Thorne, Andreas Vlachos, Christos Christodoulopoulos, and Arpit Mittal. 2018a. FEVER: a large-scale dataset for fact extraction and VERification. In *NAACL-HLT*.

James Thorne, Andreas Vlachos, Oana Cocarascu, Christos Christodoulopoulos, and Arpit Mittal. 2018b. The Fact Extraction and VERification (FEVER) shared task. In *Proceedings of the First Workshop on Fact Extraction and VERification (FEVER)*.

Sharon Weinberger. 2010. Airport security: Intent to deceive? *Nature News*, 465(7297):412–415.

Adina Williams, Nikita Nangia, and Samuel R Bowman. 2017. A broad-coverage challenge corpus for sentence understanding through inference. *arXiv preprint arXiv:1704.05426*.

Neural Multi-Task Learning for Stance Prediction

Wei Fang, Moin Nadeem, Mitra Mohtarami, James Glass
MIT Computer Science and Artificial Intelligence Laboratory
Cambridge, MA, USA
{weifang,mnadeem,mitram,glass}@mit.edu

Abstract

We present a multi-task learning model that leverages large amount of textual information from existing datasets to improve stance prediction. In particular, we utilize multiple NLP tasks under both unsupervised and supervised settings for the stance prediction task. Our model obtains state-of-the-art performance on a public benchmark dataset, Fake News Challenge, outperforming current approaches by a wide margin.

1 Introduction

For journalists and news agencies, fact checking is the task of assessing the veracity of information and claims. Due to the large volume of claims, automating this process is of great interest to the journalism and NLP communities. A main component of automated fact-checking is stance detection which aims to automatically determine the perspective (stance) of given documents with respect to given claims as *agree, disagree, discuss,* or *unrelated.*

Previous work (Riedel et al., 2017; Hanselowski et al., 2018; Baird et al., 2017; Chopra et al., 2017; Mohtarami et al., 2018; Xu et al., 2018) presented various neural models for stance prediction. One of the challenges for these models is the limited size of human-labeled data, which can adversely affect the resulting performance for this task. To overcome this limitation, we propose to supplement data from other similar Natural Language Processing (NLP) tasks. However, this is not a straightforward process due to differences between NLP tasks and data sources. We address this problem using an effective multi-task learning approach which shows sizable improvement for the task of stance prediction on the Fake News Challenge benchmark dataset. The contributions of this work are as follows:

- To the best of our knowledge, we are the first to apply multi-task learning to the problem of stance prediction across different NLP tasks and data sources.

- We present an effective multi-task learning model, and investigate the effectiveness of different NLP tasks for stance prediction.

- Our model outperforms the state-of-the-art baselines on a publicly-available benchmark dataset with a substantial improvement.

2 Multi-task Learning Framework

We propose a multi-task learning framework which utilizes the commonalities and differences across existing NLP datasets and tasks to improve stance prediction performance. More specifically, we use both unsupervised and supervised pre-training on multiple tasks, and then fine-tune the resulting model on our target stance prediction task.

2.1 Model Architecture

The architecture of our model is shown in Figure 1. We use a transformer encoder (Vaswani et al., 2017) that is shared across different tasks to encode the inputs before feeding the contextualized embeddings into task-specific output layers. In what follows, we explain different components of our model.

Input Representation The input sequence $x = \{x_1, \ldots, x_l\}$ of length l is either a single sentence or multiple texts packed together. The input is first converted to word piece sequences (Wu et al., 2016) and, in the case of multiple texts, a special token [SEP] is inserted between the tokenized sequences. Another special token [CLS] is inserted at the beginning of the sequence, which corresponds to the representation of the entire sequence.

Proceedings of the Second Workshop on Fact Extraction and VERification (FEVER), pages 13–19
Hong Kong, November 3, 2019. ©2019 Association for Computational Linguistics

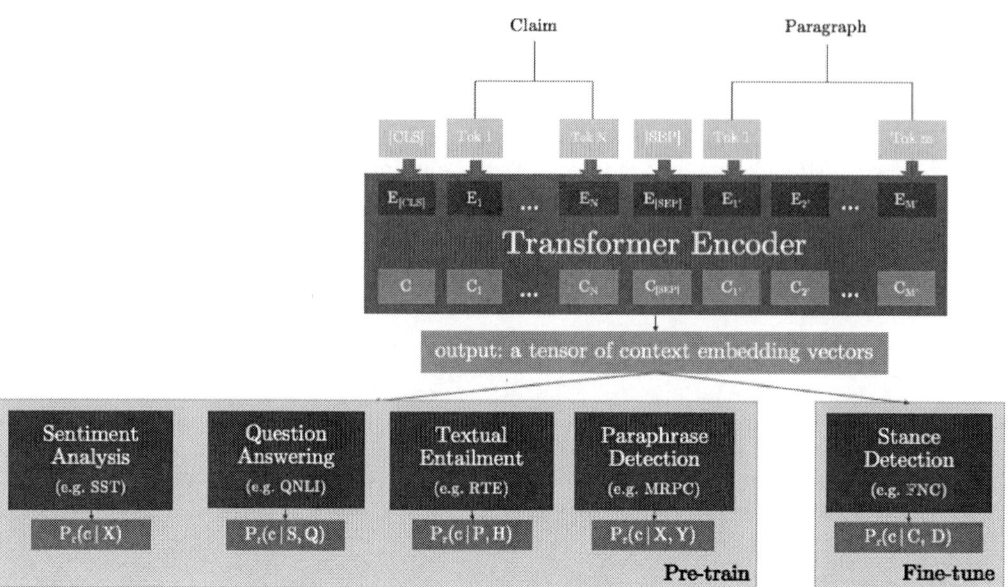

Figure 1: The architecture of our multi-task learning model for stance prediction.

Transformer Encoder We use a bidirectional Transformer encoder that takes x as input and produces contextual embedding vectors $\mathbf{C} \in \mathbb{R}^{d \times l}$ via multiple layers of self-attention (Devlin et al., 2019).

Task-specific Output Layers For single-sentence classification tasks, we take the vector from the first column in $\mathbf{C}$, corresponding to the special token [CLS], as the semantic representation of the input sentence x. We then feed this vector through a linear layer followed by softmax to obtain the prediction probabilities.

For pairwise classification tasks, we use the answer module from the stochastic answer network (SAN) (Liu et al., 2018) as the output classifier. It performs K-step reasoning over the two pieces of text with bi-linear attention and a recurrent mechanism, producing output predictions at each step and iteratively refining its predictions. At training time, some predictions are randomly discarded (stochastic dropout) before averaging, and during inference all output probabilities are utilized.

2.2 Unsupervised Pre-training

To utilize large amounts of text data, we use the BERT model which pre-trains the transformer encoder parameters with two unsupervised learning tasks: masked language modeling, for which the model has to predict a randomly masked out word in the sequence, and next sentence predic-tion, where two sentences are packed and fed into the encoder and the embedding corresponding to the [CLS] token is used to predict whether they are adjacent sentences (Devlin et al., 2019).

2.3 Multi-task Supervised Pre-training

In addition to learning contextual representations under an unsupervised setting with large data, we investigate whether existing NLP tasks that are conceptually similar to stance prediction can improve performance. We introduce four types of such tasks for pre-training:

Textual Entailment: Given two sentences, a premise and an hypothesis, the model determines whether the hypothesis is an *entailment, contradiction*, or *neutral* with respect to the premise. Since stance prediction could be cast as a textual entailment task, we investigate if the addition of this task will benefit our model.

Paraphrase Detection: Given a pair of sentences, the model should predict whether they are semantically equivalent. This task is considered because we may be able to benefit from detecting document sentences that are equivalent to claims.

Question Answering: Question answering is similar to the stance prediction task in that the model has to make a prediction given a question and a passage containing several sentences.

Sentiment Analysis: Fake claims or articles may exhibit stronger sentiment, thus we explore if pre-training on this task would be beneficial.

2.4 Training Procedure and Details

There are two stages in our training procedure: multi-task supervised pre-training, and fine-tuning on stance prediction. Before the training stages, the transformer encoder is initialized with pre-trained parameters to take advantage of knowledge learned from unlabeled data[1].

During multi-task pre-training, we randomly pick an ordering on tasks between each epoch, and train on 10% of a task's training data for each task in that order. This process is repeated 10 times in each epoch so that all the training examples are trained once. The shared encoder is learned over all tasks while each task-specific output layer is learned only for its corresponding task.

For fine-tuning, the task-specific output layers for pre-training are discarded, and a randomly initialized output layer is added for stance prediction. Then the entire model is fine-tuned over the training set for stance prediction.

For both multi-task pre-training and fine-tuning, we train with cross-entropy loss at each output layer. We use the Adam optimizer (Kingma and Ba, 2014) with learning rate of $3e\text{-}5$, $\beta_1 = 0.9$, $\beta_2 = 0.999$, and mini-batch size of 16 for 10 epochs. For the SAN answer module we set $K = 5$ and use stochastic dropout rate of 0.1.

3 Experiments

3.1 Data

The BERT model was pre-trained on the BooksCorpus (Zhu et al., 2015) and English Wikipedia. For multi-task pre-training, we use the following datasets:

SNLI Stanford Natural Language Inference is the standard entailment classification task that contains 549K training sentence pairs after removing examples with no gold labels (Bowman et al., 2015). The relation labels are *entailment*, *contradiction*, and *neutral*.

MNLI Multi-genre Natural Language Inference is a large-scale entailment classification task from a diverse set of sources with the same relation classes as SNLI (Williams et al., 2018). We use its training set that contains 393K pairs of sentences.

RTE Recognizing Textual Entailment is a binary entailment task with 2.5K training examples (Wang et al., 2019).

QQP Quora Question Pairs[2] is a QA dataset for binary classification where the goal is to predict whether two questions are semantically equivalent. We use its 364K training examples for pre-training.

MRPC Microsoft Research Paraphrase Corpus consists of automatically extracted sentence pairs from new sources, with human annotations for whether the pairs are semantically equivalent (Dolan and Brockett, 2005). The training set used for pre-training contains 3.7K sentence pairs.

QNLI Question Natural Language Inference (Wang et al., 2019) is a QA dataset which is derived from the Stanford Question Answering Dataset (Rajpurkar et al., 2016) and used for binary classification. For a given question-sentence pair, the task is to predict whether the sentence contains the answer to the question. QNLI contains 108K training pairs.

SST-2 Stanford Sentiment Treebank is used for binary classification for sentences extracted from movie reviews (Socher et al., 2013). We use the GLUE version that contains 67K training sentences (Wang et al., 2019).

IMDB The Large Movie Review Dataset contains 50K movie reviews which are categorized as either *positive* or *negative* in terms of sentiment orientation (Maas et al., 2011).

For fine-tuning on stance prediction, we use the dataset provided by the Fake News Challenge Stage 1 (**FNC-1**)[3], consisting of a total of 75K claim-document pairs collected from a variety of sources such as rumor sites and social media. The claim-document relation classes are: *agree*, *disagree*, *discuss*, and *unrelated*. The FNC-1 dataset has an imbalanced distribution over stance labels, especially lacking data for *agree* (7.3%), and *disagree* (1.7%) classes.

3.2 Evaluation Metrics

For evaluation, the standard measures of **accuracy** and **macro-F1** are used. Additionally, as per previous work, **weighted accuracy** is also reported, which is a two-level scoring scheme that gives 0.25 weight to predicting examples as *related* v.s. *unrelated* correctly, and an additional 0.75 weight to classifying related examples as *agree*, *disagree*, and *discuss* correctly.

---

[1]In this work we use the pre-trained BERT weights released by the authors.

[2]`https://data.quora.com/First-Quora-Dataset-Release-Question-Pairs`
[3]`http://www.fakenewschallenge.org`

	Model	Auxiliary Data	Weigh. Acc.	Acc.	Macro-F1
1	Gradient Boosting	-	75.2	86.3	46.1
2	TALOS	-	82.0	89.1	57.8
3	UCL	-	81.7	88.5	57.9
4	Memory Network	-	81.2	88.6	56.9
5	Adversarial Adaptation	FEVER	80.3	88.2	60.0
6	TransLinear	-	84.9	89.3	66.3
7	TransSAN	-	85.1	90.3	67.9
	Textual Entailment				
8	MTransSAN	SNLI	86.7	91.9	72.3
9	MTransSAN	MNLI	86.4	90.8	71.0
10	MTransSAN	RTE	85.6	90.7	69.3
11	MTransSAN	SNLI, MNLI, RTE	86.1	91.3	71.6
	Paraphrase Detection				
12	MTransSAN	QQP	87.6	92.1	74.1
13	MTransSAN	MRPC	87.0	92.0	73.5
14	MTransSAN	QQP, MRPC	**88.0**	**92.3**	**74.4**
	Question Answering				
15	MTransSAN	QNLI	86.5	91.2	71.9
	Sentiment Analysis				
16	MTransSAN	SST	86.7	91.8	70.0
17	MTransSAN	IMDB	85.6	91.2	70.4
18	MTransSAN	SST, IMDB	86.5	91.7	71.1
	Joint				
19	MTransSAN	SNLI, MNLI, QNLI	84.7	90.6	70.1
20	MTransSAN	MNLI, RTE, QQP, MRPC, QNLI, SST	87.0	91.6	71.8
21	MTransSAN	SNLI, MNLI, RTE, QQP, MRPC, QNLI, SST, IMDB	86.5	91.6	72.1

Table 1: Results on the FNC test data. TransLinear, TransSAN and MTransSAN show our model where the first two are based on a transformer followed by a MLP or neural model, and the later further uses multi-task learning.

3.3 Baselines

We compare our model with existing state-of-the-art stance prediction models including the top-ranked models from FNC-1 and neural models:

Gradient Boosting This baseline[4] uses a gradient-boosting classifier with hand-crafted features including n-gram features, and indicator features for polarity and refutation.

TALOS (Baird et al., 2017) An ensemble of gradient-boosted decision trees and a convolutional neural network.

UCL (Riedel et al., 2017) A Multi-Layer Perceptron (MLP) with Bag-of-Words and similarity features extracted from claims and documents.

Memory Network (Mohtarami et al., 2018) A feature-light end-to-end memory network that attends over convolutional and recurrent encoders.

Adversarial Domain Adaptation (Xu et al., 2018) This baseline uses a domain classifier with gradient reversal on top of a convolutional network and TF-IDF features to perform adversarial domain adaptation from another fact-checking dataset (Thorne et al., 2018) to FNC.

3.4 Results and Discussion

The performance of the existing models are shown in Table 1 from rows 1–5, and our models (MTransSAN) are in rows 8–21. All variants of MTransSAN consistently outperform existing models on all three metrics by a considerable margin. In particular, our best MTransSAN (row 14) **achieves 6.0 and 14.4 points of absolute improvement** in terms of weighted accuracy and macro-F1, respectively, over existing state-of-the-art results.

We also compare MTransSAN versus a model with the same architecture but without pre-training on the NLP tasks (TransSAN), shown in row 7, and another version of that model with a linear layer instead of the SAN answer module (TransLinear), shown in row 6. Using the SAN answer module improves over a linear layer for all three metrics, and generally most MTransSAN models outperform the TransSAN model. Our best MTransSAN model exceeds TransSAN by 3.1 and 6.5 points in weighted accuracy and macro-F1, respectively, justifying the effectiveness of model pre-training with NLU tasks. Note that even the TransLinear model outperforms previously state-of-the-art models by a wide margin, suggesting that a neural model pre-trained on large amounts of unlabeled data and fine-tuned on stance prediction is superior to models that require hand-crafted features.

Additionally, we conduct experiments where we use different combinations of language understanding tasks for pre-training. We pre-train with single tasks, multiple tasks with the same task type, and joint learning across multiple task types. For textual entailment (rows 8–11), we see that pre-training on SNLI gives us best improvement, and that pre-training across all three entailment tasks did not improve compared to just training on SNLI. However, for paraphrase detection (rows 12–14) the combination of QQP and MRPC gives us the best results across all MTransSAN models. This suggests that the paraphrase detection might be the most useful task type among the NLP tasks in terms of boosting stance prediction performance. Question answering and sentiment analysis (rows 15–18), on the other hand, give lower performance improvements compared to paraphrase detection. Models trained on joint tasks (rows 19–21) do not outperform our best model either.

Overall, we find that utilizing the BERT model results in large improvements compared to the baselines, which is not unexpected given the success of BERT. We also show that our multi-task learning approach gives even further improvements upon BERT by a wide margin.

4 Related Work

Stance Prediction. This task is an important component for fact checking and veracity inference. To address stance prediction, (Riedel et al., 2017) used a Multi-Layer Perceptron (MLP) with bag-of-words and similarity features extracted from input documents and claims, and (Hanselowski et al., 2018) presented a deep MLP trained using a rich feature representation, based on unigrams, non-negative matrix factorization, latent semantic indexing. (Baird et al., 2017) presented an ensemble of gradient-boosted decision trees and a deep convolutional neural network, while (Chopra et al., 2017) proposed a model based on bi-directional LSTM and attention mechanism. While, these works utilized a rich handcrafted features, (Mohtarami et al., 2018, 2019) proposed strong end-to-end feature-light memory networks for stance prediction in mono- and cross-lingual settings. Recently, (Xu et al.,

2018) presented a state-of-the-art model based on adversarial domain adaptation with more labeled data, but they limited their model to only using data from the same stance prediction task. In this work, we remove this limitation and used labeled data from other tasks that are similar to stance prediction through multi-task learning.

Multi-task and Transfer Learning. Multi-task and transfer learning have been long-studied problems in machine learning and NLP (Caruana, 1997; Collobert and Weston, 2008; Pan and Yang, 2010). More recently, numerous methods on unsupervised pre-training of deep contextualized models for transfer learning have been proposed (Peters et al., 2018; Devlin et al., 2019; Yang et al., 2019; Radford et al., 2019; Dai et al., 2019; Liu et al., 2019), and (Conneau et al., 2017; McCann et al., 2017) presented supervised pre-training methods for NLI and translation. Recent work on multi-task learning has focused on designing effective neural architectures (Hashimoto et al., 2017; Søgaard and Goldberg, 2016; Sanh et al., 2018; Ruder et al., 2017). Combining these two lines of work, (Liu et al., 2019, Clark et al., 2019) explored fine-tuning the contextualized models with multiple natural language understanding tasks. In this work, we depart from previous works by specifically studying the effects of multi-task fine-tuning for the stance prediction task with pre-trained models.

5 Conclusion and Future Work

We present an effective multi-task learning model that transfers knowledge from existing NLP tasks to improve stance prediction. Our model outperforms state-of-the-art systems by 6.0 and 14.4 points in weighted accuracy and macro-F1 respectively on the FNC-1 benchmark dataset. In future, we plan to further investigate our model to more specifically identify and illustrate its source of improvement, improve our transfer learning approach for better fine-tuning, and investigate the utility of our model in other fact-checking subproblems such as evidence extraction.

Acknowledgments

We thank the anonymous reviewers for their insightful comments, suggestions, and feedback. This research was supported in part by HBKU Qatar Computing Research Institute (QCRI) and DSTA of Singapore.

References

Sean Baird, Doug Sibley, and Yuxi Pan. 2017. Talos targets disinformation with fake news challenge victory. https://blog.talosintelligence.com/2017/06/talos-fake-news-challenge.html.

Samuel R. Bowman, Gabor Angeli, Christopher Potts, and Christopher D. Manning. 2015. A large annotated corpus for learning natural language inference. In *Proceedings of the 2015 Conference on Empirical Methods in Natural Language Processing*, pages 632–642, Lisbon, Portugal. Association for Computational Linguistics.

Rich Caruana. 1997. Multitask learning. *Mach. Learn.*, 28(1):41–75.

Sahil Chopra, Saachi Jain, and John Merriman Sholar. 2017. Towards automatic identification of fake news: Headline-article stance detection with lstm attention models.

Kevin Clark, Minh-Thang Luong, Christopher D. Manning, and Quoc V. Le. 2019. Bam! born-again multi-task networks for natural language understanding. In *ACL*.

Ronan Collobert and Jason Weston. 2008. A unified architecture for natural language processing: Deep neural networks with multitask learning. In *Proceedings of the 25th International Conference on Machine Learning*, ICML '08, pages 160–167, New York, NY, USA. ACM.

Alexis Conneau, Douwe Kiela, Holger Schwenk, Loïc Barrault, and Antoine Bordes. 2017. Supervised learning of universal sentence representations from natural language inference data. In *Proceedings of the 2017 Conference on Empirical Methods in Natural Language Processing*, pages 670–680, Copenhagen, Denmark. Association for Computational Linguistics.

Zihang Dai, Zhilin Yang, Yiming Yang, Jaime Carbonell, Quoc Le, and Ruslan Salakhutdinov. 2019. Transformer-XL: Attentive language models beyond a fixed-length context. In *Proceedings of the 57th Annual Meeting of the Association for Computational Linguistics*, pages 2978–2988, Florence, Italy. Association for Computational Linguistics.

Jacob Devlin, Ming-Wei Chang, Kenton Lee, and Kristina Toutanova. 2019. BERT: Pre-training of deep bidirectional transformers for language understanding. In *Proceedings of the 2019 Conference of the North American Chapter of the Association for Computational Linguistics: Human Language Technologies, Volume 1 (Long and Short Papers)*, pages 4171–4186, Minneapolis, Minnesota. Association for Computational Linguistics.

Bill Dolan and Chris Brockett. 2005. Automatically constructing a corpus of sentential paraphrases. In *Third International Workshop on Paraphrasing (IWP2005)*. Asia Federation of Natural Language Processing.

Andreas Hanselowski, Avinesh PVS, Benjamin Schiller, Felix Caspelherr, Debanjan Chaudhuri, Christian M. Meyer, and Iryna Gurevych. 2018. A retrospective analysis of the fake news challenge stance-detection task. In *Proceedings of the 27th International Conference on Computational Linguistics*, pages 1859–1874, Santa Fe, New Mexico, USA. Association for Computational Linguistics.

Kazuma Hashimoto, Caiming Xiong, Yoshimasa Tsuruoka, and Richard Socher. 2017. A joint many-task model: Growing a neural network for multiple NLP tasks. In *Proceedings of the 2017 Conference on Empirical Methods in Natural Language Processing*, pages 1923–1933, Copenhagen, Denmark. Association for Computational Linguistics.

Diederik P. Kingma and Jimmy Ba. 2014. Adam: A Method for Stochastic Optimization. *arXiv e-prints*, page arXiv:1412.6980.

Xiaodong Liu, Pengcheng He, Weizhu Chen, and Jianfeng Gao. 2019. Multi-task deep neural networks for natural language understanding. In *Proceedings of the 57th Annual Meeting of the Association for Computational Linguistics*, pages 4487–4496, Florence, Italy. Association for Computational Linguistics.

Xiaodong Liu, Yelong Shen, Kevin Duh, and Jianfeng Gao. 2018. Stochastic answer networks for machine reading comprehension. In *Proceedings of the 56th Annual Meeting of the Association for Computational Linguistics (Volume 1: Long Papers)*, pages 1694–1704. Association for Computational Linguistics.

Yinhan Liu, Myle Ott, Naman Goyal, Jingfei Du, Mandar Joshi, Danqi Chen, Omer Levy, Mike Lewis, Luke Zettlemoyer, and Veselin Stoyanov. 2019. RoBERTa: A Robustly Optimized BERT Pretraining Approach. *arXiv e-prints*, page arXiv:1907.11692.

Andrew L. Maas, Raymond E. Daly, Peter T. Pham, Dan Huang, Andrew Y. Ng, and Christopher Potts. 2011. Learning word vectors for sentiment analysis. In *Proceedings of the 49th Annual Meeting of the Association for Computational Linguistics: Human Language Technologies*, pages 142–150, Portland, Oregon, USA. Association for Computational Linguistics.

Bryan McCann, James Bradbury, Caiming Xiong, and Richard Socher. 2017. Learned in translation: Contextualized word vectors. In I. Guyon, U. V. Luxburg, S. Bengio, H. Wallach, R. Fergus, S. Vishwanathan, and R. Garnett, editors, *Advances in Neural Information Processing Systems 30*, pages 6294–6305. Curran Associates, Inc.

Mitra Mohtarami, Ramy Baly, James Glass, Preslav Nakov, Lluís Màrquez, and Alessandro Moschitti. 2018. Automatic stance detection using end-to-end memory networks. In *Proceedings of the 2018 Conference of the North American Chapter of the Association for Computational Linguistics: Human Language Technologies, Volume 1 (Long Papers)*, pages 767–776, New Orleans, Louisiana. Association for Computational Linguistics.

Mitra Mohtarami, James Glass, and Preslav Nakov. 2019. Contrastive language adaptation for cross-lingual stance detection. In *Proceedings of the 2019 Conference on Empirical Methods in Natural Language Processing (EMNLP)*, Hong Kong, China.

Sinno Jialin Pan and Qiang Yang. 2010. A survey on transfer learning. *IEEE Trans. on Knowl. and Data Eng.*, 22(10):1345–1359.

Matthew Peters, Mark Neumann, Mohit Iyyer, Matt Gardner, Christopher Clark, Kenton Lee, and Luke Zettlemoyer. 2018. Deep contextualized word representations. In *Proceedings of the 2018 Conference of the North American Chapter of the Association for Computational Linguistics: Human Language Technologies, Volume 1 (Long Papers)*, pages 2227–2237, New Orleans, Louisiana.

Alec Radford, Jeff Wu, Rewon Child, David Luan, Dario Amodei, and Ilya Sutskever. 2019. Language models are unsupervised multitask learners.

Pranav Rajpurkar, Jian Zhang, Konstantin Lopyrev, and Percy Liang. 2016. SQuAD: 100,000+ questions for machine comprehension of text. In *Proceedings of the 2016 Conference on Empirical Methods in Natural Language Processing*, pages 2383–2392, Austin, Texas. Association for Computational Linguistics.

Benjamin Riedel, Isabelle Augenstein, Georgios P Spithourakis, and Sebastian Riedel. 2017. A simple but tough-to-beat baseline for the Fake News Challenge stance detection task. *ArXiv:1707.03264*.

Sebastian Ruder, Joachim Bingel, Isabelle Augenstein, and Anders Søgaard. 2017. Latent multi-task architecture learning.

Victor Sanh, Thomas Wolf, and Sebastian Ruder. 2018. A hierarchical multi-task approach for learning embeddings from semantic tasks. *CoRR*, abs/1811.06031.

Richard Socher, Alex Perelygin, Jean Wu, Jason Chuang, Christopher D. Manning, Andrew Ng, and Christopher Potts. 2013. Recursive deep models for semantic compositionality over a sentiment treebank. In *Proceedings of the 2013 Conference on Empirical Methods in Natural Language Processing*, pages 1631–1642, Seattle, Washington, USA. Association for Computational Linguistics.

Anders Søgaard and Yoav Goldberg. 2016. Deep multi-task learning with low level tasks supervised at lower layers. In *Proceedings of the 54th Annual Meeting of the Association for Computational Linguistics (Volume 2: Short Papers)*, pages 231–235, Berlin, Germany. Association for Computational Linguistics.

James Thorne, Andreas Vlachos, Christos Christodoulopoulos, and Arpit Mittal. 2018. FEVER: a large-scale dataset for fact extraction and VERification. In *Proceedings of the 2018 Conference of the North American Chapter of the Association for Computational Linguistics: Human Language Technologies, Volume 1 (Long Papers)*, pages 809–819, New Orleans, Louisiana. Association for Computational Linguistics.

Ashish Vaswani, Noam Shazeer, Niki Parmar, Jakob Uszkoreit, Llion Jones, Aidan N Gomez, Ł ukasz Kaiser, and Illia Polosukhin. 2017. Attention is all you need. In I. Guyon, U. V. Luxburg, S. Bengio, H. Wallach, R. Fergus, S. Vishwanathan, and R. Garnett, editors, *Advances in Neural Information Processing Systems 30*, pages 5998–6008. Curran Associates, Inc.

Alex Wang, Amanpreet Singh, Julian Michael, Felix Hill, Omer Levy, and Samuel R. Bowman. 2019. GLUE: A multi-task benchmark and analysis platform for natural language understanding. In the Proceedings of ICLR.

Adina Williams, Nikita Nangia, and Samuel Bowman. 2018. A broad-coverage challenge corpus for sentence understanding through inference. In *Proceedings of the 2018 Conference of the North American Chapter of the Association for Computational Linguistics: Human Language Technologies, Volume 1 (Long Papers)*, pages 1112–1122.

Yonghui Wu, Mike Schuster, Zhifeng Chen, Quoc V. Le, Mohammad Norouzi, Wolfgang Macherey, Maxim Krikun, Yuan Cao, Qin Gao, Klaus Macherey, Jeff Klingner, Apurva Shah, Melvin Johnson, Xiaobing Liu, Łukasz Kaiser, Stephan Gouws, Yoshikiyo Kato, Taku Kudo, Hideto Kazawa, Keith Stevens, George Kurian, Nishant Patil, Wei Wang, Cliff Young, Jason Smith, Jason Riesa, Alex Rudnick, Oriol Vinyals, Greg Corrado, Macduff Hughes, and Jeffrey Dean. 2016. Google's Neural Machine Translation System: Bridging the Gap between Human and Machine Translation. *arXiv e-prints*, page arXiv:1609.08144.

Brian Xu, Mitra Mohtarami, and James Glass. 2018. Adversarial doman adaptation for stance detection. In *Proceedings of the Thirty-second Annual Conference on Neural Information Processing Systems (NIPS)–Continual Learning*.

Zhilin Yang, Zihang Dai, Yiming Yang, Jaime Carbonell, Ruslan Salakhutdinov, and Quoc V. Le. 2019. XLNet: Generalized Autoregressive Pretraining for Language Understanding. *arXiv e-prints*, page arXiv:1906.08237.

Yukun Zhu, Ryan Kiros, Rich Zemel, Ruslan Salakhutdinov, Raquel Urtasun, Antonio Torralba, and Sanja Fidler. 2015. Aligning books and movies: Towards story-like visual explanations by watching movies and reading books. In *The IEEE International Conference on Computer Vision (ICCV)*.

TMLab: Generative Enhanced Model (GEM) for adversarial attacks

Piotr Niewiński, Maria Pszona, Maria Janicka
Samsung R&D Institute Poland
{p.niewinski, m.pszona, m.janicka}@samsung.com

Abstract

We present our Generative Enhanced Model (GEM) that we used to create samples awarded the first prize on the FEVER 2.0 *Breakers* Task. GEM is the extended language model developed upon GPT-2 architecture. The addition of novel target vocabulary input to the already existing context input enabled controlled text generation. The training procedure resulted in creating a model that inherited the knowledge of pretrained GPT-2, and therefore was ready to generate natural-like English sentences in the task domain with some additional control. As a result, GEM generated malicious claims that mixed facts from various articles, so it became difficult to classify their truthfulness.

1 Introduction

Fact-checking systems usually consist of separate modules devoted to information retrieval (IR) and recognizing textual entailment (RTE), also known as natural language inference (NLI). First, information retrieval module searches through the database in order to find sentences related to the given statement. Next, entailment module, with respect to the extracted sentences, classifies the given claim as TRUE, FALSE or NOT ENOUGH INFO. Currently, the best results are achieved by pretrained language models that are fine-tuned with task specific data (Yang et al., 2019; Liu et al., 2019).

Our task was to provide adversarial examples to break fact-checking systems. Since many fact-checking systems are based on neural language models, they might be less resistant to attacks with samples prepared within the same approach. In line with recent advances in natural language generation, we used the GPT-2 model (Radford et al., 2019), which we modified to prepare malicious adversarial examples. GPT-2 generates subsequent sentences based on a given textual context and originally was trained on the WebText corpus. Our GEM architecture was expanded with *target* input for controlled generation, and carefully trained on the task data. During inference, the model was fed with the Wikipedia content. Simultaneously, *target* input was provided with named entities, terms and phrases extracted from Wikipedia articles.

2 FEVER *Breakers* Subtask

The second edition of Fact Extraction and Verification (FEVER 2.0) shared task was the three-phased contest utilizing the idea of adversarial training (Thorne and Vlachos, 2019). In the first phase, *Builders* had to create a fact-checking system. This system should extract evidence sentences for a given claim from Wikipedia articles that either SUPPORT or REFUTE this claim. It can also classify an example as NOT ENOUGH INFO. In the second phase, *Breakers* had to supply malicious examples to fool the existing systems. Finally, *Fixers* were obliged to improve those systems to withstand adversarial attacks. The model presented in this paper originated as a part of *Breakers* subtask. The aim of this task was to create adversarial examples that will break the majority of systems created in the *Builders* phase. Malicious claims could have been generated automatically or manually and were supposed to be balanced over three categories. The evidence sentences had to be provided in the SUPPORTS and REFUTES categories.

3 Generative Enhanced Model

3.1 Natural Language Generation with Neural Networks

Neural language models, such as GPT-2, rely on modeling conditional probability of an onco-

Proceedings of the Second Workshop on Fact Extraction and VERification (FEVER), pages 20–26
Hong Kong, November 3, 2019. ©2019 Association for Computational Linguistics

ming token for a given input sequence (context). Given the dictionary of tokens $\mathbb{D}$ and sequence $x_0 \ldots x_N \, (x_i \in \mathbb{D})$ model computes conditional probability for every token x from $\mathbb{D}$:

$$p(x) = \prod_{i=1}^{n} p(x_n | x_1, \ldots, x_{n-1}).$$

During each stage of the process, the language model outputs probability distribution of tokens from dictionary $\mathbb{D}$. There are various approaches to select a single token from output distribution. Usually, the one with the highest probability is chosen or is sampled from the distribution. This distribution may be slightly modified by parameters like temperature and top-k. However, such context-based language generation gives us very little, if any, control over the model output.

Taking that into account, our main goal was to modify the architecture of Generative Pretraining Transformer (GPT-2), and enable additional control during the generation process. Therefore, GEM samples subsequent tokens by using information from two inputs: *context* (past) and *target*.

As target words various combinations of English nouns, verbs, and named entities can be provided and their number may vary.

GEM stops generating output when the total number of consecutive tokens reaches the value of parameter *maxTokens*. As a consequence, not only the first sentence, for which target words are given, is generated. That kind of generation procedure is expected to keep the original model's ability to build sentences even without target words. The examples of first sentences from the model output are presented in Table 1.

3.2 Architecture

GEM is build upon encoder-decoder Transformer-based language model architecture (Vaswani et al., 2017) enhanced with second Transformer encoder for *target* words.

Typical autoregressive neural language model, such as GPT-2, generates the next token using representations of *context* tokens (past) and *present* tokens (previously generated). Given *context* tokens $c_1 \ldots c_n$ and *present* tokens $p_1 \ldots p_n$,

context	The main railway stations of the province are Bydgoszcz and Toruń. Both stations are served by fast PKP Intercity trains which connect them with the capital Warsaw, as well as other major Polish cities.
target	**characterized Portugal farmland numerous lakes and forests**
output	Bydgoszcz is characterized as a medium-sized city in Portugal, with its farmland and numerous lakes and forests.
context	Near the beginning of his career, Einstein thought that Newtonian mechanics was no longer enough to reconcile the laws of classical mechanics with the laws of the electromagnetic field. This led him to develop his special theory of relativity during his time at the Swiss Patent Office in Bern (1902–1909).
target	**objected quantum mechanics contrast Bohr**
output	Einstein objected to the use of quantum mechanics in contrast with Bohr's theory of gravitation, which he thought was the most superior theory of relativity.
context	The City of New York, usually called either New York City (NYC) or simply New York (NY), is the most populous city in the United States. With an estimated 2018 population of 8,398,748 distributed over a land area of about 302.6 square miles (784 km2), New York is also the most densely populated major city in the United States.
target	**realized asset establishment independent border**
output	New York City is realized as an economic, cultural, and political asset upon the establishment of an independent border country.
context	Lasse Hoile (born 1973 in Aarhus, Denmark) is an artist, photographer and film-maker. He has collaborated with musician Steven Wilson and his projects Porcupine Tree and Blackfield. He has also designed live visuals for the US progressive metal band Dream Theater.
target	**true fact Swedish progressive metal band Stockholm**
output	Hoile's true interest is in fact the Swedish progressive metal band, Stockholm.

Table 1: Examples of first sentences generated for given context and target words.

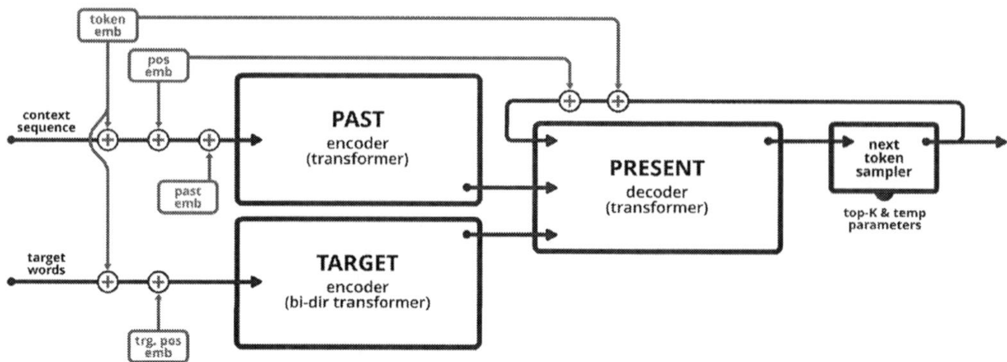

Figure 1: The architecture of GEM.

model encodes *context* representations $cr_1 \ldots cr_n$ and *present* representations $pr_1 \ldots pr_n$. With concatenated representations of *context* and *present* $cr_1 \ldots cr_n; pr1 \ldots pr_n$ model generates the next token p_{n+1}.

Both *context* and *present* representations are prepared with Transformers, using same shared parameters and embeddings. Such concept minimizes the number of parameters, and is optimal for classic generation task. Representations of *context* and *present* when concatenated are undifferentiated for decoder attention mechanism - the decoder has no information where *context* ends and *present* starts. This is not a problem for a standard task of neural language modeling.

The GEM's architecture is outlined in Figure 1. Just like GPT-2, the proposed model uses concatenated representations. However, in GEM *target* words representations $tr_1 \ldots tr_n$, prepared by target encoder, are added:

$$cr_1 \ldots cr_n; tr_1 \ldots tr_n; pr_1 \ldots pr_n.$$

In contrast to standard neural language models, GEM, in order to work properly, needs to differentiate between all three sources of representations. Both positional embeddings and Transformer weights of target encoder are not shared with past encoder and present decoder, and are initialized from scratch instead (with random normal initializer of 0.02 standard deviation). During the training, GEM learns the weights of target encoder to properly accomplish the task and distinguish *target* representations from the other two: *context* and *present*. In order to pass the information about the origin of *context* representations, we have ad-

ded *past* embedding (single trainable vector) to *context* tokens.

Past encoder and present decoder were initialized with GPT-2 checkpoint parameters. The idea was to use the knowledge of pretrained state-of-the-art English language model. Token embeddings from GPT-2 checkpoint were not updated while training. The final size of GEM is equal to 170-190% of the original GPT-2 model size (depending on GPT-2 version).

3.3 Training Procedure

The model was trained on the corpus provided by FEVER organizers. It contains a dump taken from the English-language version of Wikipedia from 2017. Each article was sentence-tokenized with spaCy tokenizer (Honnibal and Montani, 2017), and then each sentence was tokenized with BPE tokens from GPT-2 model.

Single training sample was prepared with the following procedure. First, random *target* sentence from the given Wikipedia articles was chosen. Next, the arbitrary number of words ranging from 20% to 60% was selected from *target* sentence. Selected words built *target* input. In addition, a small number of random words (up to 10%), which do not appear in *target* sentence, may be added to the set of *target* words. The intuition behind adding the noise to *target* words during the training phase was that it would prevent the model from directly 'copying' from *target* input. The model was supposed to decide whether to include the given words or not, because some of them may be irrelevant. Sentences forerunning *target* sentence established *context* input. As a result, *tar-*

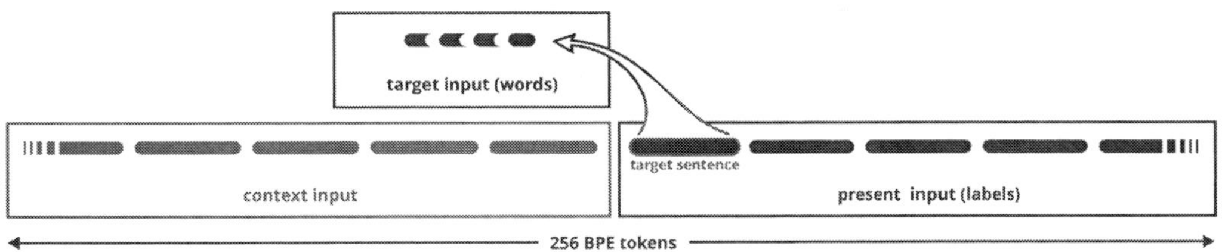

Figure 2: GEM training sample.

get sentence with the following sentences served as gold labels. In addition, single training sample was limited to 256 BPE tokens, which on average corresponds to 10 sentences. Single training sample is presented in Figure 2.

We have fine-tuned the original GPT-2 language model with the text generation task on the FEVER Wikipedia data (30M sentences). The model was fed with the Wikipedia content, and was asked to generate next sentences. GPT-2, without additional training, managed to achieve 37% accuracy on the stated task. It means that 37% of tokens generated by the model matched the gold labels from the original Wikipedia text. However, not modified GPT-2 fine-tuned with the given Wikipedia data was able to achieve 43% accuracy on a validation set.

Naturally, we expected higher accuracy with additional target words input. Though, we were afraid that adding new parameters and modifying the architecture might result in a significant loss of GPT-2 pretrained knowledge. During the training process, the initial accuracy of GEM was 3% and it raised very quickly. After the first epoch of training it achieved 47%. We trained the model with batches of 16 samples for 6 epochs, and the learning rate was set to 1e-5. The batch size of training data was limited by the memory of GPU, while other hyperparameters were chosen with the grid search evaluation. As a result, GEM finally achieved 53% accuracy while still not overfitting the data. High final accuracy of GEM states that the knowledge of GPT-2 was not forgotten, and, at the same time, the model learned to effectively use the provided target words.

We can estimate the theoretical maximum accuracy (higher bound) of GEM with stated task and training scheme. Each training sample, on average, corresponds to 10 sentences. The model generates tokens for 5 sentences. GEM additionally

fed with target words is able to achieve the maximum accuracy of 100% for the first sentence, and keep the maximum accuracy of fine-tuned GPT-2 (43%) for the remaining four sentences. With these assumptions, the average accuracy across the entire sample would reach 54.4%. Therefore, our final 53% accuracy is only a bit lower, and reversing these calculations we can get up to 93% accuracy for the first sentence when GEM is supported with target input.

4 Claims generation procedure

The procedure of generating claims was driven by the assumption that sophisticated claims contain knowledge from many sources, and cannot be checked with a single evidence sentence. To force automatic generation of such claims, we have built pipeline for input data preparation and claims selection described below. Wikipedia articles have a hypertext form with references to other articles. A single input sample (context and target words) was based on two Wikipedia articles: wiki-A and wiki-B. Wiki-A was randomly selected from the corpus. A set $\mathbb{B}$ was created from articles hyperlinked in the first five sentences of wiki-A. Then, it was filtered with the following principles. An article b was removed from $\mathbb{B}$ if:

- any words from title of b appeared in wiki-A title

- b hyperlink (string) in wiki-A was equal to b title

Finally, wiki-B article was randomly selected from $\mathbb{B}$.

The target words were randomly selected from the second sentence of wiki-B. Similar to the training procedure, their number varied from 20% to 60% of source-sentence words. Context sentences were composed of mixed wiki-A and wiki-B sentences, excluding sentences containing hyperlinks to wiki-B and the second sentence of wiki-B. Finally, the title of wiki-A article was appended to the context. GEM started generation from this point.

Generated claims were further filtered, and the ones meeting any of the listed conditions were removed:

- claims not ending with a dot (probably due to incorrect tokenization)

- claims shorter than 30 characters and longer than 200

- claims containing `<endoftext>` token

- claims too similar to the first sentence of wiki-A (measured with Levenshtein (1966) distance)

- claims containing numbers and dates not appearing in wiki-A article

- claims containing any words out-of-vocabulary, where vocabulary was built from words of all Wikipedia articles

The examples of generated claims are shown in Table 2.

The dependency between the number of provided target words and the length of generated sentence is presented in Figure 3a. The statistics of target words number is shown in Figure 3b. The presented results are based on 1917 samples generated by GEM model and clearly indicates the correlation between the length of generated sentence and number of the target words: the fewer words the system gets, the shorter sentence will be generated.

The automatically generated claims required further manual labeling as SUPPORTS, REFUTES or NOT ENOUGH INFO. Moreover, in the case of the first two classes, the evidence senten-

wiki-A	Joseph Cao
wiki-B	Republican Party (United States)
context	Ánh Quang "Joseph" Cao ([ˈɡaʊ]; Cao Quang Ánh born March 13, 1967) is a Vietnamese American politician who was the U.S. Representative for from 2009 to 2011. In April 2011, Cao announced his candidacy for the office of Attorney General of Louisiana; however, in September 2011 he pulled out of the race, and the incumbent Buddy Caldwell ran unopposed for a second term. He is the first Vietnamese American to serve in Congress, and the first and thus far only Republican from his New Orleans-based district since 1891. In December 2015, he announced that he would run for the open U.S. Senate seat being vacated by retiring fellow Republican David Vitter in 2016. The Republican Party, commonly referred to as the GOP (abbreviation for Grand Old Party), is one of the two major contemporary political parties in the United States, the other being its historic rival, the Democratic Party. He is a member of the Republican Party.
target	**The party named dominant value during**
output	Joseph Cao was elected to Congress in 2009 and has named a number of prominent Republicans to be the dominant value players during his time in the House.
wiki-A	Remmina
wiki-B	Remote Desktop Protocol
context	Remmina is a remote desktop software client for POSIX-based computer operating systems. Remmina is in the package repositories for Debian versions 6 (Squeeze) and later and for Ubuntu versions since 10.04 (Lucid Lynx). As of 11.04 (Natty Narwhal), it replaced tsclient as Ubuntu's default remote desktop client. The FreeBSD ports/package collection also contains it as a separate port and additional protocol-specific plugin ports. Remote Desktop Protocol (RDP) is a proprietary protocol developed by Microsoft, which provides a user with a graphical interface to connect to another computer over a network connection. It supports the RDP, VNC, NX, XDMCP, SPICE and SSH protocols.
target	**RDP client for must run software**
output	Remmina is a standalone RDP client for Windows and must run as a user on a Linux system, or the client software will be unavailable.

Table 2: Examples of generated sentences for given context and target words.

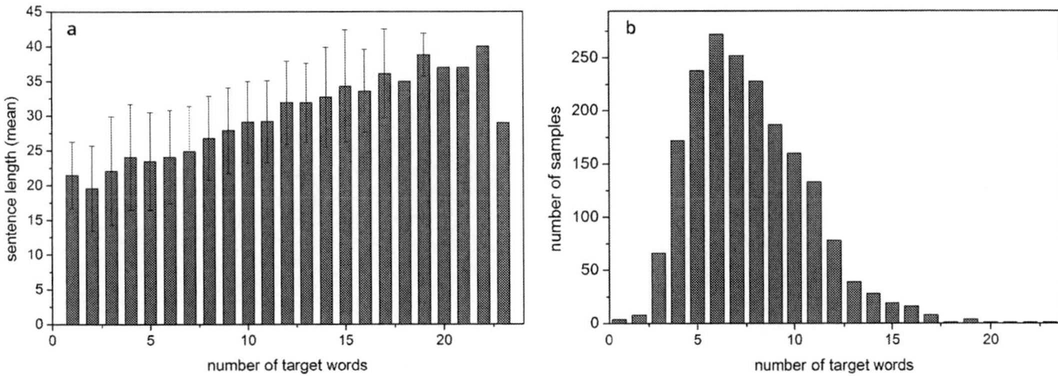

Figure 3: The dependency of the length of generated sentences on the number of target words (a) and target words statistics (b).

ces from Wikipedia were supposed to be delivered. Initially, each claim was annotated independently by two linguists. Both annotators agreed on 58.5% samples. The distribution of labels was highly unbalanced: 72.6% REFUTES, 13.7% NOT ENOUGH INFO, and 4.3% SUPPORTS. The remaining 9.4% of samples contained language errors. Finally, the supporting sentences from Wikipedia were manually extracted.

Due to a small number of claims labeled SUPPORTS in automatically generated data, there was a need to manually create some examples in this category. Malicious claims were based on several tricks, such as the usage of double negation, polysemy, comparison (of age, area, population), calculations, paraphrase (e.g. using phrases from Wikipedia articles unrelated to a claim or evidence), complex chains of reasoning, etc. The examples are provided in Table 3.

5   Results

Our adversarial attack was ranked the first place in the official FEVER 2.0 results. In total, we submitted 155 various claims (104 automatically generated and 51 written by human), which were divided into train and test sets. The quality of the test set was described by three measures: Correct Rate, Raw Potency and Potency, all defined in Thorne and Vlachos (2019). The Correct Rate, which is a percentage of positively verified samples, was 84.81%. This means that the organizers disqualified about 15% of our claims, mostly due to grammatical errors, such as word repetitions or wrong verb forms. The Raw Potency of the prepared adversarial examples, defined as the percentage of incorrect predictions, averaged over all systems was 78.80%. Finally, the main evaluation measure - Potency (the Raw Potency scaled by the Correct Rate) achieved by our samples was 66.83%.

6   Conclusions

The claims provided by GEM model appeared to be the most challenging for fact-checking systems competing in a FEVER 2.0 shared task. Our strategy was to mix Wikipedia articles, which were

double negation	It is not true that one can falsely say that double negation theorem states that "If a statement is false, than it is not the case that the statement is not false."
comparison	Łączka does not lay as close to Siedlce as Żuków.
paraphrase	Finding a theory of everything, which is considered a final theory, still remains a challenge.
polysemy	There is a fashion house with a word meaning 'sweet' in its name.
negation	K2 is not the highest mountain in the world.

Table 3: Examples of manually prepared samples.

connected to each other with a hyperlink and filtered with the established strategies. This approach led to generating cohesive, well-structured samples, which were challenging for automated verification. As GEM was developed upon GPT-2 architecture, and inherited its knowledge, the model might be biased towards factual inaccuracies. The established pipeline could just strengthen this tendency, which finally reflected in the class imbalance of automatically generated content. Automatic generation of complex claims supported by Wikipedia would require fine-tuned procedures. This issue seems to be an interesting challenge that could be addressed in further research.

The preparation of adversarial examples is a very prominent concept of modern machine learning research area. It gives the possibility of fast, automated, and massive generation of additional samples. Importantly, injecting the malicious examples into training data may result in more robust and accurate models. GEM designed for controlled text generation can also be applied in various text-driven systems, e.g. conversational agents, text summarizers or style transfer models.

References

Matthew Honnibal and Ines Montani. 2017. spaCy 2: Natural language understanding with Bloom embeddings, convolutional neural networks and incremental parsing. To appear.

VI Levenshtein. 1966. Binary Codes Capable of Correcting Deletions, Insertions and Reversals. *Soviet Physics Doklady*, 10:707.

Yinhan Liu, Myle Ott, Naman Goyal, Jingfei Du, Mandar Joshi, Danqi Chen, Omer Levy, Mike Lewis, Luke Zettlemoyer, and Veselin Stoyanov. 2019. Roberta: A robustly optimized BERT pretraining approach. *CoRR*, abs/1907.11692.

Alec Radford, Jeff Wu, Rewon Child, David Luan, Dario Amodei, and Ilya Sutskever. 2019. Language models are unsupervised multitask learners.

James Thorne and Andreas Vlachos. 2019. Adversarial attacks against fact extraction and verification. *CoRR*, abs/1903.05543.

Ashish Vaswani, Noam Shazeer, Niki Parmar, Jakob Uszkoreit, Llion Jones, Aidan N. Gomez, Lukasz Kaiser, and Illia Polosukhin. 2017. Attention is all you need. *CoRR*, abs/1706.03762.

Zhilin Yang, Zihang Dai, Yiming Yang, Jaime G. Carbonell, Ruslan Salakhutdinov, and Quoc V. Le. 2019. Xlnet: Generalized autoregressive pretraining for language understanding. *CoRR*, abs/1906.08237.

Aligning Multilingual Word Embeddings for Cross-Modal Retrieval Task

Alireza Mohammadshahi
IDIAP Research Inst.
EPFL
alireza.mohammadshahi@epfl.ch

Rémi Lebret
EPFL
remi.lebret@epfl.ch

Karl Aberer
EPFL
karl.aberer@epfl.ch

Abstract

In this paper, we propose a new approach to learn multimodal multilingual embeddings for matching images and their relevant captions in two languages. We combine two existing objective functions to make images and captions close in a joint embedding space while adapting the alignment of word embeddings between existing languages in our model. We show that our approach enables better generalization, achieving state-of-the-art performance in text-to-image and image-to-text retrieval task, and caption-caption similarity task. Two multimodal multilingual datasets are used for evaluation: Multi30k with German and English captions and Microsoft-COCO with English and Japanese captions.

1 Introduction

In recent years, there has been a huge and significant amount of research in text and image retrieval tasks which needs the joint modeling of both modalities. Further, a large number of image-text datasets have become available (Elliott et al., 2016; Hodosh et al., 2013; Young et al., 2014; Lin et al., 2014), and several models have been proposed to generate captions for images in the dataset (Lu et al., 2018; Bernardi et al., 2016; Anderson et al., 2017; Lu et al., 2016; Mao et al., 2014; Rennie et al., 2016). There has been a great amount of research in learning a joint embedding space for texts and images in order to use the model in sentence-based image search or cross-modal retrieval task (Frome et al., 2013; Kiros et al., 2014; Donahue et al., 2014; Lazaridou et al., 2015; Socher et al., 2013; Hodosh et al., 2013; Karpathy et al., 2014).

Previous works in image-caption task and learning a joint embedding space for texts and images are mostly related to English language, however, recently there is a large amount of research in other languages due to the availability of multilingual datasets (Funaki and Nakayama, 2015; Elliott et al., 2016; Rajendran et al., 2015; Miyazaki and Shimizu, 2016; Lucia Specia and Elliott, 2016; Young et al., 2014; Hitschler and Riezler, 2016; Yoshikawa et al., 2017). The aim of these models is to map images and their captions in a single language into a joint embedding space (Rajendran et al., 2015; Calixto et al., 2017).

Related to our work, Gella et al. (2017) proposed a model to learn a multilingual multimodal embedding by utilizing an image as a pivot between languages of captions. While a text encoder is trained for each language in Gella et al. (2017), we propose instead a model that learns a shared and language-independent text encoder between languages, yielding better generalization. It is generally important to adapt word embeddings for the task at hand. Our model enables tuning of word embeddings while keeping the two languages aligned during training, building a task-specific shared embedding space for existing languages.

In this attempt, we define a new objective function that combines a pairwise ranking loss with a loss that maintains the alignment in multiple languages. For the latter, we use the objective function proposed in Joulin et al. (2018) for learning a linear mapping between languages inspired by cross-domain similarity local scaling (CSLS) retrieval criterion (Conneau et al., 2017) which obtains the state-of-the-art performance on word translation task.

In the next sections, the proposed approach is called Aligning Multilingual Embeddings for cross-modal retrieval (AME). With experiments on two multimodal multilingual datasets, we show that AME outperforms existing models on text-image multimodal retrieval tasks. The code we used to train and evaluate the model is available at https://github.com/alirezamshi/AME-CMR

Proceedings of the Second Workshop on Fact Extraction and VERification (FEVER), pages 27–33
Hong Kong, November 3, 2019. ©2019 Association for Computational Linguistics

2 Datasets

We use two multilingual image-caption datasets to evaluate our model, Multi30k and Microsoft COCO (Elliott et al., 2016; Lin et al., 2014).

Multi30K is a dataset with 31'014 German translations of English captions and 155'070 independently collected German and English captions. In this paper, we use independently collected captions which each image contains five German and five English captions. The training set includes 29'000 images. The validation and test sets contain 1'000 images.

MS-COCO (Lin et al., 2014) contains 123'287 images and five English captions per image. Yoshikawa et al. (2017) proposed a model which generates Japanese descriptions for images. We divide the dataset based on Karpathy and Li (2014). The training set contains 113'287 images. Each validation and test set contains 5'000 images.

3 Problem Formulation

3.1 Model for Learning a Multilingual Multimodal Representation

Assume image i and captions c_{X_i} and c_{Y_i} are given in two languages, X and Y respectively. Our aim is to learn a model where the image i and its captions c_{X_i} and c_{Y_i} are close in a joint embedding space of dimension m. AME consists of two encoders f_i and f_c, which encode images and captions. As multilingual text encoder, we use a recurrent neural network with gated recurrent unit (GRU). For the image encoder, we use a convolutional neural network (CNN) architecture. The similarity between a caption c and an image i in the joint embedding space is measured with a similarity function $P(c, i)$. The objective function is as follows (inspired by Gella et al. (2017)):

$$
\begin{aligned}
L_R = \sum_{(c_{S_i}, i)} \Big(&\sum_{c_{S_j}} max\{0, \alpha - P(c_{S_i}, i) + P(c_{S_j}, i)\} \\
&+ \sum_{j} max\{0, \alpha - P(c_{S_i}, i) + P(c_{S_i}, j)\} \Big)
\end{aligned}
\tag{1}
$$

Where S stands for both languages, and α is the margin. c_{S_j} and j are irrelevant caption and image of the gold-standard pair (c_{S_i}, i).

3.2 Alignment Model

Each word k in the language X is defined by a word embedding $x_k \in \mathbb{R}^d$ ($y_k \in \mathbb{R}^d$ in the language Y respectively). Given a bilingual lexicon of N pairs of words, we assume the first n pairs $\{(x_i, y_i)\}_{i=1}^{n}$ are the initial seeds, and our aim is to augment it to all word pairs that are not in the initial lexicons. Mikolov et al. (2013) proposed a model to learn a linear mapping $W \in \mathbb{R}^{d \times d}$ between the source and target languages:

$$
min_{W \in \mathbb{R}^{d \times d}} \frac{1}{n} \sum_{i=1}^{n} \ell(W x_i, y_i | x_i, y_i)
\tag{2}
$$
$$
\ell(W x_i, y_i | x_i, y_i) = (W x_i - y_i)^2
$$

Where ℓ is a square loss. One can find the translation of a source word in the target language by performing a nearest neighbor search with Euclidean distance. But, the model suffers from a "hubness problem": some word embeddings become uncommonly the nearest neighbors of a great number of other words (Doddington et al., 1998; Dinu and Baroni, 2014).

In order to resolve this issue, Joulin et al. (2018) proposed a new objective function inspired by CSLS criterion to learn the linear mapping:

$$
\begin{aligned}
L_A = &\frac{1}{n} \sum_{i=1}^{n} -2x_i^T W^T y_i + \frac{1}{k} \sum_{y_j \in \mathcal{N}_Y(W x_i)} x_i^T W^T y_j \\
&+ \frac{1}{k} \sum_{W x_j \in \mathcal{N}_X(y_i)} x_j^T W^T y_i
\end{aligned}
\tag{3}
$$

Where $\mathcal{N}_X(y_i)$ means the k-nearest neighbors of y_i in the set of source language X. They constrained the linear mapping W to be orthogonal, and word vectors are $l2$-normalized.

The whole loss function is the equally weighted summation of the aforementioned objective functions:

$$
L_{total} = L_R + L_A
\tag{4}
$$

The model architecture is illustrated in Figure 1. We observe that updating the parameters in (3) every T iterations with learning rate lr_{align} obtains the best performance.

We use two different similarity functions, symmetric and asymmetric. For the former, we use the cosine similarity function and for the latter, we use the metric proposed in Vendrov et al. (2015), which encodes the partial order structure of the visual-semantic hierarchy. The metric similarity is defined as:

$$
S(a, b) = -||max(0, b - a)||^2
\tag{5}
$$

Where a and b are the embeddings of image and caption.

	Image to Text				Text to Image				Alignment
	R@1	R@5	R@10	Mr	R@1	R@5	R@10	Mr	
symmetric									
Parallel (Gella et al., 2017)	31.7	62.4	74.1	3	24.7	53.9	65.7	5	-
UVS (Kiros et al., 2014)	23.0	50.7	62.9	5	16.8	42.0	56.5	8	-
EmbeddingNet (Wang et al., 2017)	40.7	69.7	79.2	-	29.2	59.6	71.7	-	-
sm-LSTM (Huang et al., 2016)	42.5	71.9	81.5	2	30.2	60.4	72.3	3	-
VSE++ (Faghri et al., 2017)	**43.7**	71.9	82.1	2	32.3	60.9	72.1	3	-
Mono	41.4	74.2	84.2	2	32.1	63.0	73.9	3	-
FME	39.2	71.1	82.1	2	29.7	62.5	74.1	3	76.81%
AME	43.5	**77.2**	**85.3**	**2**	**34.0**	**64.2**	**75.4**	**3**	66.91%
asymmetric									
Pivot (Gella et al., 2017)	33.8	62.8	75.2	3	26.2	56.4	68.4	4	-
Parallel (Gella et al., 2017)	31.5	61.4	74.7	3	27.1	56.2	66.9	4	-
Mono	47.7	77.1	86.9	2	35.8	66.6	76.8	3	-
FME	44.9	76.9	86.4	2	34.2	66.1	77.1	3	76.81%
AME	**50.5**	**79.7**	**88.4**	**1**	**38.0**	**68.5**	**78.4**	**2**	73.10%

Table 1: Image-caption ranking results for English (Multi30k)

	Image to Text				Text to Image				Alignment
	R@1	R@5	R@10	Mr	R@1	R@5	R@10	Mr	
symmetric									
Parallel (Gella et al., 2017)	28.2	57.7	71.3	4	20.9	46.9	59.3	6	-
Mono	34.2	67.5	79.6	3	26.5	54.7	66.2	4	-
FME	36.8	69.4	80.8	2	26.6	56.2	68.5	4	76.81%
AME	**39.6**	**72.7**	**82.7**	**2**	**28.9**	**58.0**	**68.7**	4	66.91%
asymmetric									
Pivot (Gella et al., 2017)	28.2	61.9	73.4	3	22.5	49.3	61.7	6	-
Parallel (Gella et al., 2017)	30.2	60.4	72.8	3	21.8	50.5	62.3	5	-
Mono	**42.0**	72.5	83.0	2	29.6	58.4	69.6	4	-
FME	40.5	73.3	83.4	2	29.6	59.2	**72.1**	3	76.81%
AME	40.5	**74.3**	**83.4**	**2**	**31.0**	**60.5**	70.6	**3**	73.10%

Table 2: Image-caption ranking results for German (Multi30k)

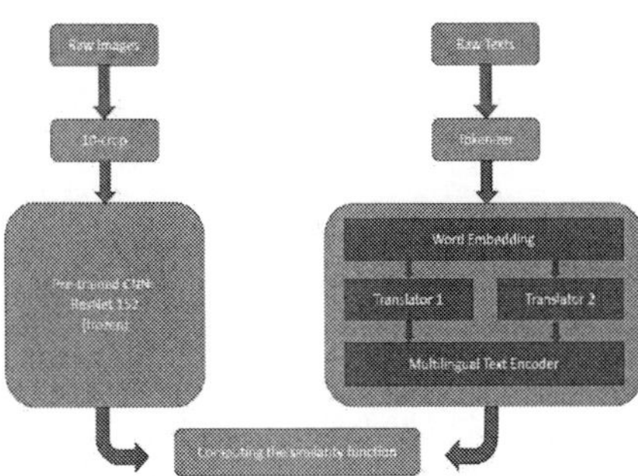

Figure 1: The AME - model architecture

4 Experiment and Results

4.1 Details of Implementation [1]

We use a mini-batch of size 128. We use Adam optimizer with learning rate 0.00011 (0.00006) and with early stopping on the validation set. We set the dimensionality of joint embedding space and the GRU hidden layer to $m = 1024$. We utilize the pre-trained aligned word vectors of FastText for the initial word embeddings. For Japanese word embedding, we use pre-trained word vectors of FastText[2], then align it to the English word embedding with the same hyper-parameters used for MS-COCO. We set the margin $\alpha = 0.2$ and $\alpha = 0.05$ for symmetric and asymmetric similarity functions respectively.

We assign k-nearest neighbors to be 5 (4). We set $T = 500$, and $lr_{align} = 2$ (5). We tokenize English and German captions with Europarl tokenizer (Koehn, 2005). For the Japanese caption, we use Mecab analyzer (Kudo et al., 2004). We train the model for 30 (20) epochs with updating the learning rate (divided by 10) on epoch 15 (10).

To extract features of images, we use a ResNet152 (He et al., 2015) CNN architecture pre-trained on Imagenet and extract the image features from FC7, the penultimate fully connected layer. We use average features from 10-crop of the re-scaled images.

For the metric of alignment, we use bilingual lexicons of Multilingual Unsupervised and Super-

---

[1]In this section, the hyper-parameters in parentheses are related to the model trained on MS-COCO.

[2]Available at https://fasttext.cc/docs/en/ crawl-vectors.html, and https://fasttext. cc/docs/en/aligned-vectors.html.

	Image to Text				Text to Image				
	R@1	R@5	R@10	Mr	R@1	R@5	R@10	Mr	Alignment
symmetric									
UVS (Kiros et al., 2014)	43.4	75.7	85.8	2	31.0	66.7	79.9	3	-
EmbeddingNet (Wang et al., 2017)	50.4	79.3	89.4	-	39.8	75.3	86.6	-	-
sm-LSTM (Huang et al., 2016)	53.2	83.1	91.5	1	40.7	75.8	87.4	2	-
VSE++ (Faghri et al., 2017)	**58.3**	**86.1**	93.3	1	**43.6**	77.6	87.8	2	-
Mono	51.8	84.8	93.5	1	40.0	77.3	89.4	2	-
FME	42.2	76.6	91.1	2	31.2	69.2	83.7	3	92.70%
AME	54.6	85	**94.3**	**1**	42.1	**78.7**	**90.3**	**2**	82.54%
asymmetric									
Mono	53.2	87.0	94.7	1	42.3	78.9	90	2	-
FME	48.3	83.6	93.6	2	37.2	75.4	88.4	2	92.70%
AME	**58.8**	**88.6**	**96.2**	**1**	**46.2**	**82.5**	**91.9**	**2**	84.99%

Table 3: Image-caption ranking results for English (MS-COCO)

	Image to Text				Text to Image				
	R@1	R@5	R@10	Mr	R@1	R@5	R@10	Mr	Alignment
symmetric									
Mono	42.7	77.7	88.5	2	33.1	69.8	84.3	3	-
FME	40.7	77.7	88.3	2	30.0	68.9	83.1	3	92.70%
AME	**50.2**	**85.6**	**93.1**	**1**	**40.2**	**76.7**	**87.8**	**2**	82.54%
asymmetric									
Mono	49.9	83.4	93.7	2	39.7	76.5	88.3	2	-
FME	48.8	81.9	91.9	2	37.0	74.8	87.0	2	92.70%
AME	**55.5**	**87.9**	**95.2**	**1**	**44.9**	**80.7**	**89.3**	**2**	84.99%

Table 4: Image-caption ranking results for Japanese (MS-COCO)

	EN → DE			DE → EN		
	R@1	R@5	R@10	R@1	R@5	R@10
FME	51.4	76.4	84.5	46.9	71.2	79.1
AME	**51.7**	**76.7**	**85.1**	**49.1**	**72.6**	**80.5**

Table 5: Textual similarity scores (asymmetric, Multi30k).

vised Embeddings (MUSE) benchmark (Lample et al., 2017). MUSE is a large-scale high-quality bilingual dictionaries for training and evaluating the translation task. We extract the training words of descriptions in two languages. For training, we combine "full" and "test" sections of MUSE, then filter them to the training words. For evaluation, we filter "train" section of MUSE to the training words. [3]

For evaluating the benefit of the proposed objective function, we compare AME with monolingual training (Mono), and multilingual training without the alignment model described in Section 3.2. For the latter, the pre-aligned word embeddings are frozen during training (FME). We add Mono since the proposed model in Gella et al. (2017) did not utilize pre-trained word embeddings for the initialization, and the image encoder is different (ResNet152 vs. VGG19).

We compare models based on two retrieval metrics, recall at position k (R@k) and Median of ranks (Mr).

4.2 Multi30k Results

In Table 1 and 2, we show the results for English and German captions. For English captions, we see 21.28% improvement on average compared to Kiros et al. (2014). There is a 1.8% boost on average compared to Mono due to more training data and multilingual text encoder. AME performs better than FME model on both symmetric and asymmetric modes, which shows the advantage of fine-tuning word embeddings during training. We have 25.26% boost on average compared to Kiros et al. (2014) in asymmetric mode.

For German descriptions, The results are 11.05% better on average compared to (Gella et al., 2017) in symmetric mode. AME also achieves competitive or better results than FME model in German descriptions too.

4.3 MS-COCO Results[4]

In Table 3 and 4, we show the performance of AME and baselines for English and Japanese captions. We achieve 10.42% improvement on aver-

---

[3] You can find the code for building bilingual lexicons on the Github link.

[4] To compare with baselines, scores are measured by averaging 5 folds of 1K test images.

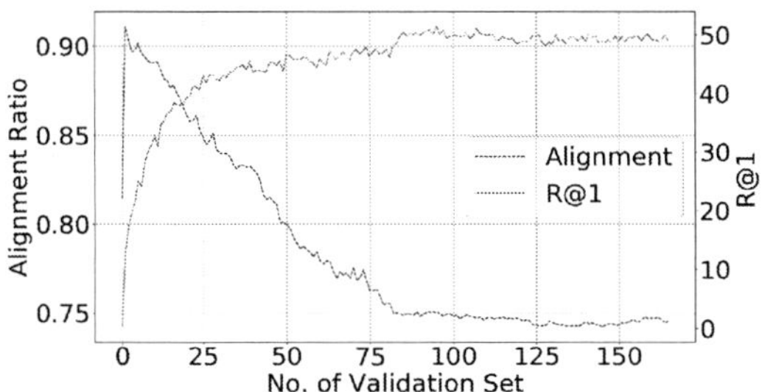

Figure 2: Alignment ratio in each validation step (asymmetric mode - image-to-text - Multi30k dataset)

age compared to Kiros et al. (2014) in the symmetric manner. We show that adapting the word embedding for the task at hand, boosts the general performance, since AME model significantly outperforms FME model in both languages.

For the Japanese captions, AME reaches 6.25% and 3.66% better results on average compared to monolingual model in symmetric and asymmetric modes, respectively.

4.4 Alignment results

In Tables 1 and 2, we can see that the alignment ratio for AME is 6.80% lower than FME which means that the translators can almost keep languages aligned in Multi30k dataset. In MS-COCO dataset, the alignment ratio for AME is 8.93% lower compared to FME.

We compute the alignment ratio and recall at position 1 (R@1) in each validation step. Figure 2 shows the trade-off between alignment and retrieval tasks. At the first few epochs, the model improves the alignment ratio since the retrieval task hasn't seen enough number of instances. Then, the retrieval task tries to fine-tune word embeddings. Finally, they reach an agreement near the half of training process. At this point, we update the learning rate of retrieval task to improve the performance, and the alignment ratio preserves constant.

Additionally, we also train AME model without adding the alignment objective function, and the model breaks the alignment between the initial aligned word embeddings, so it's essential to add the alignment objective function to the retrieval task.

4.5 Caption-Caption Similarity Scores

Given the caption in a language, the task is to retrieve the related caption in another language. In Table 5, we show the performance on Multi30k dataset in asymmetric mode. AME outperforms the FME model, confirming the importance of word embeddings adaptation.

5 Conclusion

We proposed a multimodal model with a shared multilingual text encoder by adapting the alignment between languages for image-description retrieval task while training. We introduced a loss function which is a combination of a pairwise ranking loss and a loss that maintains the alignment of word embeddings in multiple languages. Through experiments with different multimodal multilingual datasets, we have shown that our approach yields better generalization performance on image-to-text and text-to-image retrieval tasks, as well as caption-caption similarity task.

In the future work, we can investigate on applying self-attention models like Transformer (Vaswani et al., 2017) on the shared text encoder to find a more comprehensive representation for descriptions in the dataset. Additionally, we can explore the effect of a weighted summation of two loss functions instead of equally summing them together.

6 Acknowledgement

We gratefully acknowledge the support of NVIDIA Corporation with the donation of the Titan Xp GPU used for this research.

References

Peter Anderson, Xiaodong He, Chris Buehler, Damien Teney, Mark Johnson, Stephen Gould, and Lei Zhang. 2017. Bottom-up and top-down attention for image captioning and VQA. *CoRR*, abs/1707.07998.

Raffaella Bernardi, Ruket Çakici, Desmond Elliott, Aykut Erdem, Erkut Erdem, Nazli Ikizler-Cinbis, Frank Keller, Adrian Muscat, and Barbara Plank. 2016. Automatic description generation from images: A survey of models, datasets, and evaluation measures. *CoRR*, abs/1601.03896.

Iacer Calixto, Qun Liu, and Nick Campbell. 2017. Multilingual multi-modal embeddings for natural language processing. *CoRR*, abs/1702.01101.

Alexis Conneau, Guillaume Lample, Marc'Aurelio Ranzato, Ludovic Denoyer, and Hervé Jégou. 2017. Word translation without parallel data. *CoRR*, abs/1710.04087.

Georgiana Dinu and Marco Baroni. 2014. Improving zero-shot learning by mitigating the hubness problem. *CoRR*, abs/1412.6568.

George Doddington, Walter Liggett, Alvin Martin, Mark Przybocki, and Douglas Reynolds. 1998. Sheep, goats, lambs and wolves a statistical analysis of speaker performance in the nist 1998 speaker recognition evaluation. In *INTERNATIONAL CONFERENCE ON SPOKEN LANGUAGE PROCESSING*.

Jeff Donahue, Lisa Anne Hendricks, Sergio Guadarrama, Marcus Rohrbach, Subhashini Venugopalan, Kate Saenko, and Trevor Darrell. 2014. Long-term recurrent convolutional networks for visual recognition and description. *CoRR*, abs/1411.4389.

Desmond Elliott, Stella Frank, Khalil Sima'an, and Lucia Specia. 2016. Multi30k: Multilingual english-german image descriptions. *CoRR*, abs/1605.00459.

Fartash Faghri, David J. Fleet, Ryan Kiros, and Sanja Fidler. 2017. VSE++: improved visual-semantic embeddings. *CoRR*, abs/1707.05612.

Andrea Frome, Greg S Corrado, Jon Shlens, Samy Bengio, Jeff Dean, Marc Aurelio Ranzato, and Tomas Mikolov. 2013. Devise: A deep visual-semantic embedding model. In C. J. C. Burges, L. Bottou, M. Welling, Z. Ghahramani, and K. Q. Weinberger, editors, *Advances in Neural Information Processing Systems 26*, pages 2121–2129. Curran Associates, Inc.

Ruka Funaki and Hideki Nakayama. 2015. Image-mediated learning for zero-shot cross-lingual document retrieval. In *Proceedings of the 2015 Conference on Empirical Methods in Natural Language Processing*, pages 585–590. Association for Computational Linguistics.

Spandana Gella, Rico Sennrich, Frank Keller, and Mirella Lapata. 2017. Image pivoting for learning multilingual multimodal representations. *CoRR*, abs/1707.07601.

Kaiming He, Xiangyu Zhang, Shaoqing Ren, and Jian Sun. 2015. Deep residual learning for image recognition. *CoRR*, abs/1512.03385.

Julian Hitschler and Stefan Riezler. 2016. Multimodal pivots for image caption translation. *CoRR*, abs/1601.03916.

Micah Hodosh, Peter Young, and Julia Hockenmaier. 2013. Framing image description as a ranking task: Data, models and evaluation metrics. In *J. Artif. Intell. Res.*

Yan Huang, Wei Wang, and Liang Wang. 2016. Instance-aware image and sentence matching with selective multimodal LSTM. *CoRR*, abs/1611.05588.

Armand Joulin, Piotr Bojanowski, Tomas Mikolov, Hervé Jégou, and Edouard Grave. 2018. Loss in translation: Learning bilingual word mapping with a retrieval criterion. In *Proceedings of the 2018 Conference on Empirical Methods in Natural Language Processing*.

Andrej Karpathy, Armand Joulin, and Li F Fei-Fei. 2014. Deep fragment embeddings for bidirectional image sentence mapping. In Z. Ghahramani, M. Welling, C. Cortes, N. D. Lawrence, and K. Q. Weinberger, editors, *Advances in Neural Information Processing Systems 27*, pages 1889–1897. Curran Associates, Inc.

Andrej Karpathy and Fei-Fei Li. 2014. Deep visual-semantic alignments for generating image descriptions. *CoRR*, abs/1412.2306.

Ryan Kiros, Ruslan Salakhutdinov, and Richard S. Zemel. 2014. Unifying visual-semantic embeddings with multimodal neural language models. *CoRR*, abs/1411.2539.

Philipp Koehn. 2005. Europarl: A Parallel Corpus for Statistical Machine Translation. In *Conference Proceedings: the tenth Machine Translation Summit*, pages 79–86, Phuket, Thailand. AAMT, AAMT.

Taku Kudo, Kaoru Yamamoto, and Yuji Matsumoto. 2004. Applying conditional random fields to japanese morphological analysis. In *In Proc. of EMNLP*, pages 230–237.

Guillaume Lample, Ludovic Denoyer, and Marc'Aurelio Ranzato. 2017. Unsupervised machine translation using monolingual corpora only. *CoRR*, abs/1711.00043.

Angeliki Lazaridou, Nghia The Pham, and Marco Baroni. 2015. Combining language and vision with a multimodal skip-gram model. *CoRR*, abs/1501.02598.

Tsung-Yi Lin, Michael Maire, Serge J. Belongie, Lubomir D. Bourdev, Ross B. Girshick, James Hays, Pietro Perona, Deva Ramanan, Piotr Dollár, and C. Lawrence Zitnick. 2014. Microsoft COCO: common objects in context. *CoRR*, abs/1405.0312.

Jiasen Lu, Caiming Xiong, Devi Parikh, and Richard Socher. 2016. Knowing when to look: Adaptive attention via A visual sentinel for image captioning. *CoRR*, abs/1612.01887.

Jiasen Lu, Jianwei Yang, Dhruv Batra, and Devi Parikh. 2018. Neural baby talk. *CoRR*, abs/1803.09845.

Khalil Simaan Lucia Specia, Stella Frank and Desmond Elliott. 2016. A shared task on multimodal machine translation and cross-lingual image description.

Junhua Mao, Wei Xu, Yi Yang, Jiang Wang, and Alan L. Yuille. 2014. Deep captioning with multimodal recurrent neural networks (m-rnn). *CoRR*, abs/1412.6632.

Tomas Mikolov, Quoc V. Le, and Ilya Sutskever. 2013. Exploiting similarities among languages for machine translation. *CoRR*, abs/1309.4168.

Takashi Miyazaki and Nobuyuki Shimizu. 2016. Cross-lingual image caption generation. In *Proceedings of the 54th Annual Meeting of the Association for Computational Linguistics (Volume 1: Long Papers)*, pages 1780–1790. Association for Computational Linguistics.

Janarthanan Rajendran, Mitesh M. Khapra, Sarath Chandar, and Balaraman Ravindran. 2015. Bridge correlational neural networks for multilingual multimodal representation learning. *CoRR*, abs/1510.03519.

Steven J. Rennie, Etienne Marcheret, Youssef Mroueh, Jarret Ross, and Vaibhava Goel. 2016. Self-critical sequence training for image captioning. *CoRR*, abs/1612.00563.

Richard Socher, Andrej Karpathy, Quoc V. Le, Chris D. Manning, and Andrew Y. Ng. 2013. Grounded compositional semantics for finding and describing images with sentences. *Transactions of the Association for Computational Linguistics*.

Ashish Vaswani, Noam Shazeer, Niki Parmar, Jakob Uszkoreit, Llion Jones, Aidan N. Gomez, Lukasz Kaiser, and Illia Polosukhin. 2017. Attention is all you need.

Ivan Vendrov, Ryan Kiros, Sanja Fidler, and Raquel Urtasun. 2015. Order-embeddings of images and language. *CoRR*, abs/1511.06361.

Liwei Wang, Yin Li, and Svetlana Lazebnik. 2017. Learning two-branch neural networks for image-text matching tasks. *CoRR*, abs/1704.03470.

Yuya Yoshikawa, Yutaro Shigeto, and Akikazu Takeuchi. 2017. STAIR captions: Constructing a large-scale japanese image caption dataset. *CoRR*, abs/1705.00823.

Peter Young, Alice Lai, Micah Hodosh, and Julia Hockenmaier. 2014. From image descriptions to visual denotations. *Transactions of the Association for Computational Linguistics*, 2:67–78.

Unsupervised Natural Question Answering with a Small Model

Martin Andrews
Red Dragon AI
Singapore
`martin@reddragon.ai`

Sam Witteveen
Red Dragon AI
Singapore
`sam@reddragon.ai`

Abstract

The recent demonstration of the power of huge language models such as GPT-2 to memorise the answers to factoid questions raises questions about the extent to which knowledge is being embedded directly within these large models. This short paper describes an architecture through which much smaller models can also answer such questions - by making use of 'raw' external knowledge. The contribution of this work is that the methods presented here rely on unsupervised learning techniques, complementing the unsupervised training of the Language Model. The goal of this line of research is to be able to add knowledge explicitly, without extensive training.

1 Introduction

The field of question answering has been dominated by supervised methods for competitive tasks such as the Stanford question answering dataset (SQuAD) (Rajpurkar et al., 2016). However, as discussed in Yogatama et al. (2019), some of these datasets are becoming over-optimised for, making the architectures less generally applicable.

At the other extreme, the ability of the GPT-2 (Radford et al., 2019) model to answer factoid questions, based purely on unsupervised training directed at improving its Language Model (LM) performance, was striking. But further reflection highlights the following issues :

- Questions correctly (and confidently) answered were a small fraction ($\sim$1%) of the questions asked

- Huge model size and long training periods were required before such behaviour was manifested

- This does not appear to be a practical approach to adsorbing an extensive knowledge-base

This work describes early work in aiding generalised models such as GPT-2 to answer questions, without having to embed facts directly in the model's weights. The overall direction of work is towards encouraging such generalised models to make use of external datasources (and other resources) without having to internalise all the data in models of exponentially increasing size (e.g. GPT-2-1.5B is more than 10x the size of GPT-2-117M).

2 Natural Questions Dataset

The Natural Questions (NQ) dataset (Kwiatkowski et al., 2019) is a question answering dataset containing 307,373 training examples, 7,830 development examples, and 7,842 test examples. Each example is comprised of a google.com query and a corresponding Wikipedia page. Each Wikipedia page has a passage (or long answer) annotated on the page that answers the question and one or more short spans from the annotated passage containing the actual answer. The long and the short answer annotations can however be empty. If they are both empty, then there is no answer on the page at all. If the long answer annotation is non-empty, but the short answer annotation is empty, then the annotated passage answers the question but no explicit short answer could be found. Finally, 1% of the documents have a passage annotated with a short answer that is 'yes' or 'no', instead of a list of short spans.

As reported in Radford et al. (2019), GPT-2-1.5B answers 4.1% of NQ questions correctly when evaluated by the exact match metric commonly used on reading comprehension datasets like SQuAD. In contrast, the smallest GPT-2-117M model (used as the basis for the model proposed in this work) is reported as not being capa-

Proceedings of the Second Workshop on Fact Extraction and VERification (FEVER), pages 34–38
Hong Kong, November 3, 2019. ©2019 Association for Computational Linguistics

ble of exceeding the 1.0% accuracy of the simple baseline which returns the most common answer for each question type (who, what, where, etc...). The fact that GPT-2-1.5B answered 5.3 times more questions correctly suggests that model capacity has been a major factor in the poor performance of neural systems on this kind of task as of yet.

3 Model Architecture

The model proposed here is built from several components which include (a) 876k Wikipedia sentences, addressible via embeddings; (b) a pretrained GPT-2-117M language model which was noted to be incapable of answering questions successfully in Radford et al. (2019); and (c) a scheme for incorporating 'sentence hints' into the language generation context.

3.1 Embeddings for Sentence Lookup

Three different embedding methods were used :

(i) pre-trained BERT-base (L=12, H=768, A=12, Total Parameters=110M) (Devlin et al., 2018), using the the $bert - as - service$ Python tool[1]. For a given input sentence this returns a 768-d embedding, calculated as the GlobalAveragePooling of the top-but-one layer of the pretrained BERT model;

(ii) Smooth Inverse Frequency (SIF) (Arora et al., 2017) embeddings, calculated by inverse-frequency weighting the BPE embeddings (from the GPE-2-117M model being used for the text generation task) followed by removal of the first PCA component; and

(iii) Universal Sentence Encoder (Cer et al., 2018), the training details not clear in the paper, but USE is not a purely unsupervised model : "We augment unsupervised learning with training on supervised data from the Stanford Natural Language Inference (SNLI) corpus" (Bowman et al., 2015).

Methods (i) and (ii) were not fine-tuned on the question answering task (since this would violate the spirit of this unsupervised-only system), whereas method (iii) was included to judge the benefits of adding some supervised training to the embedding stage.

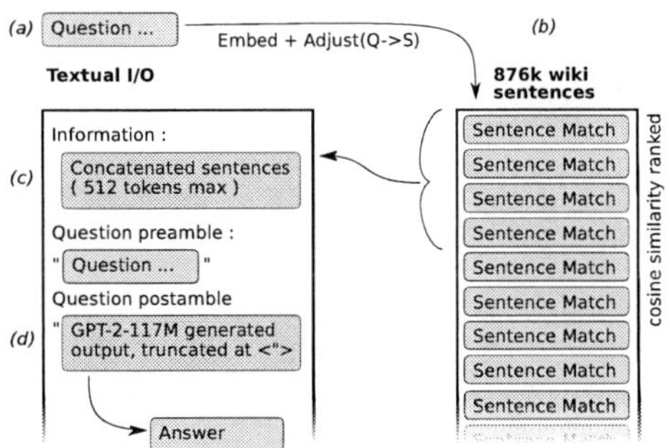

Figure 1: Proposed information flow : (a) Initial question; (b) Wiki sentence ranking; (c) hinting in preamble; (d) GPT2 output.

3.2 Embeddings for Questions

In order that facts might be supplied by external text, embeddings $e(s_n)$ were produced for each sentence s_n of the $N(= 876,645)$ wikitext sentences, and also $e(q_j)$ was calculated for each q_j of the J questions.

The search term was calculated by adding a 'question to sentence' vector, set to the mean difference between the embeddings for question phrases and those of wikitext sentences to the original question q_j :

$$search_j = e(q_j) + \frac{1}{N} \sum e(s.) - \frac{1}{J} \sum e(q.)$$

3.3 Knowledge Look-up

In order to aid the LM in retrieving factoid answers, 'hint sentences' sufficient to fill half of the LM context window were retrieved from the list of the N wikitext sentences, using a cosine distance ranking of the s_n vs $search_j$

3.4 LM Context Seeding

In order to obtain the results in Radford et al. (2019) for the NQ task, their GPT-2-1.5B model context was seeded with example question/answer pairs which helped the model infer the short answer style of the dataset.

Rather than expect the smaller GPT model to extrapolate from the Q & A format, both the 'hint sentences' and the question q_i were incorporated into the context seen by the model directly:

Information :

HintSentence[ ] *or* None

The best short answer to "q_i?" from the information above is " ...

---

[1]https://bert-as-service.readthedocs.io/

Table 1: Sample question answers with filter examples, and examples of answers where pure SQuAD accuracy did not make sense when the base data included far more information than the original (single) wiki article targetted by the Natural Questions dataset.

Question	Target	GPT-2-117M	Reject reason
Who is the richest club in the championship?	'Aston Villa', 'Manchester City'	The richest club in the championship	SMART ALEC
Are all firestone tires made in the usa?	'NO'	No	Y/N QUESTION
What is the name of manchester united stadium?	'Old Trafford'	Manchester United	WITHIN QUESTION
Who cracked the enigma code in world war 2?	'Turing'	Alan Turing	N/A : ACCEPTED
How many inches is the iphone 5s screen?	'4 - inch screen size', '4 in', '4 in (10 cm)'	4 inches	N/A : ACCEPTED

The GPT-2-117M output is then recorded up until the closing double-quote (closing quotes appears to be strongly favoured by the LM).

3.5 Sampling from the Language Model

A number of approaches to sampling from the model were tried (including Beam search, which performed poorly), and the following were found to work satisfactorially :

1. SoftMax temperature was kept at 1.0 (i.e. as trained);

2. Nucleus Sampling (Holtzman et al., 2019) was used, with only tokens that cover the first 90% of probability space being considered as choices at each step. This appears to give a good mix of diversity without 'going off the rails' - which is desirable for human-like communication (Grice, 1975);

3. A probability bias term (Murray and Chiang, 2018) was added to the log-probabilities of each sequence, whereby each token was 'awarded' a bonus of α, which was found empirically to create a more balanced spread of long and short outputs;

4. After a sorted list of 100 different sequences was created, this was further filtered (as illustrated in Table 1) to reject answers that were very unlikely to be correct:

   - answers that simply repeat the question (determined as whether the answer's bigram Jaccard similarity with the question exceeds 0.5);
   - answers that are contained within the question verbatim;
   - answers such as 'yes/no', 'i don't know', 'none', 'no one', 'it depends' - which may have been safe choices, but could not score positively on the filtered list of questions.

Further details can be found in the Supplimental Materials.

4 Experiments

The model architecture was applied to the NQ task, and results are reported for performance on the validation set (the training set was unused). Only questions that were (a) not Yes/No; and (b) had a 'short answer' were considered, resulting in 3975 triples of {question, wikitext, answer list}.

The list of 'hint sentence' candidates was set to be the aggregate of all the sentences across the 3975 wikitext pages, totalling ∼876k sentences. Importantly, the hint sentence choices weren't restricted to the wikitext corresponding to the specific question - which makes the task significantly more difficult that the BERT baseline for Natural Questions task (Alberti et al., 2019), which works on an article-by-article basis.

In the results reported, to reduce noise, the 'Yes/No' questions were removed from consideration (since scoring positively on these examples may the result of a coin-flip).

5 Results

This work is in its early stages, and the results obtained so far are encouraging, despite being low in number.

For the 3975 useful NQ development set questions, we found that the poor results of using GPT-2-117M unaided reported in Radford et al. (2019) were born out.

However, when using each question to select 'hint sentences' from the whole list of 876k wikitext sentences, the GPT-2-117M was able to make use of the extra information (without having been explicitly training to do so).

Table 2: Question answering accuracy.

EMBEDDING	DIM	α	SCORE
NO HINTS	-	0.0	0.84%
BERT-REST	768	0.0	1.08%
SIF	768	0.7	3.14%
SIF	768	0.2	3.29%
USE	512	0.0	4.45%

Note that the results in Table 2 are not directly comparable with the reported accuracy of the 1.5 billion parameter GPT-2-1.5B (4.1%), since the "Yes/No" questions have been deliberately excluded in the experimental results above, since random chance would then add approximately 1.8% (of pure noise) to the results presented here. Adjusting the reported GPT-2 figures (downward) for this effect shows that the proposed model has higher performance for a much lower parameter count, even when using purely unsupervised training methods.

6   Discussion

As mentioned in Sutskever (2019), an online video in which Radford et al. (2017) is discussed, 'higher order' capabilities seem to appear in language-related models only if the size of the model is sufficient to have captured many the basic features of the underlying language, since knowing the basic words and structures is more important to a Language Modeling objective than higher order features like sentiment and story arc (for instance).

Being able to capture such higher order features provides a natural incentive to want to scale the training of language models to as large a number of parameters as possible. And undoubtedly there will be important and interesting results to come out of these efforts.

However, it is not at all clear that embedding factoids in neural network weights is a practical way of building intelligent systems. Even humans (built on a biological neural substrate) seem to reason about facts symbolically *despite* the processing being based in neurons.

The goal of this research is to explore how to interface the extremely effective aspects of models such as GPT-2 with more accessible sources of knowledge and planning.

By using the *human readable* output of a Language Model component to direct further information gathering (or, potentially, other activities), one might imagine the system would not only become more capable (without exponentially long training), but would also have an *internal dialogue* that would be human interpretable.

6.1   Further Work

Clearly, more experimentation is needed to understand how to improve the current system. Fortunately, that can be accomplished without a huge investment in hardware.

In terms of sentence embedding techniques, one additional method was investigated, so far without encouraging results : the generation of sentence embeddings from using an additional layer for the GPT-2-117M model it its initially untrained state. This deserves further work, given the findings of Wieting and Kiela (2019).

Also interesting is the potential for training a more specific retrieval/utilisation engine in a supervised manner, such as in Bapna and Firat (2019), and then expanding the domain across which retrieval is performed to encompass a much broader range of accessible facts without further training the model. However, this is slightly contrary to the goal herein of using purely unsupervised techniques.

Beyond these initial phases, though, there is the potential for the system to achieve some level of self-improvement. As was discussed in Radford et al. (2019), the GPT-2-1.5B model could not only answer some factoid questions, but it also had a good (self-) model of confidence in its answers[2]. This implies that if a trainable embedding component were included in *this* paper's architecture it might be trainable (in a fully self-supervised way) to improve its self-hinting, and thereby achieve a self-improving positive feedback loop.

Acknowledgments

The authors would like to thank Google for access to the TFRC TPU program which was used in training and fine-tuning models during experimentation for this paper.

References

Chris Alberti, Kenton Lee, and Michael Collins. 2019. A BERT baseline for the Natural Questions. *Computing Research Repository*, arXiv:1901.08634.

---

[2] "The probability GPT-2 assigns to its generated answers is well calibrated and GPT-2 has an accuracy of 63.1% on the 1% of questions it is most confident in."

Sanjeev Arora, Yingyu Liang, and Tengyu Ma. 2017. A simple but tough-to-beat baseline for sentence embeddings. In *International Conference on Learning Representations*.

Ankur Bapna and Orhan Firat. 2019. Non-parametric adaptation for neural machine translation. *Proceedings of the 2019 Conference of the North*.

Samuel R. Bowman, Gabor Angeli, Christopher Potts, and Christopher D. Manning. 2015. A large annotated corpus for learning natural language inference. In *Proceedings of the 2015 Conference on Empirical Methods in Natural Language Processing (EMNLP)*. Association for Computational Linguistics.

Daniel Cer, Yinfei Yang, Sheng yi Kong, Nan Hua, Nicole Limtiaco, Rhomni St. John, Noah Constant, Mario Guajardo-Cespedes, Steve Yuan, Chris Tar, Yun-Hsuan Sung, Brian Strope, and Ray Kurzweil. 2018. Universal sentence encoder. *Computing Research Repository*, arXiv:1803.11175.

Jacob Devlin, Ming-Wei Chang, Kenton Lee, and Kristina Toutanova. 2018. BERT: Pre-training of deep bidirectional transformers for language understanding. *Computing Research Repository*, arXiv:1810.04805.

H Paul Grice. 1975. Logic and conversation. In Peter Cole and Jerry L. Morgan, editors, *Syntax and Semantics, Vol. 3, Speech Acts*. Academic Press, New York.

Ari Holtzman, Jan Buys, Maxwell Forbes, and Yejin Choi. 2019. The curious case of neural text degeneration. *Computing Research Repository*, arXiv:1904.09751.

Tom Kwiatkowski, Jennimaria Palomaki, Olivia Redfield, Michael Collins, Ankur Parikh, Chris Alberti, Danielle Epstein, Illia Polosukhin, Matthew Kelcey, Jacob Devlin, Kenton Lee, Kristina N. Toutanova, Llion Jones, Ming-Wei Chang, Andrew Dai, Jakob Uszkoreit, Quoc Le, and Slav Petrov. 2019. Natural Questions: a benchmark for question answering research. *Transactions of the Association of Computational Linguistics*.

Kenton Murray and David Chiang. 2018. Correcting length bias in neural machine translation.

Alec Radford, Rafal Jozefowicz, and Ilya Sutskever. 2017. Learning to generate reviews and discovering sentiment. *Computing Research Repository*, arXiv:1704.01444.

Alec Radford, Jeff Wu, Rewon Child, David Luan, Dario Amodei, and Ilya Sutskever. 2019. Language models are unsupervised multitask learners.

Pranav Rajpurkar, Jian Zhang, Konstantin Lopyrev, and Percy Liang. 2016. SQuAD: 100,000+ questions for machine comprehension of text. *arXiv preprint arXiv:1606.05250*.

Ilya Sutskever. 2019. Deep unsupervised learning.

John Wieting and Douwe Kiela. 2019. No training required: Exploring random encoders for sentence classification. *Computing Research Repository*, arXiv:1901.10444.

Dani Yogatama, Cyprien de Masson d'Autume, Jerome Connor, Tomas Kocisky, Mike Chrzanowski, Lingpeng Kong, Angeliki Lazaridou, Wang Ling, Lei Yu, Chris Dyer, et al. 2019. Learning and evaluating general linguistic intelligence. *arXiv preprint arXiv:1901.11373*.

Knowledge Graph Construction from Unstructured Text
with Applications to Fact Verification and Beyond

Ryan Clancy, Ihab F. Ilyas, and **Jimmy Lin**
David R. Cheriton School of Computer Science
University of Waterloo

Abstract

We present a scalable, open-source platform that "distills" a potentially large text collection into a knowledge graph. Our platform takes documents stored in Apache Solr and scales out the Stanford CoreNLP toolkit via Apache Spark integration to extract mentions and relations that are then ingested into the Neo4j graph database. The raw knowledge graph is then enriched with facts extracted from an external knowledge graph. The complete product can be manipulated by various applications using Neo4j's native Cypher query language: We present a subgraph-matching approach to align extracted relations with external facts and show that fact verification, locating textual support for asserted facts, detecting inconsistent and missing facts, and extracting distantly-supervised training data can all be performed within the same framework.

1 Introduction

Despite plenty of work on relation extraction, entity linking, and related technologies, there is surprisingly no scalable, open-source platform that performs end-to-end knowledge graph construction, taking as input a large text collection to "distill" a knowledge graph from it. Many enterprises today desire exactly such a system to integrate analytics over unstructured text with analytics over relational as well as semi-structured data. We are aware of a few commercial solutions for analyzing unstructured text, such as Amazon Comprehend and Refinitiv by Thomson Reuters, as well as many organizations with large internal efforts, most notably Bloomberg. However, there does not appear to be comparable open-source solutions.

This gap can be attributed, at least in part, to the fact that NLP researchers typically think about extraction in terms of sentences (or documents) and may not be interested in the engineering efforts required to scale out extraction to hundreds of thousands (or even millions) of documents. Furthermore, they are less likely equipped with the expertise (or interest) necessary to build distributed, scalable systems.

We share with the community an open-source platform for scalable, end-to-end knowledge graph construction from unstructured text called dstlr. By "end-to-end" we mean a solution that aspires to cover all aspect of the data management lifecycle: from document ingestion to relation extraction to graph management to knowledge curation to supporting downstream applications, plus integration with other systems in an enterprise's "data lake". Although other researchers have proposed solutions to knowledge graph construction (Augenstein et al., 2012; Kertkeidkachorn and Ichise, 2017), they do not appear to make open-source software artifacts available for download and evaluation.

At a high level, dstlr takes unstructured text and "distills" from it a usable knowledge graph. From a corpus stored in Apache Solr, a raw knowledge graph is populated using Stanford CoreNLP and ingested into the popular Neo4j graph database. This raw knowledge graph is further enriched with facts from an external knowledge graph, in our case, Wikidata (Vrandečić and Krötzsch, 2014). The final product can be manipulated via the declarative Cypher query language. All computations are orchestrated using Apache Spark for horizontal scaling.

On top of our platform, it is possible to build a number of applications, for example, to support business intelligence, knowledge discovery, and semantic search. In this paper, we describe an approach to align extracted relations from the corpus with external facts. We show that fact verification, locating textual support for asserted facts, detecting inconsistent and missing facts, and ex-

Proceedings of the Second Workshop on Fact Extraction and VERification (FEVER), pages 39–46
Hong Kong, November 3, 2019. ©2019 Association for Computational Linguistics

tracting distantly-supervised training data can all be formulated in terms of graph queries. As a case study, we extract and subsequently manipulate approximately 100 million triples from nearly 600K Washington Post articles on a modest cluster.

The contribution of this work is the creation of an end-to-end platform for constructing knowledge graphs from unstructured text "with minimal fuss" via the integration of four mature technologies: Apache Solr, Stanford CoreNLP, Apache Spark, and Neo4j. We demonstrate the potential of such a platform and are pleased to share our open-source project with the community.

2 Problem Formulation

We begin with a more precise formulation of the problem at hand. Given a (potentially large) collection of text documents, we wish to extract facts comprising what we call *mentions* (spans of natural language text such as named entities) and relations between them. We further assume the existence of an external knowledge graph which provides a "ground-truth" inventory of entities, and central to our task is linking *mentions* to these entities. The distinction between mentions and entities is crucial to our problem formulation, as mentions are simply spans of text that exhibit a wide range of linguistic phenomena (synonymy, polysemy, etc.), but entities are unique and have clear real-world referents. More formally:

- Documents contain zero or more mentions.

- In each document, there are zero or more relations between mentions. Mentions can participate in an arbitrary number of relations.

- Each mention has zero or exactly one link to an entity in the external knowledge graph.

- Entities participate in an arbitrary number of facts in the external knowledge graph.

The usage scenario we have in mind is the construction of enterprise-centric knowledge graphs. Most large organizations today already have internal knowledge graphs (or ongoing efforts to build them); the simplest example might be a machine-readable product catalog with product specifications. Our goal is to provide a "360-degree view" of unstructured text in an organization's "data lake"; although similar capabilities already exist for relational and semi-structured (e.g., log)

data, unstructured free text remains vastly underexplored. As we show, it is exactly this interplay between relations extracted from unstructured text and facts in the external knowledge graph that give rise to interesting applications in fact verification and related tasks. Currently, we use Wikidata as a stand-in, as our platform is designed to be enterprise and domain agnostic.

Of course, relation extraction and complementary tasks such as entity linking, coreference resolution, predicate mapping, etc. have been studied for decades. Notable efforts include the Knowledge Base Population (KBP) and Knowledge Base Acceleration (KBA) tasks in the Text Analysis Conference (TAC) series (Ji and Grishman, 2011; Getman et al., 2018), NELL (Never-Ending Language Learning) (Mitchell et al., 2015), open information extractors such as Ollie (Mausam et al., 2012), and approaches based on weak supervision such as Snorkel (Ratner et al., 2017). Our focus, however, is very different as we wish to build an end-to-end platform that not only supports extraction, but the entire data management lifecycle, as discussed in the introduction. Part of this effort is the development of various applications that exploit knowledge graphs (for example, fact verification). In this sense, our work is complementary to all these abovementioned systems and techniques, as the dstlr platform is sufficiently general to incorporate their extraction results.

3 System Overview

The overall architecture of our open-source dstlr[1] platform is shown in Figure 1. We assume the existence of a document store that holds the document collection we wish to "distill". Currently, we use Apache Solr for this role, although a good alternative would be Elasticsearch (which we are currently implementing support for).

The rationale for depending on a document store, as opposed to simply reading documents from a file system (e.g., one designed for distributed storage such as the Hadoop Distributed File System) are many: First, it is likely that users and applications of dstlr desire full-text and metadata search capabilities. A system like Solr readily provides an "industrial strength" solution. Second, a document store provides more refined mechanisms for managing incremental data ingestion, e.g., the periodic arrival of a new batch of docu-

---

[1] http://dstlr.ai/

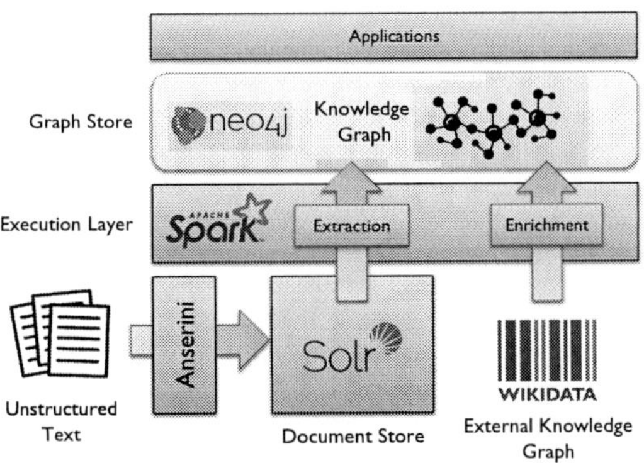

Figure 1: The overall architecture of the dstlr platform. Documents are "distilled" into a raw knowledge graph in the extraction phase, which is then enriched with facts from an external knowledge graph. Spark orchestrates execution in a horizontally scalable manner. Neo4j holds the knowledge graph, which supports applications via its query interface.

ments. Third, the integration of search capabilities with a document store allows dstlr to focus analyses on subsets of documents, as demonstrated in Clancy et al. (2019b). For convenience, our open-source search toolkit Anserini (Yang et al., 2018) provides a number of connectors for ingesting document collections into Solr (Clancy et al., 2019a), under different index architectures.

The execution layer, which relies on Apache Spark, coordinates the two major phases of knowledge graph construction: *extraction* and *enrichment*. The knowledge graph is held in the popular graph database Neo4j. Applications built on top of the dstlr platform take advantage of a declarative query language called Cypher to manipulate the contents of the knowledge graph.

The extraction phase is responsible for populating the raw knowledge graph with mentions, entities, and relations identified from unstructured text. Currently, we use Stanford's CoreNLP toolkit (Manning et al., 2014) for the JVM due to its support for many common language analysis tasks (i.e., tokenization, part-of-speech tagging, named entity recognition, etc.) that can be chained together in a pipeline. While dstlr is extractor agnostic and we have explored a number of different systems, we have found CoreNLP to be the most straightforward package to deploy from an engineering perspective. One of the contributions of our platform is the infrastructure to scale out the CoreNLP toolkit using Spark to process large document collections in an scalable manner.

At a high level, annotator output is converted into tuples (as part of Spark DataFrames) that are then ingested into the knowledge graph.

In the enrichment phase, we extract entities from the external knowledge graph (Wikidata) that are found in the unstructured text, thereby enriching the raw knowledge graph with high-quality facts from an external source. We perform this filtering step because, typically, only a portion of entities in an external source like Wikidata are referenced in a corpus; thus, for query and storage efficiency, it makes sense to only enrich entities that are mentioned in the source documents.

In what follows, we provide more details about the extraction and enrichment phases.

3.1 Extraction

For each document in the collection, we extract mentions of named entities, the relations between them, and links to entities in an external knowledge graph. Through Solr/Spark integration, extraction can be performed on all documents in the document store, or a subset that a user or an application may wish to focus on, for example, containing a particular metadata facet or the results of a keyword query (Clancy et al., 2019b).

Named Entity Extraction. We use CoreNLP's `NERClassifierCombiner` annotator to extract entity mentions of 20 different types, such as persons, organizations, locations, etc. (Finkel et al., 2005). Each mention corresponds to a row in a Spark DataFrame that contains the document id, a mention id, and a list of key–value pairs containing the mention class, mention text, and character offsets of the mention in the source document. Subsequent occurrences of the same mention in the same document are mapped to an existing mention so that character offsets can later be consolidated into an array. In this manner, we retain accurate provenance that allows us to trace back an extracted mention to its source.

Relation Extraction. CoreNLP provides two different annotators for relation extraction: the Open Information Extraction (OpenIE) annotator (Angeli et al., 2015) and the Knowledge Base Population (KBP) annotator (Surdeanu et al., 2012). The OpenIE annotator provides open-class relations based on the provided text while the KBP annotator fills slots for a fixed set of 45 relations, such as `org:city_of_headquarters`. We use the latter, as it is more appropriate for our task. As with the entities, each extracted relation corresponds to a row in a Spark DataFrame with the document id, the subject mention, the relation, the object mention, and a confidence score.

Entity Linking. In the final extraction step, we use CoreNLP's `WikidictAnnotator` to link mentions to their corresponding Wikipedia entity, which in turn allows us to map to Wikidata entities. For each entity mention, we produce a row in a Spark DataFrame that contains the document id, the mention id, and the URI of the most likely entity link. If a linked entity for a mention cannot be found, the row will contain a `null`; we made the design decision to explicitly record these cases. Note that this important step establishes correspondences between information extracted from a document and the external knowledge graph, and is critical to enabling the host of applications that we discuss later.

Pulling everything together, consider the sample sentence "Facebook is an American social media and social networking company based in Menlo Park" from document `b2c9a`. The dstlr extraction pipeline might discover the mentions "Facebook" and "Menlo Park" with a `has_hq` relation between them. Furthermore, "Facebook" is linked to the entity Q355 in Wikidata. This translates into the following knowledge graph fragment, in terms of (subject, relation, object) triples, simplified for illustrative purposes:

> (`b2c9a`, `mentions`, "Facebook")
> (`b2c9a`, `mentions`, "Menlo Park")
> ("Facebook", `subject_of`, `has_hq`)
> (`has_hq`, `object_of`, "Menlo Park")
> ("Facebook", `links_to`, Q355)

The relation itself is reified into a node to facilitate efficient querying by consumers of the knowledge graph (more details later). Following the extraction of all entity mentions, relations, and entity links as described above, the resulting rows from the Spark DataFrames are bulk-loaded into Neo4j according to the "schema" above. While it is entirely possible to construct the raw knowledge graph incrementally, we have found it to be far more efficient to perform ingestion in bulk.

3.2 Enrichment

In the enrichment phase, we augment the raw knowledge graph with facts from the external knowledge graph (Wikidata). This is accomplished by first manually defining a mapping from CoreNLP relations to Wikidata properties. For example, the "headquarters" relation from CoreNLP most closely corresponds to P159 in Wikidata.[2] Since there are only 45 relations, this did not require much effort. Then, for each distinct entity that was discovered in the document collection, we extracted the corresponding facts from Wikidata. This process, in essence, extracts subgraph fragments around referenced entities to enrich the raw knowledge graph. Currently, we only perform the augmentation with relations that are covered by CoreNLP and referenced entities in the unstructured text, but we could easily scale up (or down) the enrichment effort by "pulling in" more (or less) of Wikidata, depending on the needs of various applications. For fact verification and the related tasks that we explore in this paper, the parts of Wikidata that do not overlap with the raw knowledge graph are not needed.

As with extraction, execution of the enrichment process is coordinated by Spark via the manipulation of DataFrames. With Spark, it is easy to identify the distinct entities referenced in the corpus, which are then fed as input into the enrichment process to "pull out" the appropriate parts of Wikidata. For each entity in the corpus, we produce a row in a Spark DataFrame containing the entity URI, the relation type, and its value. These are then bulk-loaded into Neo4j; once again, this is done primarily for efficiency, just as with the extraction output.

In our running example about Facebook, this would lead to the insertion of the following triple in the graph (once again, slightly simplified):

> (Q355, `links_to`, FACT$_{34a8d}$)

where FACT$_{34a8d}$ is a node that has type `has_hq` and value "Menlo Park". Facts from Wikidata are factored according to this "schema" to facilitate efficient querying (more details below).

4 Performance Evaluation

To demonstrate the scalability of our dstlr platform, we describe an evaluation comprising both extraction and enrichment performed on a cluster comprising nine nodes. Each node has two Intel E5-2670 @ 2.60GHz (16 cores, 32 threads)

---

[2] `https://www.wikidata.org/wiki/Property:P159`

CPUs, 256GB RAM, 6×600GB 10K RPM HDDs, 10GbE networking, and runs Ubuntu 14.04 with Java 9.0.4. We utilize one node for the master services (YARN ResourceManager and HDFS NameNode); the remaining eight nodes each host a HDFS DataNode, a Solr shard, and are available for Spark worker allocation via YARN.

We ran dstlr on the TREC Washington Post Corpus,[3] which contains 595K news articles and blog posts from January 2012 to August 2017. This corpus has been used in several recent TREC evaluations and is representative of a modern newswire collection. We performed some light data cleaning before running extraction, discarding documents longer than 10,000 tokens and sentences longer than 256 tokens. These outliers were typically HTML tables that our document parser processes into very long "sentences" (concatenating all table cells together). After filtering, we arrive at a collection with 580K documents, comprising roughly 23M sentences and approximately 500M tokens.

Extraction was performed via a Spark job configured with 32 executors (four per machine), each allocated 8 CPU cores and 48GB of memory for task processing; the configuration attempts to maximize resource usage across the cluster. We extracted 97M triples from the approximately 580K documents in 10.4 hours, for a processing rate of 13K token per second. Mentions of entities and mention-to-entity links account for 92.2M triples (46.1M each) while the remaining 4.8M represent relations between mentions. Of the 46.1M mention-to-entity links, 30.7M correspond to an actual Wikidata entity (recall that we explicitly store `null` links); this represents 324K distinct entities.

Currently, dstlr uses Neo4j Community Edition, a popular open-source graph database, as the graph store. Running on a single node, we are able to insert 97M triples in 7.8 hours using a single Spark worker, co-located on the same machine as Neo4j. This translates into an ingestion rate of nearly 2.9K triples/sec, which we find acceptable for a corpus of this size. Further scale out is possible via a distributed version of Neo4j, which is available as part of the Enterprise Edition, but requires a commercial license.

Enrichment is performed by querying a local instance of Wikidata that has been ingested into

[3] https://trec.nist.gov/data/wapost/

Apache Jena Fuseki, which is an open-source RDF store that provides a REST-based SPARQL endpoint. We import the "truthy" dump, consisting of only facts, in addition to a mapping from Wikipedia to Wikidata URIs, as CoreNLP links entities to Wikipedia URIs.

For each of the 324K distinct entities found in the corpus, we fetch the corresponding facts from Wikidata using our Jena Fuseki endpoint. As with the extraction phase, the enrichment process is orchestrated by Spark. For example, for the "headquarters" relation, we are able to retrieve 11.7K corresponding facts from Wikidata in around 14 minutes. These extracted facts are then inserted into Neo4j, as described in Section 3.2. This ingestion takes only a few seconds.

5 Graph Alignment and Applications

In our case study, the "product" of dstlr is a knowledge graph constructed from a corpus of unstructured text (Washington Post articles) that has been enriched with high-quality facts extracted from an external knowledge graph (Wikidata). The knowledge graph, stored in Neo4j, can then be manipulated by different applications using Neo4j's declarative query language called Cypher.

We describe a query-driven approach to align extracted relations from CoreNLP to external facts from Wikidata. This, in essence, performs fact verification (Thorne and Vlachos, 2018) against an external knowledge source that is presumed to have high-quality facts. While fact verification using external knowledge sources is not novel (Vlachos and Riedel, 2015), the contribution of our particular case study is to illustrate how it can be recast into a query-driven subgraph alignment problem. Within this framework, fact verification, locating textual support for asserted facts, updating incorrectly-asserted facts, asserting newly-discovered facts, and data augmentation via distant supervision can all be viewed as different aspects of the same underlying task.

As an illustration of these ideas, we consider the `city_of_headquarters` relation identified by CoreNLP. Figure 2 shows a Cypher query that performs one possible subgraph alignment. A typical Cypher query has three main clauses: the MATCH clause describes, in a pseudo-graphical notation, the graph pattern being searched for; the WHERE clause specifies additional constraints on the patterns, akin to the WHERE clause in SQL; finally,

```
MATCH (d:Document)-->(s:Mention)
MATCH (s)-->(r:Relation
{ type:  "CITY_OF_HEADQUARTERS" })
MATCH (r)-->(o:Mention)
MATCH (s)-->(e:Entity)
MATCH (e)-->(f:Fact {relation:  r.type})
RETURN d, s, r, o, e, f
```

Figure 2: Cypher query to match extracted relations with external facts.

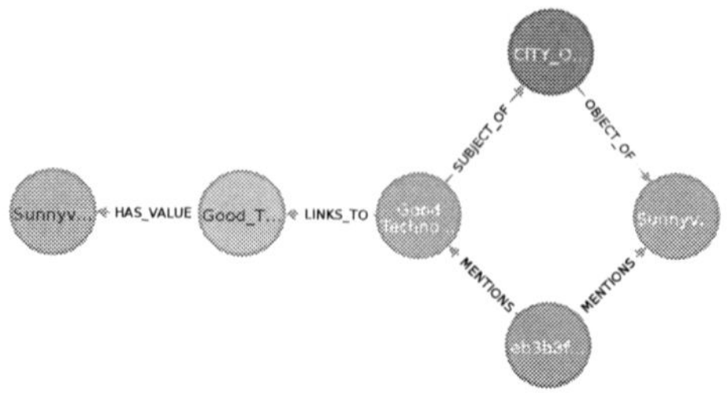

Figure 3: Example where an extracted relation matches an external fact, providing textual support for the fact.

the RETURN clause specifies the result of the query. This particular query looks for two mention nodes connected by a city_of_headquarters relation for which there exists a linked entity for the subject mention with the same fact type in Wikidata as the extracted relation, returning tuples of all matched instances. In other words, we look for all instances of extracted headquarters, and then match the headquarters with what's stored in the external knowledge graph.

We query Neo4j with its Spark connector so that the results can be integrated with subsequent distributed processing on our cluster. This particular query returns around 21K results in less than twenty seconds, where the majority of the time is spent on Spark overhead such as copying dependencies to worker nodes.

What can we do with the results? Logically, there are three possibilities: an extracted relation matches what's in the external knowledge graph, an extracted relation doesn't match what's in the external knowledge graph, and the extract relation isn't found in the external knowledge graph.[4] These correspond to identification of supporting evidence, inconsistent facts, and missing facts; we consider each of these cases in detail below.

5.1 Supporting Facts

If an extracted relation matches a fact asserted in a high-quality external source such as Wikidata, we can conclude with reasonable certainty that the information contained in the source document is indeed factual. As a specific example, our Cypher query identified Washington Post article eb3b8f as discussing the company "Good Technology", and from that article, CoreNLP was able to identify its headquarters as Sunnyvale. Figure 3 shows this subgraph, illustrating agreement on Sunnyvale between the external knowledge graph (leftmost node) and the document (rightmost node).

This forms the basis of fact verification, although there are nuanced cases that require human judgment (and thus are difficult to automate). For example, it could be the case that *both* the knowledge graph and the document are wrong, such as when a fact is outdated. Since we retain the provenance of all extracted relations, it is possible for a human to trace back evidence to its source in order to consider the broader context.

This feature allows applications to locate supporting evidence for facts in Wikidata. Existing knowledge graphs are typically constructed through a combination of different processes, ranging from manual entry to semi-automated techniques. It is frequently the case that the provenance is lost, and thus the knowledge graph cannot answer the question: how do we know this fact to be true? Our application can provide such support, and from multiple sources to boot.

5.2 Inconsistent Facts

Relations extracted from unstructured text may be inconsistent with facts in the external knowledge graph for a variety of reasons, but can be grouped into two categories, either imperfect extractors or factual errors in the documents. Distinguishing these two cases requires manual inspection, but once again, subgraph alignment provides the basis of fact verification.

Based on our own manual inspection, the overwhelming majority of inconsistencies stems from extractor errors. For example, Washington Post article b02562 contains the sentence "The company said that it will have watches to demo at department stores around the world: the Galeries Lafayette in Paris, Isetan in Tokyo, ...", from which CoreNLP asserts that Isetan has headquarter in Paris, which is obviously incorrect to a human reader. The corresponding subgraph is presented in Figure 4, which shows that the Wiki-

---

[4]This is actually the result of another query, but same idea.

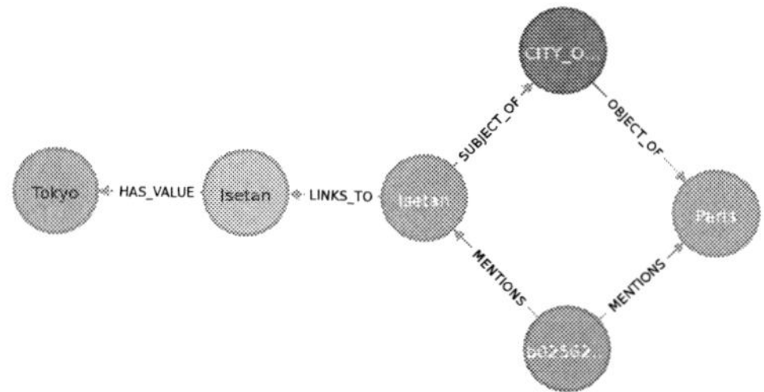

Figure 4: Example where an extracted relation is inconsistent with an external fact. In this case, the inconsistency arises from an extractor error.

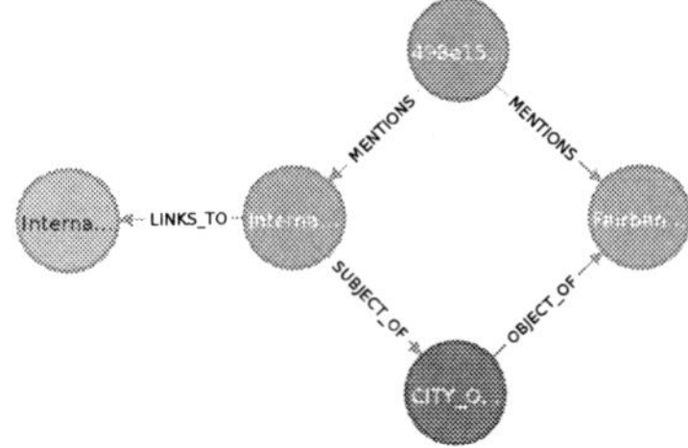

Figure 5: Example where an extracted relation does not correspond to any fact in the external knowledge graph, providing an opportunity acquire new knowledge.

data fact (leftmost node) differs from the extracted value (rightmost node).

These inconsistencies can serve as negative training data that can then be used to train better extraction models. While this is a standard technique in the literature on distant supervision for relation extraction (Smirnova and Cudré-Mauroux, 2018), we show how the process can be formulated in terms of graph queries in our dstlr platform, in essence, as a side effect of fact verification. In principle, supporting texts, such as those from the previous section, can be used as positive examples as well, although their benefits are likely to be limited as the extractor was able to correctly identify the relation to begin with.

5.3 Missing Facts

In trying to align subgraphs from extracted relations with external facts, the third possibility is that we find no corresponding fact. For example, Washington Post article `498e15` discusses a climatologist at the International Arctic Research Center in Fairbanks, Alaska. Our platform extracts Fairbanks as the headquarters of the International Arctic Research Center (see Figure 5). During the enrichment process, no value from Wikidata was present for the property P159 (based on our CoreNLP to Wikidata mapping). This can also be confirmed by noticing the lack of an infobox in the upper right-hand corner of its Wikipedia page.

In other words, we have discovered a missing fact in Wikidata, thus providing an opportunity to populate Wikidata with new knowledge. Of course, human vetting is likely needed before any facts are added to an external knowledge graph, but once again, subgraph alignment via Cypher graph queries provides the starting point for knowledge acquisition.

6 Conclusion

The contribution of dstlr is a scalable, opensource, end-to-end platform that distills a potentially large text collection into a knowledge graph. While each of the components in our architecture already exist, they have not been previously integrated in this manner to support knowledge graph construction and applications that exploit knowledge graphs.

The other interesting aspect of our work is the use of subgraph alignment to support a number of related tasks: we show that fact verification, locating textual support for asserted facts, detecting inconsistent and missing facts, and extracting distantly-supervised training data can all be performed within the same graph querying framework. The dstlr platform is under active development, with plans to integrate more extractors, particular ones based on neural networks, in support of applications in business intelligence, knowledge discovery, and semantic search.

Acknowledgments

This research was supported by the Natural Sciences and Engineering Research Council (NSERC) of Canada, with additional funding from the Waterloo–Huawei Joint Innovation Lab.

References

Gabor Angeli, Melvin Johnson Premkumar, and Christopher D. Manning. 2015. Leveraging linguistic structure for open domain information extraction. In *Proceedings of the 53rd Annual Meeting of the Association for Computational Linguistics and the 7th International Joint Conference on Natural Language Processing (Volume 1: Long Papers)*, pages 344–354, Beijing, China.

Isabelle Augenstein, Sebastian Padó, and Sebastian Rudolph. 2012. LODifier: Generating linked data from unstructured text. In *Proceedings of the 9th Extended Semantic Web Conference (ESWC 2012)*, pages 210–224, Heraklion, Crete.

Ryan Clancy, Toke Eskildsen, Nick Ruest, and Jimmy Lin. 2019a. Solr integration in the Anserini information retrieval toolkit. In *Proceedings of the 42nd Annual International ACM SIGIR Conference on Research and Development in Information Retrieval (SIGIR 2019)*, pages 1285–1288, Paris, France.

Ryan Clancy, Jaejun Lee, Zeynep Akkalyoncu Yilmaz, and Jimmy Lin. 2019b. Information retrieval meets scalable text analytics: Solr integration with Spark. In *Proceedings of the 42nd Annual International ACM SIGIR Conference on Research and Development in Information Retrieval (SIGIR 2019)*, pages 1313–1316, Paris, France.

Jenny Rose Finkel, Trond Grenager, and Christopher Manning. 2005. Incorporating non-local information into information extraction systems by Gibbs sampling. In *Proceedings of the 43rd Annual Meeting of the Association for Computational Linguistics (ACL'05)*, pages 363–370, Ann Arbor, Michigan.

Jeremy Getman, Joe Ellis, Stephanie Strassel, Zhiyi Song, and Jennifer Tracey. 2018. Laying the groundwork for knowledge base population: Nine years of linguistic resources for TAC KBP. In *Proceedings of the Eleventh International Conference on Language Resources and Evaluation (LREC-2018)*, Miyazaki, Japan.

Heng Ji and Ralph Grishman. 2011. Knowledge base population: Successful approaches and challenges. In *Proceedings of the 49th Annual Meeting of the Association for Computational Linguistics: Human Language Technologies*, pages 1148–1158, Portland, Oregon.

Natthawut Kertkeidkachorn and Ryutaro Ichise. 2017. T2KG: An end-to-end system for creating knowledge graph from unstructured text. In *Proceedings of the AAAI-17 Workshop on Knowledge-Based Techniques for Problem Solving and Reasoning*, pages 743–749, San Francisco, California.

Christopher D. Manning, Mihai Surdeanu, John Bauer, Jenny Finkel, Steven J. Bethard, and David Mc-Closky. 2014. The Stanford CoreNLP natural language processing toolkit. In *Proceedings of 52nd Annual Meeting of the Association for Computational Linguistics: System Demonstrations*, pages 55–60, Baltimore, Maryland.

Mausam, Michael Schmitz, Stephen Soderland, Robert Bart, and Oren Etzioni. 2012. Open language learning for information extraction. In *Proceedings of the 2012 Joint Conference on Empirical Methods in Natural Language Processing and Computational Natural Language Learning*, pages 523–534, Jeju Island, Korea.

Tom M. Mitchell, William Cohen, Estevam Hruschka, Partha Talukdar, Justin Betteridge, Andrew Carlson, Bhavana Dalvi Mishra, Matthew Gardner, Bryan Kisiel, Jayant Krishnamurthy, Ni Lao, Kathryn Mazaitis, Thahir Mohamed, Ndapa Nakashole, Emmanouil Antonios Platanios, Alan Ritter, Mehdi Samadi, Burr Settles, Richard Wang, Derry Wijaya, Abhinav Gupta, Xinlei Chen, Abulhair Saparov, Malcolm Greaves, and Joel Welling. 2015. Never-ending learning. In *Proceedings of the Twenty-Ninth AAAI Conference on Artificial Intelligence (AAAI-15)*, pages 2302–2310, Austin, Texas.

Alexander Ratner, Stephen H. Bach, Henry Ehrenberg, Jason Fries, Sen Wu, and Christopher Ré. 2017. Snorkel: Rapid training data creation with weak supervision. *Proceedings of the VLDB Endowment*, 11(3):269–282.

Alisa Smirnova and Philippe Cudré-Mauroux. 2018. Relation extraction using distant supervision: A survey. *ACM Computing Surveys*, 51(5):106:1–106:35.

Mihai Surdeanu, Julie Tibshirani, Ramesh Nallapati, and Christopher D. Manning. 2012. Multi-instance multi-label learning for relation extraction. In *Proceedings of the 2012 Joint Conference on Empirical Methods in Natural Language Processing and Computational Natural Language Learning*, pages 455–465, Jeju Island, Korea.

James Thorne and Andreas Vlachos. 2018. Automated fact checking: Task formulations, methods and future directions. In *Proceedings of the 27th International Conference on Computational Linguistics*, pages 3346–3359, Santa Fe, New Mexico.

Andreas Vlachos and Sebastian Riedel. 2015. Identification and verification of simple claims about statistical properties. In *Proceedings of the 2015 Conference on Empirical Methods in Natural Language Processing*, pages 2596–2601, Lisbon, Portugal.

Denny Vrandečić and Markus Krötzsch. 2014. Wikidata: A free collaborative knowledgebase. *Communications of the ACM*, 57(10):78–85.

Peilin Yang, Hui Fang, and Jimmy Lin. 2018. Anserini: Reproducible ranking baselines using Lucene. *Journal of Data and Information Quality*, 10(4):Article 16.

Relation Extraction among Multiple Entities using a Dual Pointer Network with a Multi-Head Attention Mechanism

Seongsik Park   **Harksoo Kim**

Kangwon National University, South Korea

{a163912, nlpdrkim}@kangwon.ac.kr

Abstract

Many previous studies on relation extraction have been focused on finding only one relation between two entities in a single sentence. However, we can easily find the fact that multiple entities exist in a single sentence and the entities form multiple relations. To resolve this problem, we propose a relation extraction model based on a dual pointer network with a multi-head attention mechanism. The proposed model finds n-to-1 subject-object relations by using a forward decoder called an object decoder. Then, it finds 1-to-n subject-object relations by using a backward decoder called a subject decoder. In the experiments with the ACE-05 dataset and the NYT dataset, the proposed model achieved the state-of-the-art performances (F1-score of 80.5% in the ACE-05 dataset, F1-score of 78.3% in the NYT dataset)

1   Introduction

Relation extraction is the task of recognizing semantic relations (*i.e.*, tuple structures; subject-relation-object triples) among entities in a sentence. Figure 1 shows three triples that can be extracted from the given sentence.

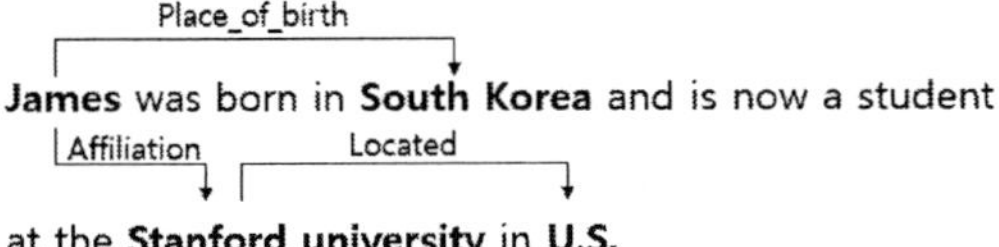

Figure 1: Subject-relation-object triples in a sentence

With significant success of neural networks in the field of natural language processing, various relation extraction models based on convolutional neural networks (CNNs) have been suggested (Kumar, 2017); the CNN model with max-pooling (Zeng et al., 2014), the CNN model with multi-sized window kernels (Nguyen and Grishman,

2015), the combined CNN model (Yu and Jiang, 2016), and the contextualized graph convolutional network (C-GCN) model (Zhang et al., 2018).

Relation extraction models based on recurrent neural network (RNNs) has been the other popular choices; the long-short term memory (LSTM) model with dependency tree (Miwa and Bansal, 2016), the LSTM model with position-aware attention mechanism (Zhang et al., 2017), and the walk-based model on entity graphs (Christopoulou et al., 2019). Most of these previous models have been focused on extracting only one relation between two entities from a single sentence. However, multiple entities exist in a single sentence, and these entities can form multiple relations. To address this issue, we propose a relation extraction model to find all possible relations among multiple entities in a sentence at once.

The proposed model is based on the pointer network (Vinyals et al., 2015). The pointer network is a sequence-to-sequence (Seq2Seq) model in which an attention mechanism (Bahdanau et al., 2015) is modified to learn the conditional probability of an output whose values correspond to positions in a given input sequence. We modify the pointer network to have dual decoders; an object decoder (a forward decoder) and a subject decoder (a backward decoder). The object decoder plays a role to extract n-to-1 relations as shown in the following example: *(James-BirthPlace-South Korea)* and *(Tom-BirthPlace-SouthKorea)* extracted from 'James and Tom was born in South Korea'. The subject decoder plays a role to extract 1-to-n relations as shown in the following example*: (James-Position-student)* and *(James-Affiliation-Stanford university)* extracted from 'James is a student at Stanford university'.

2   Dual Pointer Network Model for Relation Extraction

Proceedings of the Second Workshop on Fact Extraction and VERification (FEVER), pages 47–51

Hong Kong, November 3, 2019. ©2019 Association for Computational Linguistics

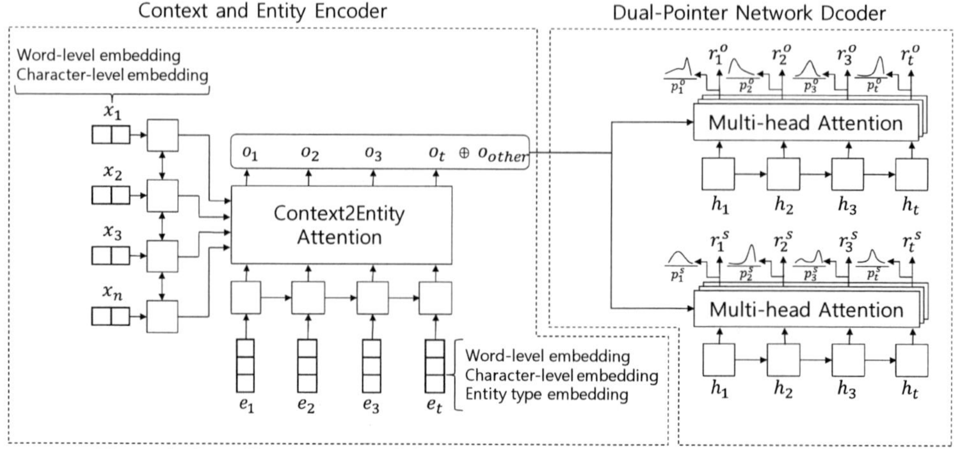

Figure 2: Overall architecture of the dual pointer networks for relation extraction

Figure 2 illustrates an overall architecture of the proposed model. As shown in Figure 2, the proposed model consists of two parts: One is a context and entity encoder, and the other is a dual pointer network decoder.

The context and entity encoder (the left part of Figure 2) computes degree of associations between words and entities in a given sentence. In the context and entity encoder, $\{x_1, x_2, ..., x_n\}$ and $\{e_1, e_2, ..., e_t\}$ are word embedding vectors and entity embedding vectors, respectively. The word embedding vectors are concatenations of two types of embeddings; word-level GloVe embeddings for representing meanings of words (Pennington et al., 2014) and character-level CNN embeddings for alleviating out-of-vocabulary problems (Park et al., 2018). The entity embedding vectors are similar to the word embedding vectors except that entity type embeddings are additionally concatenated. The entity type embeddings are vector representations associated with each entity type[1] and are initialized as random values. The word embedding vectors are input to a bidirectional LSTM network in order to obtain contextual information. The entity embedding vectors are input to a forward LSTM network because entities are listed in the order appeared in a sentence. The output vectors of the bidirectional LSTM network and the forward LSTM network are input to the context-to-entity attention layer ('Context2Entity Attention' in Figure 2) in order to compute relative degrees of associations between words and entities according to the same manner

with the Context2Query attention proposed in Seo et al. (2017).

In a pointer network, attentions show position distributions of an encoding layer. Since an attention is highlighted at only one position, the pointer network has a structural limitation when one entity forms relations with several entities (for instance, '*James*' in Figure 1). The proposed model adopts a dual pointer network decoder (the right part of Figure 2) to overcome this limitation. The first decoder called an object decoder learns the position distribution from subjects to objects. Conversely, the second decoder called a subject decoder learns the position distribution from objects to subjects. In Figure 1, 'James' should point to both 'south Korea' and 'Stanford university'. If we use a conventional forward decoder (the object decoder), this problem could not be solved because the forward decoder cannot point to multiple targets. However, the subject decoder (a backward decoder) can resolve this problem because 'south Korea' and 'Stanford university' can respectively point to 'James'.

Additionally, we adopt a multi-head attention mechanism in order to improve performances of the dual pointer network. The multi-head attention mechanism splits the input value into multiple heads and compute the attention of each head. The inputs $\{h_1, h_2, ..., h_t\}$ of multi-head attention layer are the vectors that concatenate the entity embedding vectors $\{e_1, e_2, ..., e_t\}$ and the output vectors $\{o_1, o_2, ..., o_t\}$ of the context-to-entity attention layer. The random initialized vector o_{other} is used

---

[1] We use seven entity types such as person, location, organization, facility, geo-political, vehicle and weapon in the ACE-2005 dataset. Then, we use three entity type such as person, location and organization in the NYT dataset.

for handling entities that do not have any relations with other entities. In other words, entities without any relations point to o_{other}. As shown in Figure 2, the dual pointer network decoder returns two kinds of value sequences. One is a sequence of relation labels $\{r_1, r_2, ..., r_t\}$, and the other is a sequence of pointed positions $\{p_1, p_2, ..., p_t\}$.

3 Evaluation

3.1 Datasets and Experimental Settings

We evaluated the proposed model by using the following benchmark datasets.

ACE-05 corpus: The Automatic Content Extraction dataset (ACE) includes seven major entity types and six major relation types. The ACE-05 corpus is not proper to evaluate models to extract multiple triples from a sentence. Therefore, if some triples in the ACE-05 corpus share a sentence (*i.e.*, some triples are occurred in the same sentence), we merged the triples. As a result, we obtained a data set annotated with multiple triples. Then, we divided the new data set into a training set (5,023 sentences), a development set (629 sentences), and a test set (627 sentences) by a ratio of 8:1:1.

New York Times (NYT) corpus (Riedel et al., 2010): the NYT corpus is a news corpus sampled from New York Times news articles. The NYT corpus is produced by distant supervision method. Zheng et al (2017) and Zeng et al (2018) used this dataset as supervised data. We excluded sentences without relation facts from Zheng's corpus. Finally, we obtained 66,202 sentences in total. We used 59,581 sentences for training and 6,621 for evaluate.

Optimization of the proposed model was done with the Adam optimizer (Kingma and Ba, 2014) with learning-rate = 0.001, encoder units = 128, decoder units = 256, dropout rate = 0.1.

3.2 Experimental Results

Table 1 shows performances of the proposed model and the comparison models when the ACE-05 corpus is used as an evaluation dataset. In Table 1, SPTree LSTM (Miwa and Bansal, 2016) is a model that applies the dependency information between the entities. FCM (Gormley et al., 2015) is a model in which handcrafted features are combined with word embeddings. CNN+RNN (Nguyen and Grishman, 2015) is a hybrid model of CNN and RNN. HRCNN (Kim and Choi, 2018) is hybrid model of CNN, RNN, and Fully-Connected Neural

Model	P	R	F1
SPTreeLSTM(Miwa+2016)	57.2	54.0	55.6
FCM(Gormley+2015)	71.5	49.3	58.2
CNN+RNN(Nguyen+2015)	69.3	66.3	67.7
HRCNN(Kim+2018)	-	-	74.1
WALK(Fenia+2019)	69.7	59.5	64.2
The Proposed Model	**79.1**	**81.7**	**80.5**

Table 1: Performance comparisons on ACE-05 (P: Precision, R: Recall rate, F1: F1-score in percentage)

Model	P	R	F1
NovelTag (Zheng+2017)	61.5	41.4	50.0
MultiDecoder(Zeng+2018)	61.0	56.6	58.7
The Proposed Model	**74.9**	**82.0**	**78.3**

Table 2: Performance comparisons on NYT (P: Precision, R: Recall rate, F1: F1-score in percentage)

Network (FNN). WALK is a graph-based neural network model for relation extraction (Fenia et al., 2019). As shown in Table 1, the proposed model outperformed all comparison models.

Table 2 shows performances of the proposed model and the comparison models when the NYT corpus is used as an evaluation dataset. In Table 2, NovelTag (Zheng et al., 2017) MultiDecoder (Zeng et al., 2018) are models that jointly extract entities and relations. It is not reasonable to directly compare the proposed model with NovelTag and MultiDecoder because the proposed model needs gold-labeled entities while NovelTag and MultiDecoder automatically extracts entities from sentences. Although the direct comparisons are unfair, the proposed model showed much higher performances than expected.

# of entities	# of sentences	F1
2	316	91.5
3	108	80.1
4	68	74.5
More than 5	137	75.8

Table 3: Performance changes according to the number of entities per sentence (F1: F1-score in percentage)

Table 3 shows performance changes according to the number of entities per sentence in the ACE-05 corpus. As shown in Table 3, the more the number of entities per sentence was, the lower the performances of the proposed model were. We think that the decreasing of performances is due to the increasing of complexities. The performance when the number of entities is more than five was slightly improved as compared with the performance when the number of entities is four. The reason is that many entities do not have any relations with the other entities.

4   Conclusion

We proposed a relation extraction model to find all possible relations among multiple entities in a sentence at once. The proposed model is based on a pointer network with a multi-head attention mechanism. To extract all possible relations from a sentence, we modified a single decoder of the pointer network to a dual decoder. In the dual decoder, the object decoder extracts n-to-1 subject-object relations, and the subject decoder extracts 1-to-n subject-object relations. In the experiments with the ACE-05 corpus and the NYT corpus, the proposed model showed good performances.

Acknowledgments

This work was supported by Institute of Information & Communications Technology Planning & Evaluation(IITP) grant funded by the Korea government(MSIT) (No.2013-0-00109, WiseKB: Big data based self-evolving knowledge base and reasoning platform.

References

Dzmitry Bahdanau, KyungHyun Cho and Yoshua Bengio. 2016. Neural Machine Translation by Jointly Learning to Align and Translate. *arXiv preprint arXiv:1409.0473v7*.

Fenia Christopoulou, Makoto Miwa and Sophia Ananiadou1. 2019. A Walk-based Model on Entity Graphs for Relation Extraction. *arXiv preprint arXiv:1902.07023v1*.

Matthew R. Gormley, Mo Yu and Mark Dredze. 2015. Improved Relation Extraction with Feature-Rich Compositional Embedding Models. *arXiv preprint arXiv:1505.02419v3*.

SeonWo Kim and SungPil Choi. 2018. Relation Extraction using Hybrid Convolutional and Recurrent Networks. In *Proceedings of Korea Computer Congress 2018* (KCC 2018). pages 619-621

Diederik Kingma and Jimmy Ba. 2014. Adam: A method for stochastic optimization. *arXiv preprint arXiv:1412.6980*.

Shantanu Kumar. 2017. A Survey of Deep Learning Methods for Relation Extraction. *arXiv preprint arXiv:1705.03645v1*.

Makoto Miwa and Mohit Bansal. 2016. End-to-End Relation Extraction using LSTMs on Sequences and Tree Structures. *arXiv preprint arXiv:1601.00770v3*.

Thien Huu Nguyen and Ralph Grishman. 2015. Relation extraction: Perspective from convolutional neural networks. In *Proceedings of Conference of the North American Chapter of the Association for Computational Linguistics on Human Language Technology (NAACL-HLT 2015)*. pages 39-48.

Thien Huu Nguyen and Ralph Grishman. 2015. Combining Neural Networks and Log-linear Models to Improve Relation Extraction. *arXiv preprint arXiv:1511.05926v1*.

Jeffrey Pennington, Richard Socher and Christopher D. Manning. 2014. GloVe: Global Vectors for Word Representation. In *Proceedings of the 2014 Conference on Empirical Methods in Natural Language Processing (EMNLP 2014)*. pages 1532–1543.

Sebastian Riedel, Limin Yao, and Andrew McCallum. 2010. Modeling relations and their mentions without labeled text. In *Proceedings of the European Conference on Machine Learning and Principles and Practice of Knowledge Discovery in Databases (ECML PKDD 2010)*. pages 148-163.

Minjoon Seo, Aniruddha Kembhavi, Ali Farhadi and Hananneh Hajishirz. 2017. Bi-Directional Attention Flow for Machine Comprehension. In *Proceedings of International Conference on Learning Representations (ICLR)*.

Ashish Vaswani, Noam Shazeer, Niki Parmar, Jakob Uszkoreit, Llion Jones, Aidan N. Gomez, Lukasz Kaiser and Illia Polosukhin. 2017. Attention all you need. In *Advances in Neural Information Processing Systems (NIPS 2017)*. pages 5998-6008.

Oriol Vinyals, Meire Fortunato and Navdeep Jaitly. 2015. Pointer Networks. In *Advances in Neural Information Processing Systems (NIPS 2015)*. pages 2692-2700.

Jianfei Yu and Jing Jiang. 2016. Pairwise Relation Classification with Mirror Instances and a Combined Convolutional Neural Network. In *Proceedings of the 26th International Conference on Computational Linguistics (COLING 2016)*. pages 2366-2377.

Daojian Zeng, Kang Liu, Siwei Lai, Guangyou Zhou and Jun Zhao. 2014. Relation classification via convolutional deep neural network. In *Proceedings of the 24th International Conference on Computational Linguistics (COLING 2014)*. pages 2335-2344.

Xiangrong Zeng, Daojian Zeng, Shizhu He, Kang Liu and Jun Zhao. 2018. Extracting Relational Facts by an End-to-End Neural Model with Copy Mechanism. In *Proceedings of the 56th Annual Meeting of the Association for Computational Linguistics (ACL 2018)*. pages 506-514

Suncong Zheng, Feng Wang, Hongyun Bao, Yuexing Hao,Peng Zhou and Bo Xu. Joint Extraction of Entities and Relations Based on a Novel Tagging Scheme. *arXiv preprint arXiv:1706.05075v1.*

Yuhao Zhang, Peng Qi and Christopher D. Manning. 2018. Graph Convolution over Pruned Dependency Trees Improves Relation Extraction. In *Proceedings of the 2018 Conference on Empirical Methods in Natural Language Processing (EMNLP 2018).* pages 2205-2215.

Yuhao Zhang, Victor Zhong, Danqi Chen, Gabor Angeli and Christopher D. Manning. 2017. Position-aware Attention and Supervised Data Improve Slot Filling. In *Proceedings of the 2017 Conference on Empirical Methods in Natural Language Processing (EMNLP 2017).* pages 35-45

Unsupervised Question Answering for Fact-Checking

Mayank Jobanputra
Department of Computer Science & Engineering
IIIT Delhi
New Delhi, India
mayankj@iiitd.ac.in

Abstract

Recent Deep Learning (DL) models have succeeded in achieving human-level accuracy on various natural languages tasks such as question-answering, natural language inference (NLI), and textual entailment. These tasks not only require the contextual knowledge but also the reasoning abilities to be solved efficiently. In this paper, we propose an unsupervised question-answering based approach for a similar task, fact-checking. We transform the FEVER dataset into a Cloze-task by masking named entities provided in the claims. To predict the answer token, we utilize pre-trained Bidirectional Encoder Representations from Transformers (BERT). The classifier computes label based on the correctly answered questions and a threshold. Currently, the classifier is able to classify the claims as "SUPPORTS" and "MANUAL_REVIEW". This approach achieves a label accuracy of 80.2% on the development set and 80.25% on the test set of the transformed dataset.

1 Introduction

Every day textual information is being added/updated on Wikipedia, as well as other social media platforms like Facebook, Twitter, etc. These platforms receive a huge amount of unverified textual data from all its users such as News Channels, Bloggers, Journalists, Field-Experts which ought to be verified before other users start consuming it. This information boom has increased the demand of information verification also known as Fact Checking. Apart from the encyclopedia and other platforms, domains like scientific publications and e-commerce also require information verification for reliability purposes. Generally, Wikipedia authors, bloggers, journalists and scientists provide references to support their claims. Providing referenced text against the claims makes the fact checking task a little easier as the verification system no longer needs to search for the relevant documents.

Wikipedia manages to verify all this new information with a number of human reviewers. Manual review processes introduce delays in publishing and is not a well scalable approach. To address this issue, researchers have launched relevant challenges, such as the Fake News Challenge (Pomerleau and Rao, 2017), Fact Extraction and VERification (FEVER) (Thorne et al., 2018) challenge along with the datasets. Moreover, Thorne and Vlachos (2018) released a survey on the current models for automated fact-checking. FEVER is the largest dataset and contains around 185k claims from the corpus of 5.4M Wikipedia articles. The claims are labeled as "SUPPORTS", "REFUTES", or "NOT ENOUGH INFO", based on the evidence set.

In this paper, we propose an unsupervised question-answering based approach for solving the fact-checking problem. This approach is inspired from the memory-based reading comprehension task that humans perform at an early age. As we know that kids in schools, first read and learn the syllabus content so that they can answer the questions in the exam. Similarly, our model learns a language model and linguistics features in unsupervised fashion from the provided Wikipedia pages.

To transform the FEVER dataset into the above-mentioned task, we first generate the questions from the claims. In literature, there are majorly two types of Question Generation systems: Rule-based and Neural Question Generation (NQG) model based. Ali et al. (2010) proposed a rule-based pipeline to automate the question generation using POS (Part-of-speech) tagging and Named Entity Recognition (NER) tagging from the sentences. Recently, many NQG models have been introduced to generate questions in natural lan-

Proceedings of the Second Workshop on Fact Extraction and VERification (FEVER), pages 52–56
Hong Kong, November 3, 2019. ©2019 Association for Computational Linguistics

guage. Serban et al. (2016) achieved better performance for question generation utilizing (passage, question, answer) triplets as training data and an encoder-decoder based architecture as their learning model.

Du et al. (2017) introduced a sequence-to-sequence model with an attention mechanism, outperforming rule-base question generation systems. Although the models proposed in (Kim et al., 2019; Wang et al., 2017) are effective, they require a passage to generate the plausible questions which is not readily available in the FEVER dataset. To resolve the issues and to keep the system simple but effective, we chose to generate questions similar to a Cloze-task or masked language modeling task. Such a task makes the problem more tractable as the masked entities are already known (i.e. named entities) and tight as there is only one correct answer for a given question. Later when the answers are generated, due to the question generation process, it becomes very easy to identify the correct answers.

We use the BERT's (Bidirectional Encoder Representations from Transformers) (Devlin et al., 2018) masked language model, that is pre-trained on Wikipedia articles for predicting the masked entities. Currently, neither the claim verification process nor the question generation process mandates explicit reasoning. For the same reason, it is difficult to put "REFUTES" or "NOT ENOUGH INFO" labels. To resolve this issue, we classify the unsupported claims as "MANUAL_REVIEW" instead of labeling them as "NOT ENOUGH INFO" or "REFUTES".

In the literature, the shared task has been tackled using pipeline-based supervised models (Nie et al., 2019; Yoneda et al., 2018; Hanselowski et al., 2018). To our knowledge, only Yoneda et al., 2018 has provided the confusion matrix for each of the labels for their supervised system. For the same reason, we are only providing the comparison of the label accuracy on the "SUPPORTS" label in the results section.

2   System Description

In this section, we explain the design and all the underlying methods that our system has adopted. Our system is a pipeline consisting of three stages: (1) Question Generation, (2) Question Answering, (3) Label Classification. The question generation stage attempts to convert the claims into appropri-

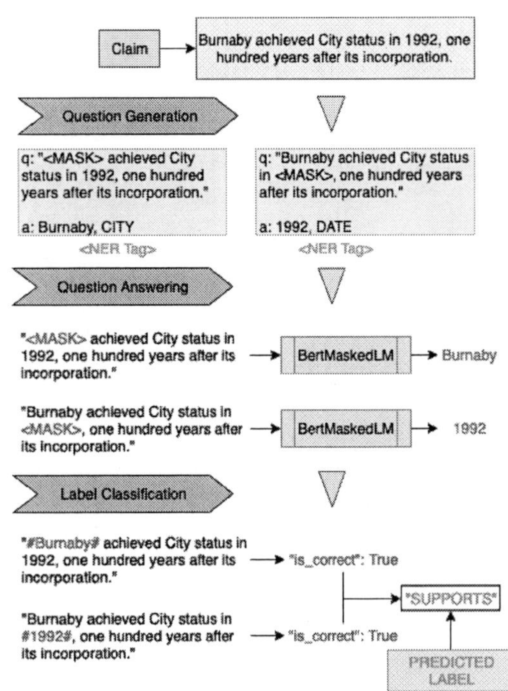

Figure 1: An overview of the model pipeline

ate questions and answers. It generates questions similar to a Cloze-task or masked language modeling task where the named entities are masked with a blank. Question Answering stage predicts the masked blanks in an unsupervised manner. The respective predictions are then compared with the original answers and exported into a file for label classification. The label classifier calculates the predicted label based on a threshold.

2.1   Question Generation

The claims generally feature information about one or more entities. These entities can be of many types such as PERSON, CITY, DATE. Since the entities can be considered as the content words for the claim, we utilize these entities to generate the questions. Although function words such as conjunctions and prepositions form relationship between entities in the claims, we currently do not make use of such function words to avoid generating complex questions. The types of entities in a sentence can be recognized by using Stanford CoreNLP (Manning et al., 2014) NER tagger.

In our case, FEVER claims are derived from Wikipedia. We first collect all the claims from the FEVER dataset along with "id", "label" and "verifiable" fields. We don't perform any normalization

Type of FEVER Set	Total Claims	Claims Converted to Questions	Conversion Accuracy	Total Questions	Questions per claim (Median)
Training Set	145449	131969	90.73	395717	3
Development Set	19998	17749	88.75	54422	3
Test Set	9999	8863	88.63	27359	3

Table 1: Performance of the question generation system on FEVER Dataset.

on the claims such as lowercasing, transforming the spaces to underscore or parenthesis to special characters as it may decrease the accuracy of the NER tagger. These claims are then processed by the NER tagger to identify the named entities and their type. The named entities are then used to generate the questions by masking the entities for the subsequent stage.

This process not only transforms the dataset but also transforms the task into a Cloze-task or masked language modeling task. Although the original masked language modeling task masks some of the tokens randomly, here we mask the named entities for generating the questions.

2.2 Question Answering

Originally inspired by the Cloze-task and developed to learn to predict the masked entities as well as the next sentence, BERT creates a deep bidirectional transformer model for the predictions. Since the FEVER claims are masked to generate the questions, we use BERT to tokenize the claims. We observed that the BERT tokenizer sometimes fails to tokenize the named entities correctly (e.g. Named entity *Taran* was tokenized as "*Tara*", "*##n*"). This is due to the insufficient vocabulary used while training the WordPiece tokenizer.

To resolve this, we use Spacy Tokenizer[1] whenever the WordPiece Tokenizer fails. Once the claim is tokenized, we use the PyTorch Implementation of the BERT[2] model (BertForMaskedLM model) to predict the vocabulary index of the masked token. The predicted vocabulary index is then converted to the actual token. We compare the predicted token against the actual answer to calculate the label accuracy based on the classification threshold.

2.3 Label Classification

In this stage, we compute the final label based on the correctness score of the predictions that we received from the previous stage. The correctness score (s) is computed as:

$$s = \frac{n_c}{N} \tag{1}$$

where n_c indicates the number of correct questions, and N is the total number of questions generated for the given claim. The label is assigned based on the correctness score (s) and the derived threshold (ϕ) as:

$$L(s) = \begin{cases} \text{SUPPORTS,} & \text{if } s \geq \phi \\ \text{MANUAL\_REVIEW,} & \text{if } s < \phi \end{cases} \tag{2}$$

Here, the classification threshold (ϕ) is derived empirically based on the precision-recall curve.

2.4 Model and Training details

We utilize standard pre-trained BERT-Base-uncased model configurations as given below:

- Layers: 12

- Hidden Units: 768

- Attention heads: 12

- Trainable parameters: 110M

We fine-tune our model (BERT) on the masked language modeling task on the wiki-text provided along with the FEVER dataset for 2 epochs.[3]

Note that Stanford CoreNLP NER tagger and the BERT model are the same for all the experiments and all the sets (development set, test set, training set). We use the same PyTorch library mentioned in Section 2.2 for the fine-tuning as well.

---

[1] https://spacy.io/api/tokenizer
[2] https://github.com/huggingface/pytorch-transformers

[3] In our experiments, after fine-tuning the model for 2 epochs there was no significant performance improvement.

3   Results

For the subtask of question generation, the results in Table 1 show that the system is able to generate questions given a claim with considerably good accuracy. The conversion accuracy is defined as the ratio of the number of claims in which the named entities are extracted to the number of claims. The results also support our assumption that the claims generally feature information about one or more entities.

Table 2 shows the performance of our Fact Checking system on the "SUPPORTS" label, the output of our system. We compare the results against two different classification thresholds. Table 1 shows that on an average there are 3 questions generated per claim. Here, $\phi = 0.76$ suggests that at least 3 out of the 4 questions have to be answered correctly while $\phi = 0.67$ suggests that at least 2 out of the 3 questions has to be answered correctly for the claim to be classified as "SUPPORTS". If only 1 question is generated,

Type of Set	Label Accuracy ($\phi = 0.76$)	Label Accuracy ($\phi = 0.67$)
Training Set	81.52	88.05
Development Set	80.20	86.7
Test Set	80.25	87.04

Table 2: Performance of the question generation system on FEVER Dataset.

then it has to be answered correctly for the claim to be classified as "SUPPORTS" in case of both the thresholds.

In contrast to the results reported in Table 2, here we consider $\phi = 0.76$ to be a better classification threshold as it improvises over False Positives considerably over the entire dataset.

Model	Label Accuracy ($\phi = 0.76$)	Label Accuracy ($\phi = 0.67$)
HexaF - UCL	80.18	80.18
Our Model (BERT)	**80.20**	**86.7**

Table 3: Comparison of the Label accuracy on Development set.

Although our unsupervised model doesn't support all the labels, to show the effectiveness of the approach, we compare the label accuracy of

"SUPPORTS" label against a supervised approach – HexaF. Results from Table 3 suggests that our approach is comparable to HexaF[4] for $\phi = 0.76$.

4   Error Analysis

4.1   Question Generation

The typical errors that we observed for the question generation system are due to the known limitations of the NER tagger. Most of the claims that the system failed to generate the questions from contain entity types for which the tagger is not trained.

For instance, the claim "A View to a Kill is an action movie." has a movie title (*i.e. A View to a Kill*) and a movie genre (*i.e. action*) but Stanford CoreNLP NER tagger is not trained to identify such type of entities.

4.2   Question Answering

We describe the most recurrent failure cases of our answering model in the description below.

Limitations of Vocabulary. Names like *"Burnaby"* or *"Nikolaj"* were not part of the original vocabulary while pre-training the BERT model, which makes it difficult to predict them using the same model. This was one of the most recurring error types.

Limitations of Tokenizer. The WordPiece tokenizer splits the token into multiple tokens. E.g. *"Taran"* into *"Tara"*, *"##n"*. In such cases, the answering system predicts the first token only which would be a substring of the correct answer. As we don't explicitly put a rule to avoid such cases, they are considered as incorrect answers.

5   Conclusion

In this paper, we presented a transformer-based unsupervised question-answering pipeline to solve the fact checking task. The pipeline consisted of three stages: (1) Question Generation (similar to a Cloze-task), (2) Question Answering, (3) Label Classification. We use Stanford CoreNLP NER tagger to convert the claim into a Cloze-task by masking the named entities. The Question Generation task achieves almost 90% accuracy in transforming the FEVER dataset into a Cloze-task. To answer the questions generated, we utilize masked language modeling approach from the BERT model. We could achieve 80.2% label

---

[4]Note that the label accuracy for HexaF is independent of the classification threshold ϕ.

accuracy on "SUPPORTS" label. From the results, we conclude that it is possible to verify the facts with the right kind of factoid questions.

6 Future Work

To date, our approach only generates two labels "SUPPORTS" and "MANUAL_REVIEW". We are working on extending this work to also generate "REFUTED" by improving our question generation framework. We will also work on generating questions using recent Neural Question Generation approaches. Later, to achieve better accuracy for tokenizing as well as answering, we plan to train the WordPiece Tokenizer from scratch.

Acknowledgments

The authors thank Dr. Amit Nanavati and Dr. Ratnik Gandhi for their insightful comments, suggestions, and feedback. This research was supported by the TensorFlow Research Cloud (TFRC) program.

References

Husam Ali, Yllias Chali, and Sadid A Hasan. 2010. Automation of question generation from sentences. In *Proceedings of QG2010: The Third Workshop on Question Generation*, pages 58–67.

Jacob Devlin, Ming-Wei Chang, Kenton Lee, and Kristina Toutanova. 2018. Bert: Pre-training of deep bidirectional transformers for language understanding. *arXiv preprint arXiv:1810.04805*.

Xinya Du, Junru Shao, and Claire Cardie. 2017. Learning to ask: Neural question generation for reading comprehension. *arXiv preprint arXiv:1705.00106*.

Andreas Hanselowski, Hao Zhang, Zile Li, Daniil Sorokin, Benjamin Schiller, Claudia Schulz, and Iryna Gurevych. 2018. Ukp-athene: Multi-sentence textual entailment for claim verification. *arXiv preprint arXiv:1809.01479*.

Yanghoon Kim, Hwanhee Lee, Joongbo Shin, and Kyomin Jung. 2019. Improving neural question generation using answer separation. In *Proceedings of the AAAI Conference on Artificial Intelligence*, volume 33, pages 6602–6609.

Christopher Manning, Mihai Surdeanu, John Bauer, Jenny Finkel, Steven Bethard, and David McClosky. 2014. The stanford corenlp natural language processing toolkit. In *Proceedings of 52nd annual meeting of the association for computational linguistics: system demonstrations*, pages 55–60.

Yixin Nie, Haonan Chen, and Mohit Bansal. 2019. Combining fact extraction and verification with neural semantic matching networks. In *Proceedings of the AAAI Conference on Artificial Intelligence*, volume 33, pages 6859–6866.

Dean Pomerleau and Delip Rao. 2017. The fake news challenge: Exploring how artificial intelligence technologies could be leveraged to combat fake news.

Iulian Vlad Serban, Alberto García-Durán, Caglar Gulcehre, Sungjin Ahn, Sarath Chandar, Aaron Courville, and Yoshua Bengio. 2016. Generating factoid questions with recurrent neural networks: The 30m factoid question-answer corpus. *arXiv preprint arXiv:1603.06807*.

James Thorne and Andreas Vlachos. 2018. Automated fact checking: Task formulations, methods and future directions. *arXiv preprint arXiv:1806.07687*.

James Thorne, Andreas Vlachos, Christos Christodoulopoulos, and Arpit Mittal. 2018. Fever: a large-scale dataset for fact extraction and verification. *arXiv preprint arXiv:1803.05355*.

Zhiguo Wang, Wael Hamza, and Radu Florian. 2017. Bilateral multi-perspective matching for natural language sentences. *arXiv preprint arXiv:1702.03814*.

Takuma Yoneda, Jeff Mitchell, Johannes Welbl, Pontus Stenetorp, and Sebastian Riedel. 2018. Ucl machine reading group: Four factor framework for fact finding (hexaf). In *Proceedings of the First Workshop on Fact Extraction and VERification (FEVER)*, pages 97–102.

Improving Evidence Detection by Leveraging Warrants

Keshav Singh[‡]   **Paul Reisert**[†,‡]   **Naoya Inoue**[‡,†]   **Pride Kavumba**[‡]   **Kentaro Inui**[‡,†]

[†] RIKEN Center for Advanced Intelligence Project   [‡] Tohoku University
`{keshav.singh29,naoya-i,pkavumba,inui}@ecei.tohoku.ac.jp`
`paul.reisert@riken.jp`

Abstract

Recognizing the implicit link between a claim and a piece of evidence (i.e. warrant) is the key to improving the performance of evidence detection. In this work, we explore the effectiveness of automatically extracted warrants for evidence detection. Given a claim and candidate evidence, our proposed method extracts multiple warrants via similarity search from an existing, structured corpus of arguments. We then attentively aggregate the extracted warrants, considering the consistency between the given argument and the acquired warrants. Although a qualitative analysis on the warrants shows that the extraction method needs to be improved, our results indicate that our method can still improve the performance of evidence detection.

1 Introduction

An argument is composed of two key components: *claim* and *a supporting piece of evidence*. Identification of these components and predicting the relationship among them forms the core of an important research area in NLP known as Argument Mining (Peldszus and Stede, 2013). Although claims can be identified with a promising level of accuracy in typical argumentative discourse (Eger et al., 2017; Stab et al., 2018), identification of a supporting evidence piece for a given claim (i.e., evidence detection) still remains a challenge (Gleize et al., 2019).

Shown in Figure 1 is an example of a given topic and claim, and three evidence candidates from Wikipedia. In this example, identification of the best supporting piece of evidence is challenging, as all three evidence are related to the topic. Although all evidence candidates appear to be semantically similar to the claim, only E_1 supports it, as it has an underlying, implicit link that can be established with the claim (i.e., *children's fun-*

Topic: This house believes that male infant circumcision is tantamount to child abuse.
Claim: Infant circumcision infringes upon individual autonomy.
Evidences:
- E_1: In Netherlands, the Royal Dutch Medical Association (KNMG) stated in 2010 that non-therapeutic male circumcision "conflicts with the child's right to autonomy and physical integrity".
- E_2: The British Medical Association states that, "Parents should determine how best to promote their children's interests".
- E_3: American Academy of Pediatrics states that, "Newborns who are circumcised without analgesia experience pain and physiologic stress".

Warrant:
- Children's fundamental right shouldn't be trumped by parental rights.

Figure 1: Three evidence candidates (E_1-E_3) for a given topic and claim, where E_1 can be considered the best evidence piece (shown in blue).

damental right shouldn't be trumped by parental rights). Thus, for detecting the best piece of evidence for a claim, it is crucial to capture such implicit reasoning between them (Habernal et al., 2018).

Existing approaches for evidence detection have often relied on lexical features extracted from argument components such as semantic similarity, adjacent sentence relation and discourse indicators (Stab and Gurevych, 2014; Rinott et al., 2015; Nguyen and Litman, 2016; Hua and Wang, 2017). However, no prior work has considered identifying the underlying, implicit reasoning, henceforth *warrants* (Toulmin, 2003), between a claim and a piece of evidence as a means for improving evidence detection. For example, if a model could establish a warrant between the claim and a piece of evidence (e.g., warrant in Figure 1 for E_1), the most plausible evidence piece could be detected.

Towards filling this reasoning gap, Boltužić and

Proceedings of the Second Workshop on Fact Extraction and VERification (FEVER), pages 57–62
Hong Kong, November 3, 2019. ©2019 Association for Computational Linguistics

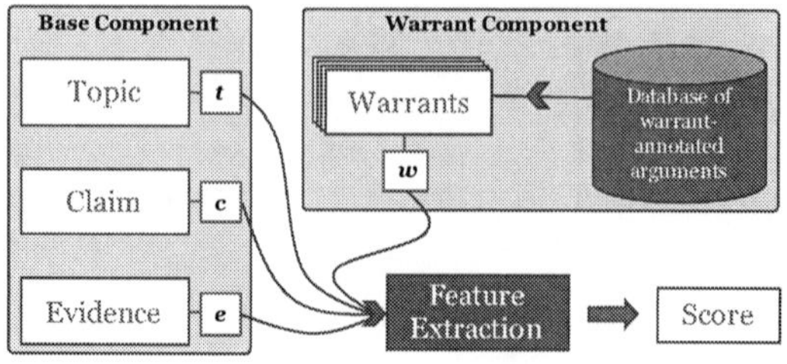

Figure 2: The proposed warrant-aware evidence detection framework.

Šnajder (2016) and Habernal et al. (2018) both created a corpus of explicit warrants for a given claim and its evidence piece. However, to the best of our knowledge, such corpora of explicit warrants have not yet been applied to the task of evidence detection.

In this paper, we explore the effectiveness of leveraging warrants for evidence detection. Given a claim and evidence, our framework first extracts relevant warrants from an existing, well-known corpus of warrant-annotated arguments (Habernal et al., 2018). It then attentively aggregates the acquired warrants, considering the consistency between the given argument and warrants. Our experiments demonstrate that exploiting warrants has the potential to help improve the performance of evidence detection.

2 Proposed Method

2.1 Overview

Given a topic, claim, and a piece of evidence as input, our framework estimates the likelihood of the claim being supported by that evidence piece. As described in Section 1, in order to identify such support relations, it is crucial to recognize the underlying, implicit link between a claim and a given piece of evidence (i.e. warrants). Our framework first extracts multiple warrants that link a given claim to an evidence piece, and later leverages the acquired warrants to estimate the score. We assume that for a given claim and a piece of evidence, there can be several possible variants of warrants for one given claim-evidence pair.

As shown in Figure 2, our proposed framework consists of: (i) *Base Component* and (ii) *Warrant Component*. The Base Component encodes a topic, claim, and an evidence piece into a corresponding vector representation $t, c, e \in \mathbb{R}^d$. The warrant component then extracts multiple warrants linking the given claim with that piece of

evidence and produces its vector representation $w \in \mathbb{R}^d$.

Finally, we generate a feature representation f of all these vectors as follows: $f = [t; c; e; w; t \odot c \odot e \odot w; i] \in \mathbb{R}^{(5d+12d)}$, where $\odot$ denotes element-wise multiplication, and i is the feature vector which captures the pairwise interaction between all ingredients. Analogously to Conneau et al. (2017), we calculate absolute difference and element-wise multiplication for all possible pairs of vectors: $i = \text{concat}(\{[|u - v|; u \odot v] \mid u, v \in \{t, c, e, w\}\})$. Finally, we feed f into a linear classifier: $y = \text{softmax}(Uf + b)$, where $U \in \mathbb{R}^{(5d+12d) \times 2}$ and $b \in \mathbb{R}^2$ are model parameters to be learned.

2.2 Base Component

The base component produces vector representations of topic, claim, and an evidence piece. This component consists of three types of layers: an embedding layer, a BiLSTM (Hochreiter and Schmidhuber, 1997) layer and a max-pooling layer.

Let $(x_1^t, x_2^t, ..., x_n^t)$ be a sequence of words in a topic. The embedding layer outputs a vector $x_i^t \in \mathbb{R}^g$ for each word x_i^t. The BiLSTM layer then takes a sequence of these vectors $(x_1^t, x_2^t, \cdots, x_n^t)$ as an input and produces a contextualized vector $z_i^t = [\vec{h}_i; \overleftarrow{h}_i]$ for each word, where $\vec{h}_i, \overleftarrow{h}_i \in \mathbb{R}^h$ are the hidden states of the forward and backward LSTM, respectively. Finally, the max pooling layer extracts the most salient word features over the words to produce a fixed-length vector, i.e. $t = \max_{i=1}^n (z_i^t) \in \mathbb{R}^{d=2h}$. In a similar fashion, we obtain vector representations c, e of claim and an evidence piece.

2.3 Warrant Component

Extracting warrants Given a claim and a piece of evidence, our goal is to extract multiple, relevant warrants that link the claim with that evidence piece. As described in Section 1, ideally, we can find plausible warrants for correct claim-evidence pieces but we cannot for wrong pieces. Instead, for wrong claim-evidence pieces, we find non-reasonable warrants that would be less convincing and irrelevant.

Let $\mathcal{D} = \{(t_i, c_i, e_i, w_i)\}_{i=1}^n$ be a database of warrant-annotated arguments, where t_i, c_i, e_i, w_i are a topic, claim, a piece of evidence, and a warrant linking c_i with e_i, respectively. Given an argument t, c, e to be analyzed, we extract warrants linking c with e via similarity search on $\mathcal{D}$. Specifically, we retrieve the top-m most similar arguments in $\mathcal{D}$ to the given argument in terms of topic, claim and an evidence piece, and then extract warrants from these similar arguments.

We define the similarity between arguments as follows: $\mathrm{sim}(\langle t, c, e \rangle, \langle t_i, c_i, e_i \rangle) = \mathrm{sim}(t, t_i) \cdot \mathrm{sim}(c, c_i) \cdot \mathrm{sim}(e, e_i)$. To calculate the similarity between components u, v, we encode each component into a vector representation $\boldsymbol{u}, \boldsymbol{v}$, and then resort to vector-based similarity. In our experiments, we use Universal Sentence Encoder as a sentence encoder and angular-based similarity as $\mathrm{sim}(\boldsymbol{u}, \boldsymbol{v})$, following Cer et al. (2018) because of its state of the art performance in various semantic textual similarity tasks.

Constructing $\mathcal{D}$ is a challenging problem. In our study, we rely on a database of arguments that have arguments which are explicitly annotated with warrants (see Section 3.1 for further details). In future work, we plan to extract warrants from web debate forums, where people frequently discuss controversial topics and ask warrants for discussion with each other.

Encoding warrants Given a set W of extracted warrants $\{w_1, w_2, ..., w_n\}$, we first encode each warrant w_i into a vector representation $\boldsymbol{w_i} \in \mathbb{R}^d$ in a similar manner to topic, claim, and a piece of evidence. Because the quality and relevance of extracted warrants may vary, we attentively aggregate sentence-level vector representations of all extracted warrants. We take a similar approach to Lin et al. (2016), which demonstrated the advantage of sentence level selective attention for multiple sentences, and take advantage of information present in multiple warrants.

Specifically, the final vector representation $\boldsymbol{v}(W) \in \mathbb{R}^d$ is computed as a weighted sum over all warrant vectors:

$$\boldsymbol{v}(W) = \sum_{i=1}^{n} \alpha_i \boldsymbol{w_i}, \tag{1}$$

where α_i is the importance of w_i (s.t. $\sum_{i=1}^{n} \alpha_i = 1$). We calculate α_i as follows:

$$\alpha_i = \frac{e^{f([\boldsymbol{t};\boldsymbol{c};\boldsymbol{e};\boldsymbol{w_i}])}}{\sum_j^n e^{f([\boldsymbol{t};\boldsymbol{c};\boldsymbol{e};\boldsymbol{w_j}])}}, \tag{2}$$

where $f(\boldsymbol{x}) = \tanh(\boldsymbol{u}^\top \boldsymbol{x} + b)$. $\boldsymbol{u} \in \mathbb{R}^{4d}$ and $b \in \mathbb{R}$ are model parameters to be learned. Analogously to attentions in neural models, f estimates

the consistency between a given topic, claim, an evidence piece, and warrant.

In our experiments, we also consider a model in which we assume that all warrants are of equal importance and have the same contribution towards the final vector representation $\boldsymbol{v}(W)$, i.e. $\forall i, \alpha_i = \frac{1}{n}$.

3 Experiments

3.1 Dataset

Benchmark of evidence detection To test the model's evidence detection ability, we use the Context Dependent Evidence Detection (CDED) dataset (Rinott et al., 2015). Each instance in CDED consists of (i) topic, (ii) claim, and (iii) a piece of evidence. To create the dataset, Rinott et al. (2015) initially selected 39 topics at random from *Debatabase*.[1] For each topic, they collected 5-7 related Wikipedia articles and then annotated sentences in each article with a claim and its piece of evidence. They also classified each evidence piece into the types *anecdotal*, *study*, and *expert*. In total, the test and training data consists of 3,057 distinct instances (anecdotal: 385, study: 1,020, and expert: 1,896[2]).

Database of warrant-annotated arguments We utilize the dataset of the Argument Reasoning Comprehension Task (ARCT) (Habernal et al., 2018), because it provides a large collection of warrant-annotated arguments that cover a wide variety of topics. The dataset contains 1,970 warrant-annotated arguments covering over 172 topics. Specifically, each instance in the dataset consists of (i) topic, (ii) claim, (iii) premise (i.e., a piece of evidence), (iv) correct warrant, and (v) wrong warrant. For our experiments, we utilize only the correct warrants. The word overlap between topics of CDED and ARCT after stemming and lemmatization was found to be approximately 15%.

3.2 Setting

Evaluation protocol We evaluate our model in the task of *evidence ranking* (Rinott et al., 2015). Specifically, given a claim and candidate evidence, the task is to rank the candidates properly. For each instance in CDED, we extract one false piece of evidence from instances with the same topic but

---

[1] https://idebate.org/debatabase
[2] Each evidence piece can consists of more than one type.

Number of warrants	Importance α_i	MQ (Anecdotal)	MQ (Study)	MQ (Expert)
None	-	0.47	0.52	0.67
$m = 1$	-	0.48	**0.56**	**0.70**
$m = 1$ (random)	-	0.47	0.51	0.56
$m = 5$	Equal	0.44	0.51	0.65
$m = 5$	Weighted	**0.49**	0.51	0.64

Table 1: Performance of evidence ranking. Results in bold indicate the best MQ score.

different claim. In general, when we have N types of claims in one topic, the task is to rank $N+1$ candidate evidence consisting of one correct and N false evidence. As an evaluation measure, we report Mean Quantile (MQ) score (Guu et al., 2015) which gives a normalized version of Mean Reciprocal Rank. Specifically, for instance, we define the quantile of a correct piece of evidence k as the fraction of incorrect evidence ranked after k. MQ is defined to be the average quantile score over all instances in the dataset, with the quantile ranging from 0 to 1 (1 being optimal).

Following Rinott et al. (2015), we use leave-one-out cross validation schema to evaluate our approach. For every topic, we train our model on instances in all other topics and then test the resulting model on the left out topic. Prior to our experiments, we exclude topics of each evidence type that had less than 3 evidence.

Hyperparameters For both base and warrant components, we use pre-trained 100-dimensional GloVe embeddings (Pennington et al., 2014) to initialize the word embedding layer ($g = 100$). For the BiLSTM layer, we set $h = 100$ (i.e. $d = 200$) and apply dropout before the linear classifier with probability of 0.5. We optimize the categorical cross-entropy loss using Adagrad (Duchi et al., 2011) with a learning rate of 0.01 and the batch size of 32. We choose the model that performs best on the validation set.

3.3 Results

The results are shown in Table 1. The results indicate that incorporating warrant information is effective for ranking evidence across all evidence types. Among warrant-aware models, we found that using a single warrant is more effective overall. We attribute this to the fact that extracted warrants are not of high quality (see Section 3.4), which introduces noisy information into the model. Our future work includes developing a more sophisticated method for extracting war-

Type	α	A_1	A_2
Anecdotal	0.50	2.05	2.30
Study	0.50	1.60	2.10
Expert	0.26	1.35	1.95
Overall	0.39	1.60	2.10

Table 2: Results of qualitative evaluation of automatically acquired warrants.

rants. The results also indicate that estimating the importance of each warrant is effective on the anecdotal type evidence.

To see the importance of the quality of extracted warrants, we experimented with randomly extracted warrants from the database. The results (i.e. "$m = 1$ (random)") show that the performance does not improve or degrade over the non-warrant-aware model. This indicates that extracting relevant warrants is indeed crucial, and that our improvement is attributed to relevant warrants.

3.4 Qualitative Analysis of Warrants

To investigate the quality of the extracted warrants, two annotators (A_1, A_2) experienced in the field of argumentation were asked to score 20 randomly sampled positive instances for each evidence type. Depending on the degree to which a warrant helped them understand the relation between a claim and a piece of evidence, they were asked to score each instance in the range of 1-5. A score of 1 indicates that the given warrant is unrelated to the evidence piece and its paired claim, and 5 indicates that the relationship between the claim and its piece of evidence pair is easy to understand with the warrant. For calculating the agreement scores, we used Krippendorff's α (Krippendorff, 2011). We also show the average scores given by each annotator.

The results of the analysis are shown in Table 2. Although the anecdotal and study agreement scores can be considered fair, the average scores given by both annotators was low, which indicates that the extracted warrants might not be as useful in linking the claim to its evidence piece.

One successful example of an automatically extracted warrant is shown in Figure 1. As described in Section 1, a warrant gives good support for the link between the claim and a piece of evidence. Additionally, our framework extracted the warrant "a doctor has a responsibility to treat patients problems at all costs", which does not support the link and is irrelevant.

4 Conclusion and Future Work

In this paper, we have explored an approach for exploiting warrant information for the task of evidence detection. Our experiments demonstrated that leveraging warrants even at the coarse-grained sentence-level can improve the overall performance of evidence detection. However, in our future work, we will focus on a fine-grained level to capture a better reasoning structure of warrants. Furthermore, instead of using separate sentence encoders, we will experiment with using a single general sentence encoder. In our qualitative analysis, we found that the automatically acquired warrants are not of high-quality on average. This can be attributed due to the low lexical overlap between the topics of the two datasets used in our experiments. To address this, we will focus on finding relevant warrants from online web discussion portals, in addition to the current structured database of arguments. Simultaneously, we will explore methods for acquiring warrants at a large-scale, such as crowdsourcing.

References

Filip Boltužić and Jan Šnajder. 2016. Fill the gap! analyzing implicit premises between claims from online debates. In *Proceedings of the Third Workshop on Argument Mining (ArgMining2016)*, pages 124–133, Berlin, Germany. Association for Computational Linguistics.

Daniel Cer, Yinfei Yang, Sheng-yi Kong, Nan Hua, Nicole Limtiaco, Rhomni St. John, Noah Constant, Mario Guajardo-Cespedes, Steve Yuan, Chris Tar, Brian Strope, and Ray Kurzweil. 2018. Universal sentence encoder for English. In *Proceedings of the 2018 Conference on Empirical Methods in Natural Language Processing: System Demonstrations*, pages 169–174, Brussels, Belgium. Association for Computational Linguistics.

Alexis Conneau, Douwe Kiela, Holger Schwenk, Loïc Barrault, and Antoine Bordes. 2017. Supervised learning of universal sentence representations from natural language inference data. In *Proceedings of the 2017 Conference on Empirical Methods in Natural Language Processing*, pages 670–680, Copenhagen, Denmark. Association for Computational Linguistics.

John Duchi, Elad Hazan, and Yoram Singer. 2011. Adaptive subgradient methods for online learning and stochastic optimization. *J. Mach. Learn. Res.*, 12:2121–2159.

Steffen Eger, Johannes Daxenberger, and Iryna Gurevych. 2017. Neural end-to-end learning for computational argumentation mining. In *Proceedings of the 55th Annual Meeting of the Association for Computational Linguistics (Volume 1: Long Papers)*, pages 11–22, Vancouver, Canada. Association for Computational Linguistics.

Martin Gleize, Eyal Shnarch, Leshem Choshen, Lena Dankin, Guy Moshkowich, Ranit Aharonov, and Noam Slonim. 2019. Are you convinced? choosing the more convincing evidence with a Siamese network. In *Proceedings of the 57th Annual Meeting of the Association for Computational Linguistics*, pages 967–976, Florence, Italy. Association for Computational Linguistics.

Kelvin Guu, John Miller, and Percy Liang. 2015. Traversing knowledge graphs in vector space. *CoRR*, abs/1506.01094.

Ivan Habernal, Henning Wachsmuth, Iryna Gurevych, and Benno Stein. 2018. The argument reasoning comprehension task: Identification and reconstruction of implicit warrants. In *Proceedings of the 2018 Conference of the North American Chapter of the Association for Computational Linguistics: Human Language Technologies, Volume 1 (Long Papers)*, pages 1930–1940, New Orleans, Louisiana. Association for Computational Linguistics.

Sepp Hochreiter and Jürgen Schmidhuber. 1997. Long short-term memory. *Neural Comput.*, 9(8):1735–1780.

Xinyu Hua and Lu Wang. 2017. Understanding and detecting supporting arguments of diverse types. In *Proceedings of the 55th Annual Meeting of the Association for Computational Linguistics (Volume 2: Short Papers)*, pages 203–208, Vancouver, Canada. Association for Computational Linguistics.

Klaus Krippendorff. 2011. Computing krippendorff's alpha-reliability.

Yankai Lin, Shiqi Shen, Zhiyuan Liu, Huanbo Luan, and Maosong Sun. 2016. Neural relation extraction with selective attention over instances. In *Proceedings of the 54th Annual Meeting of the Association for Computational Linguistics (Volume 1: Long Papers)*, pages 2124–2133, Berlin, Germany. Association for Computational Linguistics.

Huy Nguyen and Diane Litman. 2016. Context-aware argumentative relation mining. In *Proceedings of the 54th Annual Meeting of the Association for Computational Linguistics (Volume 1: Long Papers)*, pages 1127–1137, Berlin, Germany. Association for Computational Linguistics.

Andreas Peldszus and Manfred Stede. 2013. From argument diagrams to argumentation mining in texts: A survey. *Int. J. Cogn. Inform. Nat. Intell.*, 7(1):1–31.

Jeffrey Pennington, Richard Socher, and Christopher Manning. 2014. Glove: Global vectors for word representation. In *Proceedings of the 2014 Conference on Empirical Methods in Natural Language Processing (EMNLP)*, pages 1532–1543, Doha, Qatar. Association for Computational Linguistics.

Ruty Rinott, Lena Dankin, Carlos Alzate Perez, Mitesh M. Khapra, Ehud Aharoni, and Noam Slonim. 2015. Show me your evidence - an automatic method for context dependent evidence detection. In *Proceedings of the 2015 Conference on Empirical Methods in Natural Language Processing*, pages 440–450, Lisbon, Portugal. Association for Computational Linguistics.

Christian Stab and Iryna Gurevych. 2014. Identifying argumentative discourse structures in persuasive essays. In *Proceedings of the 2014 Conference on Empirical Methods in Natural Language Processing (EMNLP)*, pages 46–56, Doha, Qatar. Association for Computational Linguistics.

Christian Stab, Tristan Miller, Benjamin Schiller, Pranav Rai, and Iryna Gurevych. 2018. Cross-topic argument mining from heterogeneous sources. In *Proceedings of the 2018 Conference on Empirical Methods in Natural Language Processing*, pages 3664–3674, Brussels, Belgium. Association for Computational Linguistics.

Stephen E. Toulmin. 2003. *The Uses of Argument*. Cambridge University Press.

Hybrid Models for Aspects Extraction without Labelled Dataset

Wai-Howe Khong
Faculty of Computing and Informatics
Multimedia University, Malaysia.
`swordmasterex@hotmail.com`

Lay-Ki Soon
School of Information Technology
Monash University Malaysia
`soon.layki@monash.edu`

Hui-Ngo Goh
Faculty of Computing and Informatics
Multimedia University, Malaysia.
`hngoh@mmu.edu.my`

Abstract

One of the important tasks in opinion mining is to extract aspects of the opinion target. Aspects are features or characteristics of the opinion target that are being reviewed, which can be categorised into explicit and implicit aspects. Extracting aspects from opinions is essential in order to ensure accurate information about certain attributes of an opinion target is retrieved. For instance, a professional camera receives a positive feedback in terms of its functionalities in a review, but its overly high price receives negative feedback. Most of the existing solutions focus on explicit aspects. However, sentences in reviews normally do not state the aspects explicitly. In this research, two hybrid models are proposed to identify and extract both explicit and implicit aspects, namely TDM-DC and TDM-TED. The proposed models combine topic modelling and dictionary-based approach. The models are unsupervised as they do not require any labelled dataset. The experimental results show that TDM-DC achieves F_1-measure of 58.70%, where it outperforms both the baseline topic model and dictionary-based approach. In comparison to other existing unsupervised techniques, the proposed models are able to achieve higher F_1-measure by approximately 3%. Although the supervised techniques perform slightly better, the proposed models are domain-independent, and hence more versatile.

1 Introduction

Opinion holds positive or negative view, attitude, emotion or appraisal on entity. An entity can be a product, person, event, organization, or topic. Aspect, also known as feature, is the various distinctive attributes on the entity itself (Liu, 2010, 2012). For example, for a product review on mobile phone, the mobile phone is the entity and its aspects may include battery life, design, screen size, and charging time. Being able to identify the specific aspects of an opinion target is crucial as it gives more accurate analysis of the opinion. Aspects can be categorised into explicit and implicit aspects. Explicit aspect is explicitly stated in the review while the latter is not. For instance, given this review *"This is an affordable smartphone with a very long battery life."*, *battery life* is explicitly stated with the associated opinion but the aspect of *price* is implicitly denoted by *affordable*.

Most of the existing research works focus on explicit aspects identification and extraction (Hu and Liu, 2004). Few models have been proposed to identify implicit aspect from the dataset using supervised or semi-supervised approaches (Fei et al., 2012; Wang et al., 2013; Xu et al., 2015). Supervised approaches requires annotated training dataset, which is laborious to label. Furthermore, models produced by supervised model are domain-dependent. Supervised models need to be trained with domain-specific dataset. To the best of our knowledge, unsupervised approach has yet to be proposed to identify both explicit and implicit aspects. Hence, in this research work, the main objective is to propose unsupervised models, which are domain-independent, and able to extract both explicit and implicit aspects, without using any labelled training dataset.

The remainder of this paper is organised as follows: Section 2 discusses some relevant related works. Section 3 presents the proposed models. The experimental setup and results are discussed in Section 4. Finally, the paper is concluded in Section 5.

2 Related Work

Aspect extraction for opinion mining has three main approaches, namely the supervised, semi-supervised and unsupervised approach. Models

Proceedings of the Second Workshop on Fact Extraction and VERification (FEVER), pages 63–68
Hong Kong, November 3, 2019. ©2019 Association for Computational Linguistics

from supervised approach are trained using annotated corpus. The resultant models are normally domain-dependent. In other words, a supervised model trained in one domain often performs poorly in another domain. An example of supervised approach uses Lexicalized Hidden Markov Models (HMM) to learn patterns to extract aspects and opinion expressions through part-of-speech and surrounding contextual clues in the document (Jin et al., 2009). Jakob and Gurevych used Conditional Random Fields (CRF) to train review sentences from different domains for domain independent extraction (Jakob and Gurevych, 2010). Toh and Su trained their Sigmoidal Feedforward Neural Network (FNN) with one hidden layer with a training set to predict the aspect categories (Toh and Su, 2015). Repaka, Palleira et al. used Linear Support Vector Machine (SVM) model with Bag-of-Words (BoW) as features and trained it using the multi-class classification method (Repaka et al., 2015). Table 1 summarises the techniques used, whether it extracts implicit aspect or otherwise, and their limitations.

3 Proposed Models

In this research, two domain-independent models are proposed to identify and extract both explicit and implicit aspects. The proposed models are topic dictionary model - direct combine (TDM-DC) and topic dictionary model - topic extended with dictionary model (TDM-TED). Both TDM-DC and TDM-TED combine topic modelling and dictionary-based approach to identify the aspects from a given corpus. Every review is segmented into sentences. Each sentence is used as a document. Part-of-speech (POS) tagged documents are used for topic modelling. Stop words and unused part-of-speech (for example, determiner and conjunction) are filtered from the POS-tagged documents. For dictionary-based approach, noun and opinionated word pairings are extracted as candidate aspects, which is notated as $< N, Ow >$, where N represents the noun extracted from the dataset and Ow represents the opinionated word associated with the noun N in the corpus. Nouns are identified using TreeTagger. Opinionated words are identified using word sense disambiguation (WSD) and sentiment tagging. Sentiment tags are obtained using SentiWordNet (Baccianella et al., 2010). The pairings are identified through pairing noun and opin-

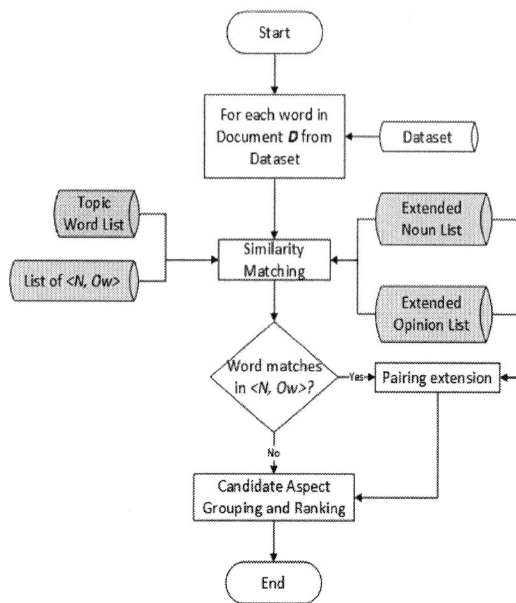

Figure 1: The process of TDM-DC grouping and identifying candidate aspects.

ionated words in the same sentence segment. $< N, Ow >$ notations are then extended using different sets of semantic relations from the dictionary. Extended noun list consists of hypernym and hyponym of nouns, while extended opinion list consists synonym and antonym of the opinionated words. The extended lists are constructed to enlarge the pool of nouns and opinionated words, which in return increases the coverage of aspect candidates. Eventually, each model generates a ranked list of candidate aspects. The details of TDM-DC and TDM-TED are presented in the following subsections.

3.1 Topic Dictionary Model - Direct Combine (TDM-DC)

TDM-DC is a direct search and match of words from the given dataset to the words generated from both models. As shown in Figure 1, every word from the document will be matched with the words in four generated lists, which are the topic word list, $< N, Ow >$ notation list, extended noun and extended opinion lists. For topic model, it will find a match of word $w1$ from document D in topic model T, if a match is found in topic $T1$, every word in topic $T1$ will be extracted and labelled with the same aspect as $T1$. For dictionary model, it will find a match of word $w1$ from document D in $< N, Ow >$ notation list P. If $w1$ is matched

Models	Approach	Explicit Aspect	Implicit Aspect	Limitation
HMMs (Jin et al., 2009)	supervised	Yes	No	laborious data pre-processing step
CRF (Jakob and Gurevych, 2010)	supervised	Yes	Yes	dependant on labelled data
Dictionary Based	supervised	Yes	Yes	highly dependent on dictionary definitions
FNN (Toh and Su, 2015)	supervised	Yes	No	requires a variety of features
Linear SVM (Repaka et al., 2015)	supervised	Yes	No	does not work on sentences without noun
Double Propagation (Hu and Liu, 2004)	semi-supervised	Yes	Yes	only identify adjectives
PSWAM (Liu et al., 2013, 2015)	semi-supervised	Yes	No	does not identify implicit aspects
Topic Model (Blei et al., 2003)	unsupervised	Yes	No	groups unrelated words together
Word2Vec (Mikolov et al., 2013) (Pablos et al., 2015)	unsupervised	Yes	No	require representative seed words

with a notation, all its extended noun Pn and opinion Po words will be labelled with the same aspect, as its parent $< N, Ow >$ notation $P1$. It will also search from the extended list, Pn and Po and extract all the matched words. To reduce duplicate entry of the same word (same word, with same aspect and same POS), duplicates will be eliminated from the final list, after aggregating all the candidate words from all models. TDM-DC ranks candidate aspect list as follow:

1. If a word from the document is matched with a word from the topic model, extract the candidate aspect of the topic model and add a count equivalent to the number of words in the topic.

2. If a word from the document is matched with a word from the $< N, Ow >$ notation, extract the candidate aspect of the notation and add two counts to the candidate aspect because there are two words in the pair.

3. If a duplicate match is found in both $< N, Ow >$ notation list and extended list, it will not add to the count for the candidate aspect.

4. With the parent $< N, Ow >$ notation from the matched notation, add the count for every words matching the parent notation in the extended word lists. Duplicates are excluded in the process.

5. If there is a match in the extended list, extract the word's parent candidate aspect, and add one count to it.

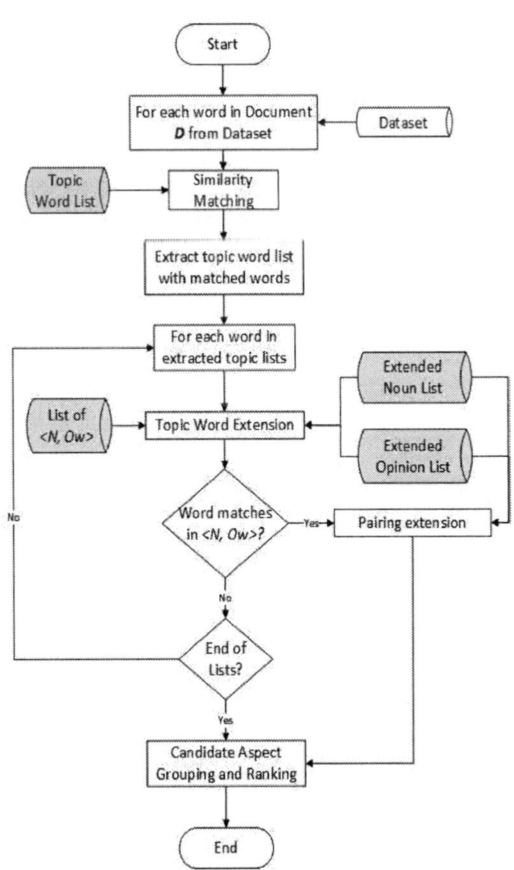

Figure 2: The process of TDM-TED grouping and identifying candidate aspects.

6. Aggregate all the matched candidate aspect count in a ranked list of candidate aspects identified for the provided document.

3.2 Topic Dictionary Model - Topic-Extended (TDM-TED)

Similar to TDM-DC, this proposed model, as illustrated in Figure 2 will search and match the similar words in a document. TDM-TED is different from TDM-DC where it will directly search for similar words in the topic word list and indirectly on other word lists. If a word in document D, $w1$ is matched in a single topic $T1$, all its words will be extracted from the topic. Then, for every word list in the topic T, it will search for its matched word in the $< N, Ow >$ notation list P, together with its extended words from both Extended Noun Pn and Extended Opinion Po list. Furthermore, for every words in Topic T, it will also directly search for its match in both Extended Noun Pn, and Extended Opinion Po lists. Finally, similar to TDM-DC, duplicate entries will be removed from the aggregated list of words. TDM-TED ranks candidate aspect list as follow:

1. If a word from the document matched with a word from the topic model, extract the candidate aspect of the topic model and add a count equivalent to the number of words in the topic. Extract the list of words in that topic.

2. For every words in the topic, if there is a match from the $< N, Ow >$ notation, extract the candidate aspect of the notation and add two counts to the candidate aspect for every candidate notation found because there are two words in the pair.

3. If a duplicate match is found in both $< N, Ow >$ notation list and extended list, it will not add to the count for the candidate aspect.

4. With the parent word from $< N, Ow >$ notation, add the count for every words matching the parent notation in the extended list to the parent's candidate aspect. Each candidate aspect extracted from the candidate extended word lists will add a count. Duplicates are excluded in the process.

5. For every words in the topic, if there is a match in the extended list, extract the word's

parent candidate aspect, and add one count to it.

6. Aggregate all the matched candidate aspect count in a ranked list of candidate aspects identified for the provided document.

4 Experimental Design

The dataset used for this experimentation was downloaded from SemEval-2015 Task 12: Aspect Based Sentiment Analysis [1]. It contains multiple complete reviews breakdown into pre-labelled sentences with potentially out of context sentences about Restaurants. Their aspect category contains both entity labels (e.g. Restaurant, Service, Food) and attribute labels (e.g. prices, quality). To evaluate against other existing models, the entity and attributes of the entity are notated together to form the aspect tuple for the restaurant dataset. Data pre-processing steps have been implemented on the dataset prior to constructing the models, which include POS-tagging using Tree-Tagger and word sense disambiguation (WSD). Sentiment tagging is subsequently carried out to assign sentiment tags to every word based on SentiWordNet (Baccianella et al., 2010). For the weighted sentiment on SentiWordNet, sentiment with the largest weight and with the matched POS attached to the word sense were taken into account. For example, given a row in SentiWordNet of $< a, 0.5, 0.125, living\#3 >$, a is the part-of-speech of the word (living), *0.5* is the positive weight and *0.125* is the negative weight and *living#3* is the word sense. Since *0.5* is more than *0.125*, the word will be considered as positive. In case of same weight, it will be tagged as neutral. For example, *living#a#3* will be tagged as *living#p* where *p* represents the positive sentiment for the word *living* in that sentence.

For words that are not included in SentiWordNet, they were checked against a compiled list of opinion lexicon (Hu and Liu, 2004) to determine the sentiment polarity of a word. The words were then tagged as *p, g* or *n* respectively, where *p* represent positive, *g* represents negative and *n* represents neutral. As sentiment tagging assigns sentiment on a word-by-word basis, a sentence with negation (e.g. no, not, never etc.) will give the opposite sentiment instead. To solve this, the sentiment of opinionated words are flipped if a negation

---

[1] http://alt.qcri.org/semeval2015/task12/

word is detected in the sentence. Once data preprocessing is completed, LDA was implemented. Baseline LDA model was chosen because it outperforms complex models of LDA when there is more than two hundred reviews (Moghaddam and Ester, 2012). Complex models of LDA include topic models which are built using phrases or grammatical dependencies (Moghaddam and Ester, 2012). The topics in the resultant model come from the labels provided by the dataset. In other words, the number of topics are set based on the number of labels from the dataset. For the dictionary model, WordNet [2] and Wordnik [3] are used to extract words in the selected semantic relations.

5   Results and Discussion

Precision, recall and F_1-measure are used to evaluate the experimental results. Due to space limitation, only F_1-measure is presented in this paper. Table 2 shows that among the four models, which include two baseline models and two proposed models, TDM-DC has the highest score. The performance of TDM-DC and TDM-TED are very close, with TDM-DC leading on all three columns of comparison. This is unexpected as TDM-TED generates more candidate aspects compared to TDM-DC. Dictionary-based approach has the lowest score. Dictionary-based approach is good in generating a vast amount of candidate aspects using semantic relations. However, if the defined relations are lacking or none to be found, it will highly affect the candidate aspect count.

Table 2: Baseline model and topic dictionary model F_1 comparison by percentage

Model	F_1	Explicit F_1	Implicit F_1
Topic Model	55.80	57.47	32.53
Dictionary Model	54.67	56.56	21.71
TDM-DC	**58.70**	**60.51**	**33.15**
TDM-TED	58.34	60.15	32.34

The performance of TDM-DC and TDM-TED are also compared against other existing models based on F_1-measure obtained in identifying implicit and explicit aspects, as presented in Table 3. NLANGP represents Sigmoidal Feedforward Network (FNN) with one hidden layer implemented by Toh et. al. (Toh and Su, 2015). It is the best supervised approach for both datasets. UMDuluthC uses Linear Support

[2] https://wordnet.princeton.edu/
[3] https://www.wordnik.com/

Table 3: F_1 comparison by percentage with other approaches. * indicate unconstrained systems.

Approach	Model	F_1
Supervised	NLANGP	62.68*
Supervised	NLANGP	61.94
Unsupervised	**TDM-DC**	**58.70**
Unsupervised	**TDM-TED**	**58.34**
Unsupervised	Topic Model	55.80
Unsupervised	Dictionary Model	54.67
Supervised	UMDuluthC	57.19
Unsupervised	V3	41.85*
Supervised	Baseline	51.32

Vector Machine (SVM) Model for both dataset (2015). Finally, V3 uses Word2Vec to identify the aspect from both dataset, which is the only unsupervised approach used on this dataset (Pablos et al., 2015). By comparing with the baseline approach, which is a Support Vector Machines (SVM) with a trained linear kernel (Pontiki et al., 2015), most approaches outperform it excluding V3. For TDM-DC and TDM-TED, both proposed models are able to outperform UMDuluthC by a small margin, but lost to NLANGP model; both constrained (using only the provided training set of the corresponding domain) and unconstrained approaches. Baseline, NLANGP and UMDuluthC run on supervised classification, which require labelled datasets, while TDM-DC and TDM-TED use unsupervised approach. Among the unsupervised approaches, the proposed TDM-DC and TDM-TED outperform V3 by more than 10%.

6   Conclusion

The main strength of the proposed models is its ability in identifying both explicit and implicit aspects without any labelled dataset. Although the result is not the best when compared to state-of-the-art supervised approach, it is a huge step forward for unsupervised approach in identifying both explicit and implicit aspect. In future, the proposed models will be experimented on opinions that have more implicit aspects to verify its effectiveness at a greater measure.

Acknowledgements

This work is funded by Fundamental Research Grant Scheme (FRGS) by Malaysia Ministry of Higher Education (Ref: FRGS/2/2013/ICT07/MMU/02/2).

References

Stefano Baccianella, Andrea Esuli, and Fabrizio Sebastiani. 2010. Sentiwordnet 3.0: An enhanced lexical resource for sentiment analysis and opinion mining. In *LREC*, volume 10, pages 2200–2204.

David M Blei, Andrew Y Ng, and Michael I Jordan. 2003. Latent dirichlet allocation. *Journal of machine Learning research*, 3(Jan):993–1022.

Geli Fei, Bing Liu, Meichun Hsu, Malu Castellanos, and Riddhiman Ghosh. 2012. A dictionary-based approach to identifying aspects im-plied by adjectives for opinion mining. In *24th international conference on computational linguistics*, page 309.

Minqing Hu and Bing Liu. 2004. Mining and summarizing customer reviews. In *Proceedings of the tenth ACM SIGKDD international conference on Knowledge discovery and data mining*, pages 168–177. ACM.

Niklas Jakob and Iryna Gurevych. 2010. Extracting opinion targets in a single-and cross-domain setting with conditional random fields. In *Proceedings of the 2010 conference on empirical methods in natural language processing*, pages 1035–1045. Association for Computational Linguistics.

Wei Jin, Hung Hay Ho, and Rohini K Srihari. 2009. A novel lexicalized hmm-based learning framework for web opinion mining. In *Proceedings of the 26th annual international conference on machine learning*, pages 465–472. Citeseer.

Bing Liu. 2010. Sentiment analysis and subjectivity. *Handbook of natural language processing*, 2:627–666.

Bing Liu. 2012. Sentiment analysis and opinion mining. *Synthesis lectures on human language technologies*, 5(1):1–167.

Kang Liu, Heng Li Xu, Yang Liu, and Jun Zhao. 2013. Opinion target extraction using partially-supervised word alignment model. In *IJCAI*, volume 13, pages 2134–2140.

Kang Liu, Liheng Xu, and Jun Zhao. 2015. Co-extracting opinion targets and opinion words from online reviews based on the word alignment model. *IEEE Transactions on knowledge and data engineering*, 27(3):636–650.

Tomas Mikolov, Ilya Sutskever, Kai Chen, Greg S Corrado, and Jeff Dean. 2013. Distributed representations of words and phrases and their compositionality. In *Advances in neural information processing systems*, pages 3111–3119.

Samaneh Moghaddam and Martin Ester. 2012. On the design of lda models for aspect-based opinion mining. In *Proceedings of the 21st ACM international conference on Information and knowledge management*, pages 803–812. ACM.

Aitor García Pablos, Montse Cuadros, and German Rigau. 2015. V3: Unsupervised aspect based sentiment analysis for semeval2015 task 12. In *Proceedings of the 9th International Workshop on Semantic Evaluation (SemEval 2015)*, pages 714–718.

Maria Pontiki, Dimitris Galanis, Haris Papageorgiou, Suresh Manandhar, and Ion Androutsopoulos. 2015. Semeval-2015 task 12: Aspect based sentiment analysis. In *Proceedings of the 9th International Workshop on Semantic Evaluation (SemEval 2015)*, pages 486–495.

Ravikanth Repaka, Ranga Reddy Pallelra, Akshay Reddy Koppula, and Venkata Subhash Movva. 2015. Umduluth-cs8761-12: A novel machine learning approach for aspect based sentiment analysis. In *Proceedings of the 9th International Workshop on Semantic Evaluation (SemEval 2015)*, pages 742–747.

Zhiqiang Toh and Jian Su. 2015. Nlangp: Supervised machine learning system for aspect category classification and opinion target extraction. In *Proceedings of the 9th International Workshop on Semantic Evaluation (SemEval 2015)*, pages 496–501.

Wei Wang, Hua Xu, and Xiaoqiu Huang. 2013. Implicit feature detection via a constrained topic model and svm. In *Proceedings of the 2013 Conference on Empirical Methods in Natural Language Processing*, pages 903–907.

Hua Xu, Fan Zhang, and Wei Wang. 2015. Implicit feature identification in chinese reviews using explicit topic mining model. *Knowledge-Based Systems*, 76:166–175.

Extract and Aggregate: A Novel Domain-Independent Approach to Factual Data Verification

Anton Chernyavskiy and **Dmitry Ilvovsky**

Faculty of Computer Science
National Research University Higher School of Economics
Moscow, Russia
`aschernyavskiy_1@edu.hse.ru, dilvovsky@hse.ru`

Abstract

Triggered by Internet development, a large amount of information is published in online sources. However, it is a well-known fact that publications are inundated with inaccurate data. That is why fact-checking has become a significant topic in the last 5 years. It is widely accepted that factual data verification is a challenge even for the experts. This paper presents a domain-independent fact checking system. It can solve the fact verification problem entirely or at the individual stages. The proposed model combines various advanced methods of text data analysis, such as BERT and Infersent. The theoretical and empirical study of the system features is carried out. Based on FEVER and Fact Checking Challenge test-collections, experimental results demonstrate that our model can achieve the score on a par with state-of-the-art models designed by the specificity of particular datasets.

1 Introduction

With the development of online technologies, people tend to receive information mainly through the Internet. Nevertheless, Internet sources have a tendency to spread unauthentic information. In some cases, it can be done intentionally. So that to achieve, for instance, some political advantages, or to obtain a financial benefit through advertising or product promotion. In particular, the analysis conducted by Shao et al. (2017) demonstrated that, during the 2016 US presidential election on Twitter, social bots spread a lot of misinformation. Moreover, even statements about the falseness of some information in its turn can appear to be fake claims.

This paper discusses how modern approaches to the analysis of text information, such as BERT (Qiao et al., 2019), CatBoost[1] and pre-trained con-textual embeddings, can assist in a fact-checking problem. We developed a model that is universal in relation to the data to be checked. Our model is based on the automatic information extraction from sources and combines best techniques from the modern approaches. Verified information can be either confirmed or refuted by each source subject to the presence of the necessary data. The collection of such results allow us to make a general conclusion about the truth or falsity of the fact.

Investigated sub-tasks are the following:

- extract qualitative information from the authoritative sources

- find the relationship between the extracted information and the verifiable claim

Due to the domain-independence of the proposed system, the problem of determining any fake information can be solved both completely or with the further study by experts. In this aspect, the task will be significantly simplified (in fact, experts just need to make the right conclusion based on the model predictions).

In our work, we combine the most successful ideas of solving each step of the fact-checking problem to build a *domain-independent pipeline* that surpasses all of the previous ones. We additionally focus on the *independence of the components* in its development (each component is not allowed to use the scores of the others). We also analyze in details the effect of natural language preprocessing (stemming, stop-words filtering, normalization, keyword highlighting, coreference resolution) and text embeddings selection. Based on this, we make some improvements at each stage[2].

---

[1] https://catboost.ai

[2] The source code is available online at https://github.com/aschern/FEVER

Proceedings of the Second Workshop on Fact Extraction and VERification (FEVER), pages 69–78
Hong Kong, November 3, 2019. ©2019 Association for Computational Linguistics

The paper is organized as follows. First, we review the relevant methods and approaches used in recent fact-checking studies and shared tasks. Then, the baseline model architecture is presented. After that, the components of the developed model are described. This is followed by quantitatively comparative analysis with the state-of-the-art models on the several datasets (FEVER and Fake News Challenge). The paper ends with a summary and directions for further research.

2 Related Work

The fact-checking problem can be solved by various approaches. The majority of the most successful ones are based on information extraction from the authoritative sources. All of them were proposed in the framework of various competitions. Approaches that do not consider any additional information, achieve significantly lower results (Oshikawa et al., 2018).

FEVER competition for factual data verification with the help of information extraction from Wikipedia was held in 2018 (Thorne et al., 2018b).

A 3-stage model consisting of a sequential application of document retrieval (DR), sentence retrieval (SR) and natural language inference (NLI) components was proposed as a baseline (Thorne et al., 2018a). The first and second components select relevant articles from Wikipedia and sentences from them respectively using the part of DrQA (Chen et al., 2017) system combined with the TF-IDF metric. Then the Decomposable Attention Model (DAM) (Parikh et al., 2016) is used as the Recognizing Textual Entailment (RTE) module.

Most of the participants used the same multi-stage model structure. An additional aggregation step was often added at the last stage instead of combining all sentences into one paragraph as the entrance of the RTE module (Hanselowski et al., 2018b; Luken et al., 2018).

For relevant documents selection search API was widely used (Wikipedia Search, Google, Search, Solr, Lucene, etc.). UCL Machine Reading Group (Yoneda et al., 2018) and Athene UKP (Hanselowski et al., 2018b) teams searched for the noun phrases extracted from the statement; Columbia NLP (Chakrabarty et al., 2018) and GESIS Cologne (Otto, 2018) teams searched for the named entities.

So far, various techniques have been proposed for sentence retrieval: Word Mover's Distance and TF-IDF (Chakrabarty et al., 2018), supervised models such as logistic regression purposefully trained on the specific features (for instance, sentence numbers accounting has a big impact for the FEVER dataset – evidence is often placed at the beginning of the documents) (Yoneda et al., 2018). Thus, the model presented by Yoneda et al. (top-2 result in the competition) is not domain-independent.

Leaders of the competition UNC-NLP reformulated all of the sub-tasks in terms of neural semantic matching and solved each of them with the same architecture, based on bi-LTSM (Nie et al., 2018). Their NLI component used scores from the SR component and the SR used scores from the DR step. For this reason, this model is not task-independent.

UCL Machine Reading Group, Athene UKP, Columbia NLP used Enhanced Sequential Inference Model (ESIM) or DAM as RTE module and their variations as SR component. Sweeper team conducted joint SR and RTE components training, adapting ESIM (Hidey and Diab, 2018).

At present, other current and completed competitions related to fact-checking are also held: RumourEval[3], Fact Checking in Community Question Answering Forums[4], Fake News Challenge[5], Fast & Furious Fact Check Challenge[6].

In Fake News Challenge participants used conventional well-established machine learning models: gradient boosting, Multilayer Perceptron (MLP). These models were applied to the set of features, based on TF-IDF and word embeddings (Riedel et al., 2017; Sean Baird and Pan, 2017). Masood and Aker (2018) proposed a new state of the art model after the competition. It also utilized standard machine learning methods for manually extracted features (n-grams; similarity of embeddings, tf-idf and WordNet[7]; BoW; length of sentences, etc.).

3 Model Description

The implemented model comprises four components, like the FEVER competition baseline (it is illustrated in Figure 1).

First, document retrieval selects the set of relevant documents $\{d_1, ..., d_m\}$ for each claim c from

---

[3]http://alt.qcri.org/semeval2017/task8/
[4]https://competitions.codalab.org/competitions/20022
[5]http://www.fakenewschallenge.org/
[6]https://www.herox.com/factcheck/community
[7]https://mitpress.mit.edu/books/wordnet

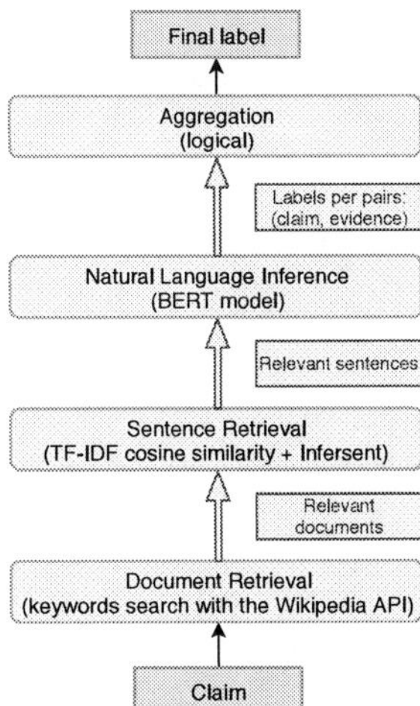

Figure 1: Four-stage model structure. Outputs of the model in each step are shown in grey boxes near the arrows.

the corpus D (if it is not initially specified). Then sentence retrieval extracts sentences $\{s_1, ..., s_n\}$ from these documents, which will help in verification. Afterwards, the NLI model f analyzes the extracted sentences in pairs with the statements and issues a verdict for each pair. Ultimately, aggregation step is implemented to obtain the final forecast: $agg(f(c, s_1), ..., f(c, s_n))$.

3.1 Document Retrieval

Search in the corpus (Wikipedia): Here we have implemented the Document Retrieval stage from (Hanselowski et al., 2018b). We applied Python Wikipedia API[8] to retrieve relevant documents from Wikipedia corpus. The following list of keywords and phrases from the claim has been taken to construct search queries: noun phrases, named entities, part of the sentence up to the "head" word. For each query, the top-k results were selected for the final list. Because sometimes there are many search queries for each claim, additionally, the filtering of results was performed. We applied Porter Stemmer to all titles of the found documents. Then we selected those documents that fully contained an initial query.

Determining document relevance: We proposed the following algorithm. Initially, the keywords (noun phrases and named entities) are highlighted from the claim. If the document contains none of them (after stemming), it is considered as "unrelated". Otherwise, an additional examination

is conducted. The cosine distance between TF-IDF embeddings of the claim and each sentence in the document is calculated. If the maximum is lower than some fixed bound, the document is also considered as "unrelated".

3.2 Sentence Retrieval

We chose the combination of the TF-IDF approach and Infersent[9] for the SR stage. To find the similarity between two texts we calculated the cosine between their TF-IDF representations with the weight 0.45 and the cosine between Infersent embeddings (built on the Glove) with the weight 0.55. These weights were selected using the validation. The set of top-k sentences closest to the statement by this measure was selected.

We have also experimented with other encoding options (Glove, Word2vec), ranked by variations of BM25 (Trotman et al., 2014) and further re-ranked with BERT. But the final quality for these options was lower (see chapter 5 for the details).

3.3 Natural Language Inference

NLI component determines a relationship between the statement and each retrieved sentence from the previous step. Bidirectional Embedding Representations from Transformers (BERT) model was employed, as it had high results for several Glue dataset tasks (Devlin et al., 2018). Sentences from the evidence set (combined into one paragraph or stand-alone) and claim statement were involved as the "premise" and the "hypothesis" in terms of RTE. The evidence set here is the set of sentences from the SR stage.

3.4 Aggregation

In case of training BERT model on separate sentences, we applied an additional aggregation step to obtain the final prediction.

CatBoost gradient boosting model was applied as the main algorithm at this step. It was trained on the stacked predictions from the NLI step.

It is also possible to use the logical aggregation (if there is not enough training data). If all predicted labels are "NOT ENOUGH INFO", the result is the same. Otherwise, a vote between the number of "SUPPORTS" and "REFUTES" labels is taken. In the case of equality, the answer is given according to the label with the highest NLI component score. Another variant is to use the sum of

---

[8]https://wikipedia.readthedocs.io/en/latest/

[9]https://github.com/facebookresearch/InferSent

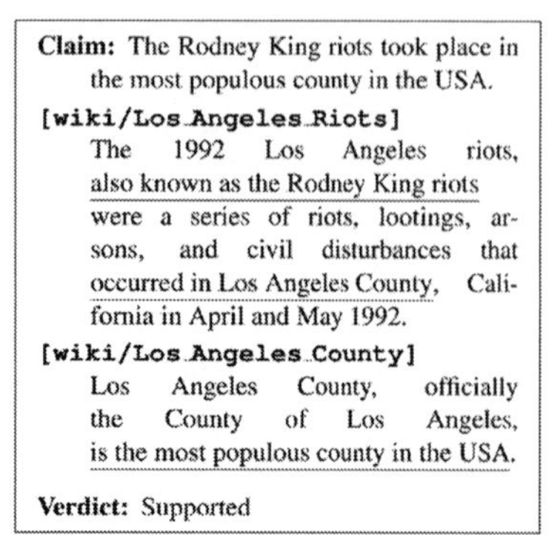

Figure 2: Example of FEVER task from (Thorne et al., 2018a). The required evidence set for the claim consists of two sentences.

class probabilities for voting.

4 Evaluation Setup

To assess the quality and verify domain-independence of our approach we tested the proposed model on several datasets and several tasks.

4.1 Datasets

Fact Extraction and VERification: The dataset from the FEVER competition (Thorne et al., 2018a) was selected as the main collection for the analysis of the presented model. Its corpus includes approximately 5.4M Wikipedia articles. All statements (about 220K) are split into 3 classes: "SUPPORTS", "REFUTES", "NOT ENOUGH INFO", depending on the presence of the corresponding evidence in the corpus. Evidence is a sentence (or set of sentences), which allows making a conclusion about the truth or falsity of the claim.

The organizers of the competition proposed the special "FEVER score" metrics. It awards points for accuracy only if the correct evidence is found. Thus, the goal is not only to identify the label correctly but also to highlight relevant evidence. Nowadays, FEVER collection is the only large collection for fact-checking with the usage of additional information.

Fake News Challenge: The Fake News Challenge competition was held in 2017 with the aim of automating the Stance Detection task. It contains 4 classes of headers paired with the articles' bodies: "agrees" (the text is in agreement with the title), "disagrees" (the text is in disagreement with the title), "discusses" (the text describes the

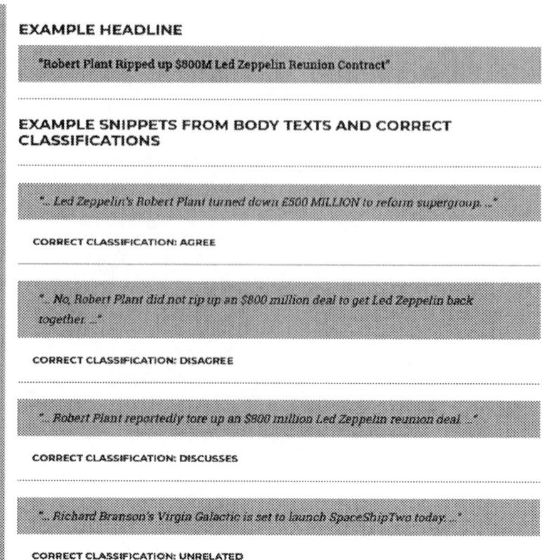

Figure 3: Example of Fake News Challenge task

same topic, but does not take any position related with the title), "unrelated" (the text and the title describe different topics). The dataset consists of around 75k such pairs for about 2587 texts.

In this competition, a special metrics was developed. It awards 0.25 for the correct separation of the class "unrelated" from "related" (the rest) and an additional 0.75 for the correct assignment of the first three labels. The maximum score on the test part is 11651.25.

4.2 Implementation and Training Details

Fact Extraction and VERification: The following model hyperparameters were fixed: Wikipedia API returns top-3 results for each query; the Sentence Retrieval selects top-20 sentences.

All words and phrases utilized to identify relevant documents were extracted using the Constituency Parsing, Named Entity Recognition, and Dependency Parsing implemented in the AllenNLP library. We applied Porter Stemmer from NLTK for stemming.

The first two parts (Sentence Retrieval and Document Retrieval) do not require a training step. We trained NLI component on examples of classes "SUPPORTS" and "REFUTES" from the training sample. As for statements with the "NOT ENOUGH INFO" label there is no ground truth evidence, we took the top-3 sentences from the retrieval part of the model. This number was chosen to balance "NOT ENOUGH INFO" and "SUPPORTS" classes. BERT Large was trained from the official baseline[10] for 1 epoch on mini-batches of size 32 with the learning rate 3e-5.

We used a part of the validation sample (random 70%) to train the CatBoost aggregation method. CatBoost was trained on trees of depth 9 for 500 iterations (other parameters were taken by default).

Fake News Challenge: In this case, we applied the second variant of the Document Retrieval (determining the relevance of a particular document). Keywords for filtering were selected with the Constituency Parsing and Named Entity Recognition modules from AllenNLP. The filtering threshold for TF-IDF in the Document Retrieval component was chosen 0.05. The Sentence Retrieval highlighted top-5 sentences for each title.

The dataset was divided into training and validation samples according to the official competition repository[11].

To train BERT we used all three classes ("agrees", "disagrees", "discusses"). We chose the BERT Base version because the dataset is small. In contrast to FEVER, here the full paragraph composed of 5 separate sentences for each statement was submitted as the input because there is no ground-truth markup for the correct evidence. Thus, the aggregation stage is not required (the final result is obtained directly from BERT). The model was trained for 5 epochs on mini-batches of size 32 with the learning rate 2e-5.

5   Results and Analysis

5.1   Fact Extraction and VERification

The proposed model has many modifications: hyperparameters of TF-IDF (binarization, stop-words filtering, lower case conversion, idf usage, sublinear tf usage); application of coreference resolution (replacement of pronouns on representational entities or their addition to the beginning of the corresponding sentences); aggregation variants (boosting or logical).

5.1.1   Document Retrieval

We achieved the quality 0.908 on the validation set for the Document Retrieval component. Here the predicted set of the documents was considered as correct if it contained full evidence for the examined claim.

Sentence Retrieval	Score
Jaccard	0.8574
Glove	0.8548
Infersent (on Glove)	0.9025
TF-IDF, n-grams range (1, 2)	0.8930
+ lowercase	0.8934
+ max df (0.85)	0.8947
+ sublinear tf	0.8976
+ traditional stop-words filtration	0.8889
TF-IDF, n-grams range (1, 1)	0.8926
+ lowercase	0.8930
+ max df, sublinear tf	0.8997
+ binary	0.9024
+ weighted Infersent	**0.9081**

Table 1: Results of Sentence Retrieval on the validation set for the selection of the top-5 sentences. For TF-IDF cumulative results for applied techniques are provided. tf/df - term/document frequency, sublinear tf = 1 + log(tf), max df - all words with df higher, than threshold are considered as stop-words.

5.1.2   Sentence Retrieval

The results of the Sentence Retrieval for finding top-5 sentences are presented in Table 1. The most successful variant was the TF-IDF search by unigrams with the filtering of stop-words selected in each document, binarization and lower case conversion in the combination with Infersent embeddings. Again, the predicted set was considered as correct if it contained entire evidence set.

We considered all words whose proportion in a particular document is higher than 0.85 as stop-words. The importance of using such stop-words follows from the fact that in case of determining the most significant sentences *inside* the document, they do not play an important role. The term frequency binarization has a significant impact because only the availability of information is important but not the number of references.

We also experimented with FastText embeddings, but Glove achieved higher results in all cases (see Figure 4).

In addition, we tried different BM25 modifications: BM25L, BM25+, BM25Okapi. The optimal combination was stop-words filtering, lower case conversion and Krovetz stemming. The results for the selection of the top-20 sentences are presented in Table 2.

---

[10]https://github.com/google-research/bert
[11]https://github.com/FakeNewsChallenge/fnc-1-baseline

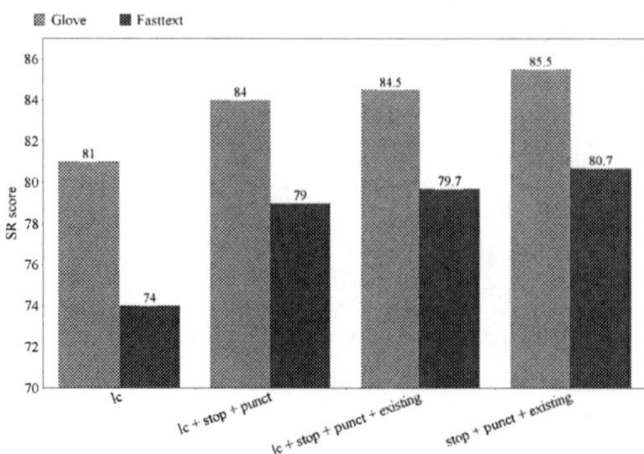

Figure 4: SR-score for Glove and FastText embeddings. lc – lowercase; stop + punct – filtering stopwords and punctuation for embeddings calculation; existing – averaging only by words from the dictionary (otherwise zero vectors were considered for OOV).

algorithm	lc + stop	lc + stop + Krovetz
BM25Okapi	0.93389	0.93414
BM25+	0.93314	0.93419
BM25L	0.94124	0.94224

Table 2: The results of SR component on the validation sample for the top 20 sentences selection. lc – lowercase, stop – stop-words filtering, Krovertz – Krovetz stemming.

As it was mentioned above, we utilized the top-20 extracted sentences for each claim in our solution (the results are fully correlated with Table 1 for top-5 sentences). We chose this value for two reasons: a relatively high quality ($\sim$94.7) should be achieved, and the number itself should not be very large to simplify further analysis and aggregation. Thus, the quality changed faintly starting with the top-20 and reached $\sim$95.1 for the top-50.

Coreference resolution gave us 0.9041 for the top-5 sentences extraction. We used Stanford NLP Coreference parser (we also experimented with the Co-reference Resolution module from AllenNLP). Here, we appended representative mentions of pronouns to the beginning of the sentences. But it did not improve the quality. This can be explained by the fact that the fixed document refers to exactly one entity (mentioned in its title) very often. Therefore, additional mentioning does not make sense for the relevancy evaluation.

5.1.3 Natural Language Inference

The quality of the BERT model according to the accuracy metrics was 0.834 (classification of the individual sentences into 3 classes) on a balanced subset of the validation sample. In this case, to solve the coreference problem, we added the titles of the documents to the beginning of the sentences through the separator. In contrast with the relevance assessment, it is important to have a comprehension of what entity is considered.

5.1.4 Aggregation

For 30% of the validation sample, we achieved accuracy 74.81 for the CatBoost aggregation and 73.47 for the logical aggregation. In the case of CatBoost, the model was trained on 70% of the validation set and was tested on the remaining 30

Confusion matrices for logical aggregation on the full validation sample and CatBoost aggregation on its test part are presented in tables 3 and 4 respectively. In the first case, the "NOT ENOUGH INFO" label is the greatest difficulty for the model. In the second case, the classes have approximately equal complexity, but the main fraction of errors also occurs due to the separation of "NOT ENOUGH INFO" from the rest.

For the second variant of logical aggregation (voting by the sum of the class probabilities predicted by BERT model), the maximum accuracy was 72.98. It is lower than 73.47 for the first case.

Our model achieves the accuracy 71.72 for labels and F1-score 70.20 for retrieved evidence on the test set (the results are presented in Table 5).

We tried two prediction options for the evidence. In the first case, only those sentences whose labels match with the final prediction were added to the answer. In the second case, we complemented this set to 5 sentences, according to the ranking of the Sentence Retrieval. This raises the FEVER score (a key metrics for the competition) on the test set from 66.69 to 67.68. However, precision falls significantly (from 71.66 to 41.36), and, respectively, the F1 score for the evidence decreases too.

Additionally, we trained BERT for binary classification into classes "NOT ENOUGH INFO"/"ENOUGH INFO" and re-ranked sentences by the probability of "ENOUGH INFO" label. Thus, the order of relevant sentences from the Sequence Retrieval component was replaced by the order according to this BERT model. However, it did not give positive results – the FEVER score on the test sample even slightly decreased (down to 67.62).

	predicted labels		
	SUPPORTS	REFUTES	NOT ENOUGH INFO
SUPPORTS	**5734**	229	703
REFUTES	599	**4856**	1211
NOT ENOUGH INFO	1465	1238	**3963**

Table 3: Confusion matrix for logical aggregation

	predicted labels		
	SUPPORTS	REFUTES	NOT ENOUGH INFO
SUPPORTS	**1595**	65	347
REFUTES	110	**1395**	434
NOT ENOUGH INFO	250	346	**1458**

Table 4: Confusion matrix for CatBoost aggregation

Team name	Evidence F1 (%)	Label Accuracy (%)	FEVER Score
DREAM (MSRA+MSNews)*	39.33	**76.42**	**69.76**
a.soleimani.b*	38.61	71.86	69.66
abcd_zh*	39.14	72.81	69.40
cunlp*	37.65	72.47	68.80
dominiks*	36.26	71.54	68.46
own*	36.80	72.03	67.56
GEAR*	36.87	71.60	67.10
UNC-NLP	52.96	68.21	64.23
UCL Machine Reading Group	34.97	67.62	62.52
Athene UKP TU Darmstadt	36.97	65.46	61.58
Papelo	64.85	61.08	57.36
Our model	70.20	71.72	66.69
Our model (all 5)	53.21	71.72	*67.68*

Table 5: Results on the FEVER test dataset (top teams)
* - after competition (up to 19.08.2019)

5.1.5 Error Analysis

Document Retrieval: Errors in the DR component are often caused by the misspelling of entities in statements: "Homer *Hickman* wrote some historical fiction novels." vs. "Homer *Hickam*" or "2015 was the year of the Disaster *Aritst* film (film) started." vs. "The Disaster *Artist*".

Another popular mistake is the lack of keywords from the title in the claim. For example, the evidence set for the statement "Christian Gottlob Neefe was an *opera writer*" includes the document "Composer".

The third type of error is dividing one entity into several. For instance, in the claim "The Food Network is a channel that ran *Giada at Home*." our model highlights two entities: "Giada" and "Home" and selects documents with that titles.

Sentence Retrieval: The SR component works mostly correctly since 20 sentences are selected for each claim. Errors often occur in the case of composite evidence where one sentence clarifies some information from another.

Natural Language Inference: The main source of errors is cases with very similar concepts. For example, claim "Wildfang is a US-based women's apparel company featuring *pants* that are tomboyish in style" has "NOT ENOUGH INFO" label. But the model selects evidence "Wildfang is a US-based women 's apparel company featuring *clothing* that is tomboyish in style" and classifies this claim as "SUPPORTS".

There are also opposite cases where words with

different meanings don't have a key impact. So, for the claim "Michigan is a *stop destination* for recreational boating within the U.S." the correct label is "SUPPORTS" with the evidence "Michigan # As a result, it is one of the leading *U.S. states* for recreational boating.". Our model predicts "REFUTES" due to the words "stop destination" vs. "state". Another interesting example: the statement "Seohyun was *only born on July* 28, 1991." has ground truth label "SUPPORTS" with the corresponding evidence "Seo Ju-hyun -LRB- *born June* 28 , 1991 -RRB- ...". Our model predicts the label "REFUTES" focusing on the words "June" and "July" and not the word "only".

Also, the BERT model makes predictions for separate sentences. For the claim "Papua comprised all of a country" the correct label is "SUPPORTS" with the evidence comprising "Papua is the largest and easternmost province of Indonesia, comprising most of western New Guinea" and the document "Western_New_Guinea". But this evidence separately is not enough to make the right conclusion.

5.2 Fake News Challenge

The TF-IDF approach calculated by unigrams and bigrams with filtering of standard stop-words was optimal for the relevance determination (after evaluation by keywords). These parameters differ from the TF-IDF parameters in the Sentence Retrieval. In this case, we filtered standard stop-words (we utilized the list from NLTK), as they do not affect the global assessment of the complete document.

BERT achieved 0.822 accuracy for the classification into one of three classes. We also tried to apply coreference resolution. However, as for the FEVER dataset, no improvement was received. We achieved accuracy 0.815 as maximum among all the cases under consideration (unrepresentative mentions replacement, addition to beginning of the sentences, using of pronouns only). This can be explained by the fact that all 5 sentences are submitted to the NLI component as a single text. And this text already contains representative references to the pronouns with a high probability.

We also estimated the contribution of the features of retrieval components. It was detected that the filtering of the documents by keywords for the binary definition of the type "related"/"unrelated" improves the quality of the final model from 9430

Team name	FNC score
Zhang et al. (2018)	**10097.00**
Masood and Aker (2018)	9565.70
SOLAT in the SWEN	9556.50
Athene	9550.75
UCLMR	9521.50
Chips Ahoy!	9345.50
CLUlings	9289.50
Our model	*9808.00*

Table 6: Results on the FNC test dataset. FNC-score - relative competition score

	predicted labels			
	unrel.	discuss	agree	disagree
unrelated	**6416**	368	69	45
discuss	123	**1499**	130	48
agree	55	172	**504**	31
disagree	12	50	20	**80**

Table 7: Confusion matrix on the FNC validation set

to 9592 points. The reason is that the method has high precision 0.9776 for the class "unrelated". This approach has a relatively small recall 0.5581, but combining with TF-IDF rises it to 0.9668 (it is higher than 0.95 for the separate TF-IDF usage). This observation demonstrates that a preliminary analysis of the presence of the keywords is important for document relevance determination. Discarding the traditional stop-words increases the total score from 9592.0 to 9808.0 (or 0.8417 of max) with the total accuracy at 0.883. The results are presented in Table 6.

Confusion matrix (Table 7) on the validation part shows that the class "disagree" is the hardest one for the model. The reason is that its proportion in the training sample is only 2.8%. Nevertheless, the macro-averaged class-wise F1 score is high - 0.709. It is a very important metric in this case (Hanselowski et al., 2018a) and models of competition participants achieve only $\sim$0.60.

It should be noted that fewer examples started to belong to the class "unrelated" when we reduced the hyperparameter in the TF-IDF filtering (that is, the model separated only the most explicit articles). It increased the probability of the correct classification into the remaining 3 classes (which has a great significance in this competition). The highest score of 3799.75 (or 0.8541) on the validation set was obtained with the filtration hyperparameter value 0.05. It is also worth to notice that BERT model demonstrated here significantly higher performance (in terms of accuracy) than on the test part: 0.822 vs. 0.783.

6 Conclusion

The paper presents a domain-independent model for checking factual information using automatic information extraction. The presented model was inspired by the FEVER baseline but has significant improvement at all 4 stages (document retrieval, sentence retrieval, natural language inference, aggregation). Experimental and theoretical analysis of all new features was carried out.

The proposed model exploits no data-specific features. Moreover, it can solve all of the sub-tasks (perform at all 4 steps) independently because none of the components use the scores of the others. We experimentally demonstrated that the model can perform at the same level as the current state-of-the-art models on the two most popular tasks and datasets.

While the model already demonstrates good results, an important further improvement is its integration with the methods that take into account additional linguistic features (for instance, discourse information for an evidence set creation).

7 Acknowledges

The article was prepared within the framework of the HSE University Basic Research Program and funded by the Russian Academic Excellence Project '5-100'.

References

Tuhin Chakrabarty, Tariq Alhindi, and Smaranda Muresan. 2018. Robust document retrieval and individual evidence modeling for fact extraction and verification. In *Proceedings of the First Workshop on Fact Extraction and VERification (FEVER)*, pages 127–131, Brussels, Belgium. Association for Computational Linguistics.

Danqi Chen, Adam Fisch, Jason Weston, and Antoine Bordes. 2017. Reading wikipedia to answer open-domain questions. *CoRR*, abs/1704.00051.

Jacob Devlin, Ming-Wei Chang, Kenton Lee, and Kristina Toutanova. 2018. BERT: pre-training of deep bidirectional transformers for language understanding. *CoRR*, abs/1810.04805.

Andreas Hanselowski, Avinesh PVS, Benjamin Schiller, Felix Caspelherr, Debanjan Chaudhuri, Christian M. Meyer, and Iryna Gurevych. 2018a. A retrospective analysis of the fake news challenge stance-detection task. In *Proceedings of the 27th International Conference on Computational Linguistics*, pages 1859–1874, Santa Fe, New Mexico, USA. Association for Computational Linguistics.

Andreas Hanselowski, Hao Zhang, Zile Li, Daniil Sorokin, Benjamin Schiller, Claudia Schulz, and Iryna Gurevych. 2018b. UKP-athene: Multi-sentence textual entailment for claim verification. In *Proceedings of the First Workshop on Fact Extraction and VERification (FEVER)*, pages 103–108, Brussels, Belgium. Association for Computational Linguistics.

Christopher Hidey and Mona Diab. 2018. Team SWEEPer: Joint sentence extraction and fact checking with pointer networks. In *Proceedings of the First Workshop on Fact Extraction and VERification (FEVER)*, pages 150–155, Brussels, Belgium. Association for Computational Linguistics.

Jackson Luken, Nanjiang Jiang, and Marie-Catherine de Marneffe. 2018. QED: A fact verification system for the FEVER shared task. In *Proceedings of the First Workshop on Fact Extraction and VERification (FEVER)*, pages 156–160, Brussels, Belgium. Association for Computational Linguistics.

Razan Masood and Ahmet Aker. 2018. The fake news challenge: Stance detection using traditional machine learning approaches.

Yixin Nie, Haonan Chen, and Mohit Bansal. 2018. Combining fact extraction and verification with neural semantic matching networks. *CoRR*, abs/1811.07039.

Ray Oshikawa, Jing Qian, and William Yang Wang. 2018. A survey on natural language processing for fake news detection. *CoRR*, abs/1811.00770.

Wolfgang Otto. 2018. Team GESIS cologne: An all in all sentence-based approach for FEVER. In *Proceedings of the First Workshop on Fact Extraction and VERification (FEVER)*, pages 145–149, Brussels, Belgium. Association for Computational Linguistics.

Ankur P. Parikh, Oscar Täckström, Dipanjan Das, and Jakob Uszkoreit. 2016. A decomposable attention model for natural language inference. In *EMNLP*.

Yifan Qiao, Chenyan Xiong, Zheng-Hao Liu, and Zhiyuan Liu. 2019. Understanding the behaviors of BERT in ranking. *CoRR*, abs/1904.07531.

Benjamin Riedel, Isabelle Augenstein, Georgios P. Spithourakis, and Sebastian Riedel. 2017. A simple but tough-to-beat baseline for the fake news challenge stance detection task. *CoRR*, abs/1707.03264.

Doug Sibley Sean Baird and Yuxi Pan. 2017. Talos targets disinformation with fake news challenge victory.

Chengcheng Shao, Giovanni Luca Ciampaglia, Onur Varol, Alessandro Flammini, and Filippo Menczer. 2017. The spread of fake news by social bots. *CoRR*, abs/1707.07592.

James Thorne, Andreas Vlachos, Christos Christodoulopoulos, and Arpit Mittal. 2018a. FEVER: a large-scale dataset for fact extraction and VERification. In *NAACL-HLT*.

James Thorne, Andreas Vlachos, Oana Cocarascu, Christos Christodoulopoulos, and Arpit Mittal. 2018b. The Fact Extraction and VERification (FEVER) shared task. In *Proceedings of the First Workshop on Fact Extraction and VERification (FEVER)*.

Andrew Trotman, Antti Puurula, and Blake Burgess. 2014. Improvements to bm25 and language models examined. In *Proceedings of the 2014 Australasian Document Computing Symposium*, ADCS '14, pages 58:58–58:65, New York, NY, USA. ACM.

Takuma Yoneda, Jeff Mitchell, Johannes Welbl, Pontus Stenetorp, and Sebastian Riedel. 2018. Ucl machine reading group: Four factor framework for fact finding (hexaf). In *Proceedings of the First Workshop on Fact Extraction and VERification (FEVER)*, pages 97–102. Association for Computational Linguistics.

Qiang Zhang, Emine Yilmaz, and Shangsong Liang. 2018. Ranking-based method for news stance detection. In *Companion Proceedings of the The Web Conference 2018*, WWW '18, pages 41–42, Republic and Canton of Geneva, Switzerland. International World Wide Web Conferences Steering Committee.

Interactive Evidence Detection:
train state-of-the-art model out-of-domain
or simple model interactively?

Chris Stahlhut

Ubiquitous Knowledge Processing Lab (UKP-TUDA)
Research Training Group KRITIS
Department of Computer Science, Technische Universitt Darmstadt
`https://www.ukp.tu-darmstadt.de/`

Abstract

Finding evidence is of vital importance in research as well as fact checking and an evidence detection method would be useful in speeding up this process. However, when addressing a new topic there is no training data and there are two approaches to get started. One could use large amounts of out-of-domain data to train a state-of-the-art method, or to use the small data that a person creates while working on the topic. In this paper, we address this problem in two steps. First, by simulating users who read source documents and label sentences they can use as evidence, thereby creating small amounts of training data for an interactively trained evidence detection model; and second, by comparing such an interactively trained model against a pre-trained model that has been trained on large out-of-domain data. We found that an interactively trained model not only often out-performs a state-of-the-art model but also requires significantly lower amounts of computational resources. Therefore, especially when computational resources are scarce, e.g. no GPU available, training a smaller model on the fly is preferable to training a well generalising but resource hungry out-of-domain model.

1 Introduction

Evidence is a crucial prerequisite for research, forming an opinion, and fact checking. Scholars spend vast amounts of time reading through countless books and other documents to find evidence relevant to their research; fact checkers read through innumerable documents to find evidence to (in)validate popular claims.

Evidence Detection (ED) aims at supporting these activities by finding textual evidence and thereby reducing the amount of reading required by a human. In this paper, we define evidence similar to Shnarch et al. (2018) as a sentence that either supports or contradicts a controversial topic,

e.g. *we should ban gambling* and is categorisable as *expert opinion, anecdote,* or *study data* (figure 1). This is similar to premise detection in argument mining, but requires the additional filtering for these particular types.

> *A 2010 Australian hospital study found that 17% of suicidal patients admitted to the Alfred Hospital's emergency department were problem gamblers.*

Figure 1: An example piece of evidence.

In this paper, we focus on the following scenario. Suppose a group of fact checkers is evaluating a set of claims that are gaining popularity. They start by distributing the claims among each other and downloading relevant articles from Wikipedia. They then intend to use an ED method to help them collect the evidence but are faced with the question of where to get the training data from. First, they could use the data that has been compiled for previous claims; or second, train a model interactively. The former approach introduces a domain shift, while the latter turns ED into a small data problem.

From this we developed our research questions

(1) Does a simple but interactively trained model out-perform a state-of-the-art model that was trained on out-of-domain data?

(2) What amount of in-domain training data is required to out-perform the state-of-the-art model trained on out-of-domain data?

We investigated the first research question by comparing the results of static models that have been trained on out-of-domain data with ones that learn on the in-domain data. As out-of-domain model we chose BERT (Devlin et al., 2018) because it performs well on both ED and Argument Mining (AM) (Reimers et al., 2019). As in-domain trained model we chose a topic agnostic

Proceedings of the Second Workshop on Fact Extraction and VERification (FEVER), pages 79–89
Hong Kong, November 3, 2019. ©2019 Association for Computational Linguistics

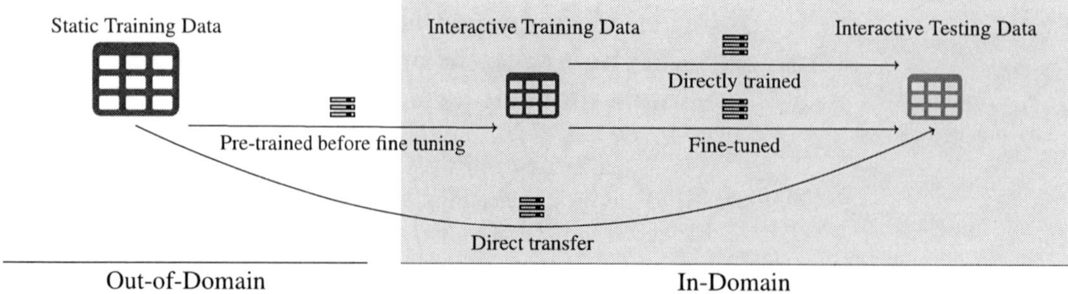

Figure 2: The relation between the out-of-domain and in-domain datasets and different training setups.

BiLSTM which performed well in in-domain experiments in AM (Stab et al., 2018). We chose a topic agnostic model because each user is working on only one topic which doesn't change between samples and therefore contains no additional information. To address the cold-start problem, we also evaluated a similar topic agnostic model that has been pre-trained on the out-of-domain data and was then fine-tuned on the in-domain data. We did not fine-tune BERT on the in-domain data, because we consider the datasets too small. Figure 2 shows the relationship between the different domains and models. To investigate our second research question, we used simulated users who each trained a personalised ED model interactively. We then compared the quality of the interactively trained or fine-tuned models with the static BERT trained on out-of-domain data. We also investigated the robustness of our results interactively fine-tuning a model for AM. We chose AM, because it is similar in that it contains arguments (pro and contra) on a controversial topic, such as *nuclear energy*.

The contributions of this paper are three fold. (1) A much simpler model can out-perform a state-of-the-art model when given in-domain training data, (2) that often only a few documents for training are required, and (3) a more realistic evaluation interactive ED than random downsampling and the datasets used in our experiments.

2   Related Work

This paper touches three areas of research, namely the overarching field of claim validation, the task domain (ED and AM) with small data, and the interaction of Natural Language Processing (NLP) components with users.

Claim Validation   Reasoning about the validity of a particular claim can be separated into three sub-tasks: document retrieval to find documents related to the claim, ED to find the relevant pieces of evidence that support or contradict the claim, and Textual Entailment (TE) to determine whether the claim follows from the evidence. The FEVER shared tasks follows this approach (Thorne et al., 2018; Thorne and Vlachos, 2019). Other approaches, such as TwoWingOS (Yin and Roth, 2018) and DeClarE (Popat et al., 2018) combine the ED and TE models into a single end-to-end method. Ma et al. (2019) used two pre-trained models, one for ED and one for TE which are then jointly fine-tuned. While presenting promising results, all of these approaches rely on static models that are trained beforehand and do not learn from the user.

Evidence detection and argument mining   Much focus of ED has been in on supporting decision making (Hua and Wang, 2017) or to find evidence for debating (Rinott et al., 2015; Aharoni et al., 2014). Evidence detection can be seen as a sub-task of AM. Argument mining is an established task within NLP with different foci, e.g. parsing arguments from student essays (Stab and Gurevych, 2017) or extracting topic related argumentative sentences from Wikipedia articles (Levy et al., 2018). Still, the cold-start problem for new domains and topics remains and multiple approaches have been suggested to address it. One approach is to increase the generalisability of a learned AM model, either by adding topic information (Stab et al., 2018) or by using distant supervision with automatically extracted data from debate portals (Al-Khatib et al., 2016). A similar method was used by Shnarch et al. (2018) who combined weakly and strongly labeled data to reduce the necessary amount of expensive to create strongly labeled data for ED. Schulz et al. (2018a) on the other hand, used multi-task learning with artificially shrunk target datasets. However, artificially shrinking a dataset to a pre-defined number of samples is not a realistic simulation method for interactive learning because it does not take the content of a document and resulting bias in the training data into account. While the previous approaches mostly worked with large amounts of data, some work with smaller datasets was conducted in the medical domain. For instance finding and classifying evidence in the abstracts of research articles (Shardlow et al., 2018; Mayer et al., 2018). However, neither of these approaches consider learning interactively from users.

Interactive NLP Combining NLP components with direct human interactions generally serves either the system or the user. Focussing on the system side is generally done to support the process of annotation for a dataset, such as improving dependency parsing of historical documents (Eckhoff and Berdicevskis, 2016) via pre-annotation. Moreover, learning directly from users is beneficial from the first sentence on in dependency parsing (Ulinski et al., 2016). Another common approach is to use active learning to reduce the amount of data to train a model (Kasai et al., 2019; Lin et al., 2019). While these approaches are beneficial in creating annotated data or speeding up the training of a model, they focus on the goal of the system. Focussing on the goal of the users, on the other hand, is all about benefiting the user, for instance supporting teachers in evaluating the diagnostic reasoning abilities of students (Schulz et al., 2018b). The INCEpTION (Klie et al., 2018) platform also focusses on the user's goals by learning from users to assist them in their annotation work. However, all these approaches assume the task to be independent from the individual user, which Stahlhut et al. (2018) showed to not be the case for ED. This is especially important, because the system's recommendations do influence what the user annotates (Fort and Sagot, 2010). The SHERLOCK system (P.V.S. et al., 2018) does does offer user specific results, but is not focussed on ED but multi-document summarisation.

3 Interactive Evidence Detection

For our experiments, we defined ED as extracting sentences from a collection of documents D that are evidential[1] regarding a controversial topic. Interactive ED considers the same task in combination with a user who provides the documents and order in which they are processed, as well as corrections of the predictions of the ED model m.

3.1 User simulation

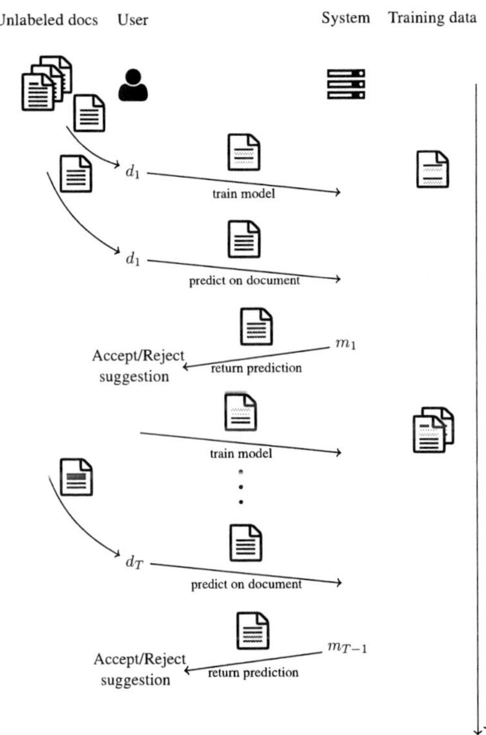

Figure 3: The user picks one unlabeled document and annotates the evidential sentences. After processing the document, it gets added to the training data for a newly trained model. Afterwards, the user picks the next document which contains suggestions from the model.

Each user sorts all documents that are relevant to their topic in alphabetical order and proceeds to read one document at a time. While reading the first document $d_1 \in D$, the user labels each sentence they find evidential regarding the topic as evidence. After reading the entire document d_1 they proceed to the next one d_2 without returning to the

---

[1]For simplicity, we are referring to arguments also as evidence.

previous one d_1. The document d_1 is then added to the training data and the interactive training begins with the training of the model m_1.

When the user opens the next document d_2, it already contains suggestions regarding evidential sentences by the model m_1. The user then accepts correct suggestions of evidential sentences, rejects incorrect suggestions, and labels missed pieces of evidence. After the user finishes reading and correcting the labels of all sentences, the amount of training data again increases and a new model m_2 is trained on them. This cycle continues until the user opens the last document d_T, $T = |D|$ which shows suggestions made by the previously trained model m_{T-1}. Figure 3 illustrates our simulation and interactive training.

3.2 Measure of work-load

In our simulation, we also required a measure that allows us to compare the amount of work a user has to perform to correct the suggestions of different models. This includes not only the incorrectly suggested evidential sentences, but also the missing ones. We therefore defined an error rate that accounts for incorrect, as well as missing suggestions of evidence. Formally, we defined the *error rate E* as the sum of the *false discovery rate* and *false omission rate*, or

$$E = (1 - P) + (1 - R), \tag{1}$$

with P being the precision and R being the recall on the evidence class.

3.3 Measurement of minimal amount of training data

To answer our second research question, we needed to measure the minimum amount of training documents μ required to out-perform a static model, which we defined as

$$\mu = \begin{cases} \min \{t \mid \forall i \in \{t, \ldots, |\mathcal{R}|\} : \mathcal{R}_i < \mathcal{B}\} & , \exists t : \mathcal{R}_t < \mathcal{B} \\ |\mathcal{R}| & , \text{otherwise,} \end{cases} \tag{2}$$

where $\mathcal{R}$ is the sequence of error-rates through time $t \in \{1, \ldots, T\}$ and $\mathcal{B}$ is the average error-rate of the baseline.

4 Data and Models

4.1 Datasets and data preparation

We used three different datasets as in-domain data for our evaluation. For ED we used two datasets, namely *ED-ACL-2014* published by Aharoni et al.

(2014) and *ED-EMNLP-2015* published by Rinott et al. (2015). As out-of-domain data, we used a dataset published by Shnarch et al. (2018), named *ED-ACL-2018*.[2] For AM, we used the dataset provided by Stab et al. (2018).

Data preparation To run the user simulation, we needed to convert the data from collections of evidential sentences to documents with sentences labeled as evidential or not.[3] We converted all three datasets into topic related collections of documents with sentential annotations. That means we took all documents that are relevant to a particular topic and labeled all sentences that are evidential towards this topic in each of these documents. For evidential sequences that are more than one sentence long, we first segmented them into individual sentences via NLTK.[4] To avoid problems due to errors in the sentence segmentation, we ignored all evidential sentences with a length of less than three tokens. The resulting datasets are highly biased towards non-evidential sentences.

ED-ACL-2014 The first ED dataset contains 12 topics and 315 articles from Wikipedia as source with 143 containing evidence. The individual pieces of evidence can be up to 16 sentences long with about half being exactly one sentence and about 90% being up to three sentences in length.

ED-EMNLP-2015 The second dataset consists of 58 topics, 19 of which are for development purposes, and 2.3k hypotheses. Of these hypotheses, 1.4k are supported by at least one piece of evidence from Wikipedia articles. The dataset uses 1.3k Wikipedia articles as source for the evidence, of which 547 contain at least one piece of evidence. We decided to exclude twelve of the test topics due to their large overlap with the ED-ACL-2014 dataset, leaving 27 test topics.

ED-ACL-2018 As out-of-domain data for the pre-trained ED models we chose the dataset presented by Shnarch et al. (2018). It contains 4k topic evidence pairs as training data and 1.7k pairs as testing data. We pre-trained models exclusively on the training data so that we could use the testing data for comparison with published literature.

---

[2]The topics and number of documents for each topic can found in the supplementary material

[3]The source code for the data preparation and experiments can be found under `https://github.com/UKPLab/fever2019-interactive-evidence-detection`.

[4]`https://www.nltk.org/`

Table 1 shows an overview of the statistics of all three ED datasets.

	Documents	Sentences	Evidence
ED-ACL-2014			
train test	143	20649	1318
ED-EMNLP-2015			
train dev	170	28540	2300
train test	234	35877	2646
ED-ACL-2018			
train	–	4065	1499
test	–	1718	683

Table 1: Statistics on the ED datasets.

Argument mining The AM corpus consists of about 25k sentences that are evidential (distinguishing supporting from contradicting evidence) or non-evidential regarding one of eight topics. The sentences of each topic were extracted from the 50 highest ranking documents retrieved by an external search engine. In our processing, we labeled the evidential sentences in the original documents. This lead to a change in number of sentences and pieces of evidence as table 2 shows. When separated into in- and out-of-domain data, we selected all documents of one topic as in-domain data, and the training data of the other seven as out-of-domain data.

	Documents	Sentences	Evidence
Original	–	25492	11139
Converted	400	39577	11538[5]

Table 2: Statistics on the AM dataset before and after the data preparation.

4.2 Models

We built two interactively trained models, $bilstm_{direct}$ and $bilstm_{fine}$, and used BERT as static model trained on the out-of-domain data. We refer to the $bilstm_{fine}$ after its pre-training but before additional fine tuning as $bilstm_{pre}$. Table 3 shows the models and which data they are trained on, ouf-of-domain, in-domain, or both. We decided to use a BiLSTM with 100 nodes, a dense layer for classification, and no input for the topic for these experiments because the in-domain training data is small and always specific to a single topic. All interactively trained models used 100-dimensional GloVe embeddings (Pennington et al., 2014) as input features and a dropout of 0.5 after the embedding layer and before the classification layer. We addressed the class imbalance by weighting the classes similar to King and Zeng (2001) using the implementation provided by scikit-learn.[6] To reduce the effect of the random initialisation, we repeated all experiments with 10 different randomisation seeds.

	Training domain	
	Out-of-Domain	In-Domain
$bilstm_{direct}$	no	yes
$bilstm_{pre}$	yes	no
$bilstm_{fine}$	yes	yes
BERT	yes	no

Table 3: Model label depending on the training data.

$bilstm_{direct}$ The directly trained model was trained as described above and received no additional input. We trained this model for 10 epochs in each iteration with one additional training document.

$bilstm_{pre}$ The pre-trained model uses the same architecture than the directly trained one. We changed no hyper-parameter except the number of epochs compared to the directly trained model. That means, we trained the $bilstm_{pre}$ model for five epochs on the out-of-domain training data and used a learning rate of 0.001 with a dropout of 0.5.

$bilstm_{fine}$ For fine-tuning, we replaced the classification layer of the $bilstm_{pre}$ model with a new one and trained this new layer for five epochs with a learning rate of 0.001. Afterwards, we unfroze the other layers and trained the complete network for five more epochs with a learning rate of 0.001. This is similar to gradual unfreezing, presented by Howard and Ruder (2018).

BERT Short for Bidirectional Encoder Representations from Transformers. We chose the BERT base model (Devlin et al., 2018) as static model, since it outperforms previously published models on both tasks (Reimers et al., 2019). We fine-tuned it for three epochs on the out-of-domain data. We provided the model with the candidate sentence, as well as the topic, because we fine-tuned the model across multiple topics of the training data and used the same model for prediction

---

[5]The number varies due to duplicated evidential sentences. There are 11128 unique pieces of evidence in the converted dataset.

[6]https://scikit-learn.org/

	Macro values across both classes			Evidence only		
	F1	Precision	Recall	F1	Precision	Recall
ED-ACL-2014						
bilstm$_{direct}$	0.509 (0.033)	0.514 (0.028)	0.526 (0.039)	0.117 (0.058)	0.091 (0.055)	0.183 (0.053)
bilstm$_{fine}$	0.481 (0.043)	0.518 (0.018)	**0.553 (0.047)**	**0.139 (0.064)**	0.088 (0.045)	**0.373 (0.118)**
BERT	**0.540 (0.052)**	**0.590 (0.055)**	0.538 (0.048)	0.118 (0.098)	**0.238 (0.105)**	0.094 (0.096)
ED-EMNLP-2015						
bilstm$_{direct}$	**0.572 (0.062)**	0.566 (0.050)	0.613 (0.075)	**0.225 (0.133)**	0.176 (0.114)	0.340 (0.160)
bilstm$_{fine}$	0.544 (0.063)	0.553 (0.046)	**0.631 (0.089)**	0.212 (0.132)	0.145 (0.101)	**0.453 (0.212)**
BERT	0.550 (0.060)	**0.596 (0.084)**	0.558 (0.081)	0.143 (0.118)	**0.251 (0.169)**	0.143 (0.171)
Argument Mining						
bilstm$_{fine}$	0.681 (0.021)	0.698 (0.014)	0.739 (0.021)	0.620 (0.027)	0.490 (0.034)	**0.848 (0.015)**
BERT	**0.754 (0.016)**	**0.747 (0.015)**	**0.779 (0.015)**	**0.676 (0.023)**	**0.599 (0.033)**	0.780 (0.038)

Table 4: The results are macro-averaged across all topics with the standard deviations shown in parenthesis.

5 Experiments

5.1 Evaluation of pre-trained models

We evaluated the pre-trained models on the testing data of their pre-training domain. That means that in the case of ED, we trained and evaluated the models on the ED-ACL-2018 dataset. For AM, we conducted a leave-one-topic-out evaluation, training on the training data of the training topics and evaluated on the testing data of the left-out topic.

	F1	Precision	Recall	Accuracy
ED-ACL-2018				
bilstm$_{pre}$	0.609	0.620	0.608	0.639
BERT	0.781	0.809	0.770	0.802
Argument Mining				
bilstm$_{pre}$	0.624	0.647	0.632	–
BERT	0.795	0.800	0.800	–

Table 5: Results of the pre-trained models on their respective training domain test data. The results are macro-averaged for F1, Precision, and Recall.

The table 5 shows the quality of the pre-trained models for both the ED and AM experiments with macro-averaged F1, precision, and recall. BERT clearly out-performed the topic agnostic model bilstm$_{pre}$ by a margin of almost 18pp macro F1 score for ED. For AM, BERT also clearly out-performed the topic agnostic model by about

17pp macro-F1 score in binary classification of evidence/no-evidence.

5.2 Static evaluation

In the static evaluation, we compared the performance of the static model with the interactively trained ones after having been trained with all training documents. We conducted the experiments in a leave-one-document-out fashion for each topic separately. Table 4 shows the results of the static evaluation. We found that although BERT reached the highest macro F1 score on the ED-ACL-2014 dataset, it did not perform better than the fine-tuned model when looking at the evidence F1 score due to its lower recall. On the ED-EMNLP-2015 dataset, all three models improved compared to the ED-ACL-2014 dataset. Furthermore, both interactively trained models improved more than BERT, increasing the gap when performing better.

We conducted the experiments on the AM data also in a leave-one-document-out fashion for each interactively processed topic, using the training data of the other topics for pre-training. We found that BERT out-performed bilstm$_{fine}$ by about 7pp macro F1 score, which is a considerable smaller margin than before fine-tuning. Moreover, the difference varies between the individual metrics, being closer in evidence F1 score and in evidence recall the bilstm$_{fine}$ model even out-performs BERT.

5.3 Interactive evaluation

To avoid irregularities due to changes in number of pieces of evidence and length of a document between different amounts of training data, we cal-

across all topics in the in-domain data. We used a PyTorch based implementation provided by Huggingface[7].

---

[7] https://github.com/huggingface/pytorch-pretrained-BERT

culated the error-rate in a leave-one-document out fashion. This means, instead of calculating the error-rate, defined by (1), on the next document the user opens which might have a different number of pieces of evidence, we calculated it on a left-out one. The left-out document then remains the same across the experiment with increasing number of training documents. We then repeated this process with each document being left-out once. As before, we repeated the experiments with ten different randomisation seeds.

Table 6 shows that the $bilstm_{fine}$ model reached a lower error-rate and therefore requires less work for the user to correct than BERT on the ED-ACL-2014 dataset. It already did so after few training documents.

Id	Docs	$bilstm_{fine}$		BERT
		μ	E	E
0	6	6.000	1.761	**1.230**
1	19	3.800	**1.526**	1.677
2	10	10.000	1.752	**1.617**
3	11	1.000	**1.288**	1.742
4	13	6.300	**1.655**	1.737
5	10	5.200	**1.612**	1.772
6	13	1.000	**1.535**	1.898
7	6	1.300	**1.665**	1.830
8	13	5.500	**1.525**	1.681
9	15	10.200	**1.307**	1.426
10	20	6.200	**1.397**	1.560
11	7	1.000	**1.445**	1.846

Table 6: Number of documents and minimum number of training documents μ to reach a smaller error-rate E than BERT for the $bilstm_{fine}$ model for each topic on the ED-ACL-2014 dataset. The values for μ and E are averaged across all left-out documents and repeated experiments.

On the ED-EMNLP-2015 dataset (table 7), we found that both interactively trained models generally out-perform the static BERT and that they reach a lower error-rate often already after one or two training documents. When comparing the interactively trained models, we found that the $bilstm_{fine}$ often reaches slightly better results than the $bilstm_{direct}$ model. BERT reached the lowest overall error-rate on topic 6 which contained only two documents. We selected the topics 1, 5, 18 and 8 for a more detailed analysis with a focus on the amount of work a user would have to do to correct the suggestions of a model. Figure 4 shows that for topic 1 (figure 4a the $bilstm_{fine}$ model out-performed the $bilstm_{direct}$ model. In the case of the topics 18 and 5 (figures 4b and 4c), we found that the both interactively trained model learned at a

similar rate. For topic 8 (figure 4d), on the other hand, neither interactively trained model reached the performance of BERT.

Id	Docs	$bilstm_{direct}$		$bilstm_{fine}$		BERT
		μ	E	μ	E	E
0	5	5.000	1.739	5.000	1.837	**1.586**
1	11	1.000	1.194	1.000	**0.932**	1.373
2	4	4.000	1.932	4.000	1.981	**1.226**
3	4	1.000	**1.432**	1.200	1.474	1.793
4	3	1.000	**1.235**	1.000	1.247	1.799
5	13	1.000	1.643	1.000	**1.591**	1.829
6	2	2.000	2.000	2.000	2.000	**0.723**
7	14	1.000	1.123	1.000	**1.011**	1.472
8	4	4.000	1.805	4.000	1.592	**1.289**
9	4	1.000	1.244	1.000	**1.182**	1.607
10	17	17.000	1.592	5.000	**1.268**	1.385
11	8	1.400	**1.307**	1.000	1.329	1.636
12	15	14.000	1.554	4.800	**1.433**	1.543
13	9	8.800	1.486	6.500	**1.405**	1.416
14	12	2.200	1.484	1.200	**1.297**	1.683
15	12	3.100	1.500	1.000	**1.366**	1.643
16	14	1.000	1.213	1.000	**1.049**	1.724
17	3	2.300	1.449	1.700	**1.401**	1.490
18	25	1.000	1.190	1.000	**1.152**	1.517
19	5	4.700	1.960	5.000	2.000	**1.903**
20	4	2.600	1.862	2.200	**1.688**	1.949
21	10	1.000	1.039	1.000	**1.019**	1.606
22	12	1.100	1.240	1.000	**1.147**	1.431
23	6	3.000	1.585	3.000	**1.478**	1.990
24	6	1.000	1.456	1.000	**1.350**	1.965
25	7	2.700	1.590	3.800	**1.461**	1.923
26	5	1.000	1.217	1.000	**1.151**	1.871

Table 7: Number of documents and minimum number of training documents μ to reach a smaller error-rate E then BERT for the $bilstm_{direct}$ and $bilstm_{fine}$ models for each topic on the ED-EMNLP-2015 dataset. The values for μ and E are averaged across all left-out documents and repeated experiments.

6 Discussion

To understand the difference in quality between the ED-ACL-2014 and ED-ACL-2015 dataset we hypothesise that the annotators gained more experience which lead to a more consistent evidence annotation. This might also beneficial for machine learning. When creating the ED-ACL-2014 dataset, Aharoni et al. (2014) stated that they used five annotators that searched Wikipedia independently from each other for evidence on the same topic. Afterwards, they used five different annotators to accept or reject these annotations. Rinott et al. (2015) used the same process, although not for twelve but 58 topics. This means that the same annotator had the opportunity to work on many more topics than when constructing the ED-ACL-2014 dataset.

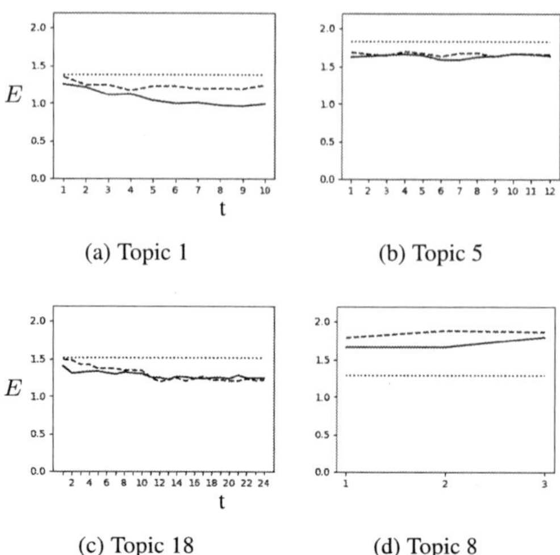

(a) Topic 1   (b) Topic 5

(c) Topic 18   (d) Topic 8

Figure 4: The average error-rates E of the bilstm$_{\text{fine}}$ (solid lines), bilstm$_{\text{direct}}$ (dashed lines), and BERT (dotted lines) through time t.

To evaluate this hypothesis, we chose the twelve topics from the ED-EMNLP-2015 dataset which we excluded due to their large overlap with the topics of the ED-ACL-2014 dataset. While being very similar in topic and using the same Wikipedia articles as sources, they are not identical. Some hypotheses were added and others were removed. The bilstm$_{\text{fine}}$ and bilstm$_{\text{direct}}$ models improved considerable ($\approx$9pp and $\approx$13pp respectively in evidence F1 score) on the later created dataset compared to the previously created one. To our surprise however, we found that in stark contrast to the other models, BERT's performance decreased. We assume that due to the larger number of topics, the annotators gained more experience and created more consistent annotations, making the ED-EMNLP-2015 dataset more machine learning friendly.

	F1	Precision	Recall
bilstm$_{\text{direct}}$	0.243 [+0.126]	0.195 [+0.104]	0.345 [+0.162]
bilstm$_{\text{fine}}$	0.233 [+0.094]	0.155 [+0.067]	0.509 [+0.136]
BERT	0.110 [−0.008]	0.290 [+0.052]	0.073 [−0.021]

Table 8: The results of the evidence class scores and are macro-averaged across the previously held out topics of the ED-EMNLP-2015 dataset. The values in the brackets are the difference the to ED-ACL-2014 dataset.

While BERT performed very well on the ED-ACL-2018 dataset, when tested on the ED-ACL-2014 and ED-EMNLP-2015 datasets, its perfor-

mance dropped significantly. We developed two hypotheses that might explain this drop.

The topic labels used in the ED-EMNLP-2015 dataset are worded as debate motions which is different from the wording in the ED-ACL-2018 dataset. In the latter dataset, the topics are worded directly as a controversial statement, e.g. *We should ban gambling*, which is different from the wording as a debate motion *This house would ban gambling*. To test this hypothesis, we selected three topics from the ED-EMNLP-2015 dataset which also appear in ED training domain for BERT. We then updated the topic label to be the same as the one used in the training data for BERT and evaluated the effect this had on the performance. We found that the modification of the topic label to be more like the one used while training BERT increased the evidence F1 score by 1pp (table 9); the wording of the topic label therefore cannot be the reason for the low performance of BERT.

	F1	Precision	Recall
in-domain topic label	0.077	0.213	0.050
out-of-domain topic label	0.087	0.262	0.060

Table 9: The results show only the evidence class and are macro-averaged across the three selected topics.

In our second hypothesis, we suggest that the sentence segmentation into partial evidence caused the dramatic drop in recall between the ED-ACL-2018 and other ED datasets. If so, then using the complete pieces of evidence that consist of multiple sentences would be classified correctly with much higher probability. We therefore also evaluated the recall that BERT reached on the multiple sentence long pieces of evidence on the previously selected three topics. We found that not segmenting the evidence increased the performance by almost 4pp to 0.098. This is too small to explain the observed drop in performance.

A possible influence on the minimum number of training documents μ is also the order in which the documents are processed. The error-rate of topic 1 in the ED-EMNLP-2015 dataset first decreased with the first four training documents and then varied. For topic 8, the error-rate increased with the amount of increasing training data. It is therefore possible that can also be dependent on the order of documents. However, as we defined the minimum number of training documents μ as the first document after which it out-performs the baseline, which means that there will be no subsequent reduction in performance below the baseline, we think that the influence is small and can be treated as additional noise. We decided to use an alphabetical order, because it is deterministic and does not add additional degrees of freedom which an ranking based order would, e.g. by using term frequency versus TF-IDF.

7 Conclusion

In this paper we investigated the question of whether to use large amounts of out-of-domain data or small amounts of interactively generated data to train an ED or AM model. To answer this question, we simulated users who read documents relevant to a particular topic and while doing so, generated training data for the interactively trained models. We also converted three existing datasets, two ED and one AM dataset, into collections of topic relevant documents of labeled sentences. We then used the simulated users working on the newly created corpora to interactively train a model and compared it to a state-of-the-art static model, in our case BERT, that was fine-tuned on the out-of-domain data. We found that especially for ED the interactively trained models out-performed BERT in evidence F1 score. We also found that it would take the user less work to correct the predictions of an interactively trained model. Moreover, it often does so after only a few iterations. In AM, we found that although BERT performed best, it does so by a small margin.

We conclude from these results that unless computational resources are abundant, e.g. a GPU is available for training as well as prediction, it is better to train a model interactively, even if it is no longer state-of-the-art. This is especially important when considering constraints placed on interactive system that are used by multiple users in parallel. In the future, we intend apply these results to support real users in finding evidence by interactively training an ED model.

Acknowledgements

This work has been supported by the German Research Foundation (DFG) as part of the Research Training Group KRITIS No. GRK 2222/1. Calculations for this research were conducted on the Lichtenberg high performance computer of the TU Darmstadt.

References

Ehud Aharoni, Anatoly Polnarov, Tamar Lavee, Daniel Hershcovich, Ran Levy, Ruty Rinott, Dan Gutfreund, and Noam Slonim. 2014. A Benchmark Dataset for Automatic Detection of Claims and Evidence in the Context of Controversial Topics. In *Proceedings of the First Workshop on Argumentation Mining*, pages 64–68. Association for Computational Linguistics.

Khalid Al-Khatib, Henning Wachsmuth, Matthias Hagen, Jonas Köhler, and Benno Stein. 2016. Cross-Domain Mining of Argumentative Text through Distant Supervision. In *Proceedings of the 2016 Conference of the North American Chapter of the Association for Computational Linguistics: Human Language Technologies*, pages 1395–1404, San Diego, California. Association for Computational Linguistics.

Jacob Devlin, Ming-Wei Chang, Kenton Lee, and Kristina Toutanova. 2018. BERT: Pre-training of Deep Bidirectional Transformers for Language Understanding. *arXiv:1810.04805 [cs]*.

Hanne Martine Eckhoff and Aleksandrs Berdicevskis. 2016. Automatic parsing as an efficient pre-annotation tool for historical texts. In *Proceedings of the Workshop on Language Technology Resources and Tools for Digital Humanities (LT4DH)*, pages 62–70, Osaka, Japan. The COLING 2016 Organizing Committee.

Karën Fort and Benoît Sagot. 2010. Influence of Pre-Annotation on POS-Tagged Corpus Development. In *Proceedings of the Fourth Linguistic Annotation Workshop*, pages 56–63, Uppsala, Sweden. Association for Computational Linguistics.

Jeremy Howard and Sebastian Ruder. 2018. Universal Language Model Fine-tuning for Text Classification. *arXiv:1801.06146 [cs, stat]*.

Xinyu Hua and Lu Wang. 2017. Understanding and Detecting Supporting Arguments of Diverse Types. In *Proceedings of the 55th Annual Meeting of the Association for Computational Linguistics (Volume 2: Short Papers)*, pages 203–208, Vancouver, Canada. Association for Computational Linguistics.

Jungo Kasai, Kun Qian, Sairam Gurajada, Yunyao Li, and Lucian Popa. 2019. Low-resource Deep Entity Resolution with Transfer and Active Learning. In *Proceedings of the 57th Annual Meeting of the Association for Computational Linguistics*, pages 5851–5861, Florence, Italy. Association for Computational Linguistics.

Gary King and Langche Zeng. 2001. Logistic Regression in Rare Events Data. *Political Analysis*, 9(2):137–163.

Jan-Christoph Klie, Michael Bugert, Beto Boullosa, Richard Eckart de Castilho, and Iryna Gurevych.

2018. The INCEpTION Platform: Machine-Assisted and Knowledge-Oriented Interactive Annotation. In *Proceedings of the 27th International Conference on Computational Linguistics: System Demonstrations*, pages 5–9, Santa Fe, New Mexico. Association for Computational Linguistics.

Ran Levy, Ben Bogin, Shai Gretz, Ranit Aharonov, and Noam Slonim. 2018. Towards an argumentative content search engine using weak supervision. In *Proceedings of the 27th International Conference on Computational Linguistics*, pages 2066–2081, Santa Fe, New Mexico, USA. Association for Computational Linguistics.

Bill Yuchen Lin, Dong-Ho Lee, Frank F. Xu, Ouyu Lan, and Xiang Ren. 2019. AlpacaTag: An Active Learning-based Crowd Annotation Framework for Sequence Tagging. In *Proceedings of the 57th Annual Meeting of the Association for Computational Linguistics: System Demonstrations*, pages 58–63, Florence, Italy. Association for Computational Linguistics.

Jing Ma, Wei Gao, Shafiq Joty, and Kam-Fai Wong. 2019. Sentence-Level Evidence Embedding for Claim Verification with Hierarchical Attention Networks. page 12.

Tobias Mayer, Elena Cabrio, and Serena Villata. 2018. Evidence Type Classification in Randomized Controlled Trials. In *Proceedings of the 5th Workshop on Argument Mining*, pages 29–34, Brussels, Belgium. Association for Computational Linguistics.

Jeffrey Pennington, Richard Socher, and Christopher D. Manning. 2014. GloVe: Global Vectors for Word Representation. In *Empirical Methods in Natural Language Processing (EMNLP)*, pages 1532–1543.

Kashyap Popat, Subhabrata Mukherjee, Andrew Yates, and Gerhard Weikum. 2018. DeClarE: Debunking Fake News and False Claims using Evidence-Aware Deep Learning. In *Proceedings of the 2018 Conference on Empirical Methods in Natural Language Processing*, pages 22–32, Brussels, Belgium. Association for Computational Linguistics.

Avinesh P.V.S., Benjamin Hättasch, Orkan Özyurt, Carsten Binnig, and Christian M. Meyer. 2018. Sherlock: A system for interactive summarization of large text collections. *Proceedings of the VLDB Endowment*, 11(12):1902–1905.

Nils Reimers, Benjamin Schiller, Tillman Beck, Johannes Daxenberger, and Iryna Gurevych. 2019. Classification and Clustering of Arguments with Contextualized Word Embeddings. In *Proceedings of the 57th Annual Meeting of the Association for Computational Linguistics*, page to appear, Florence, Italy. Association for Computational Linguistics.

Ruty Rinott, Lena Dankin, Carlos Alzate Perez, Mitesh M. Khapra, Ehud Aharoni, and Noam Slonim. 2015. Show Me Your Evidence – an Automatic Method for Context Dependent Evidence Detection. In *Proceedings of the 2015 Conference on Empirical Methods in Natural Language Processing*, pages 440–450, Lisbon, Portugal. Association for Computational Linguistics.

Claudia Schulz, Steffen Eger, Johannes Daxenberger, Tobias Kahse, and Iryna Gurevych. 2018a. Multi-Task Learning for Argumentation Mining in Low-Resource Settings. In *Proceedings of the 2018 Conference of the North American Chapter of the Association for Computational Linguistics: Human Language Technologies, Volume 2 (Short Papers)*, pages 35–41, New Orleans, Louisiana. Association for Computational Linguistics.

Claudia Schulz, Christian M. Meyer, Michael Sailer, Jan Kiesewetter, Elisabeth Bauer, Frank Fischer, Martin R. Fischer, and Iryna Gurevych. 2018b. Challenges in the Automatic Analysis of Students' Diagnostic Reasoning. *arXiv:1811.10550 [cs]*.

Matthew Shardlow, Riza Batista-Navarro, Paul Thompson, Raheel Nawaz, John McNaught, and Sophia Ananiadou. 2018. Identification of research hypotheses and new knowledge from scientific literature. *BMC Medical Informatics and Decision Making*, 18(1):46.

Eyal Shnarch, Carlos Alzate, Lena Dankin, Martin Gleize, Yufang Hou, Leshem Choshen, Ranit Aharonov, and Noam Slonim. 2018. Will it Blend? Blending Weak and Strong Labeled Data in a Neural Network for Argumentation Mining. In *Proceedings of the 56th Annual Meeting of the Association for Computational Linguistics (Volume 2: Short Papers)*, pages 599–605, Melbourne, Australia. Association for Computational Linguistics.

Christian Stab and Iryna Gurevych. 2017. Parsing Argumentation Structures in Persuasive Essays. *Computational Linguistics*, 43(3):619–659.

Christian Stab, Tristan Miller, Benjamin Schiller, Pranav Rai, and Iryna Gurevych. 2018. Cross-topic Argument Mining from Heterogeneous Sources. In *Proceedings of the 2018 Conference on Empirical Methods in Natural Language Processing*, pages 3664–3674, Brussels, Belgium. Association for Computational Linguistics.

Chris Stahlhut, Christian Stab, and Iryna Gurevych. 2018. Pilot Experiments of Hypothesis Validation Through Evidence Detection for Historians. In *Proceedings of the First Biennial Conference on Design of Experimental Search & Information Retrieval Systems*, volume 2167 of *CEUR Workshop Proceedings*, pages 83–89, Bertinoro, Italy.

James Thorne and Andreas Vlachos. 2019. Adversarial attacks against Fact Extraction and VERification. *arXiv:1903.05543 [cs]*.

James Thorne, Andreas Vlachos, Oana Cocarascu, Christos Christodoulopoulos, and Arpit Mittal. 2018. The Fact Extraction and VERification (FEVER) Shared Task. In *Proceedings of the First Workshop on Fact Extraction and VERification (FEVER)*, pages 1–9, Brussels, Belgium. Association for Computational Linguistics.

Morgan Ulinski, Julia Hirschberg, and Owen Rambow. 2016. Incrementally Learning a Dependency Parser to Support Language Documentation in Field Linguistics. In *Proceedings of COLING 2016, the 26th International Conference on Computational Linguistics: Technical Papers*, pages 440–449, Osaka, Japan. The COLING 2016 Organizing Committee.

Wenpeng Yin and Dan Roth. 2018. TwoWingOS: A Two-Wing Optimization Strategy for Evidential Claim Verification. In *Proceedings of the 2018 Conference on Empirical Methods in Natural Language Processing*, pages 105–114, Brussels, Belgium. Association for Computational Linguistics.

Veritas Annotator: Discovering the Origin of a Rumour

Lucas Azevedo
Insight Centre for Data Analytics
`lucas.azevedo`
`@insight-centre.org`

Mohamed Moustafa
National University of Ireland, Galway
`m.moustafa1`
`@nuigalway.ie`

Abstract

Defined as the intentional or unintentional spread of false information (K et al., 2019) through context and/or content manipulation, fake news has become one of the most serious problems associated with online information (Waldrop, 2017). Consequently, it comes as no surprise that Fake News Detection has become one of the major foci of various fields of machine learning and while machine learning models have allowed individuals and companies to automate decision-based processes that were once thought to be only doable by humans, it is no secret that the real-life applications of such models are not viable without the existence of an adequate training dataset. In this paper we describe the Veritas Annotator, a web application for manually identifying the origin of a rumour. These rumours, often referred as claims, were previously checked for validity by Fact-Checking Agencies.

1 Introduction

"As an increasing amount of our lives is spent interacting online through social media platforms, more and more people tend to seek out and consume news from social media rather than traditional news organizations." (Shu et al., 2017). This change in societal behaviour has made it much easier for some malicious authors to confuse the public opinion through lies and deception. Articles, tweets, blog posts, and other media used for spreading fake news usually include URLs(Uniform Resource Locators) to fake news websites that are often heavily biased or satirical in nature. Such content is created either for propaganda and political attacks (Waldrop, 2017), or for entertainment purposes by the infamous "trolls", individuals who aim to disrupt communication and influence consumers into emotional distress.

To better understand the necessity of improvements in the automatic fact-checking field, add to the above described scenario the fact that when it comes to identifying a false claim, we, humans cannot perform a simple binary classification over deceptive statements with an accuracy much better than chance, In fact, "just 4% better, based on a meta-analysis of more than 200 experiments." (Bond Jr and DePaulo, 2006) and typically find only one-third of text-based deceptions (George and Keane, 2006; Hancock et al., 2004). This reflects the so-called 'truth bias' or the notion that people are more apt to judge communications as truthful (Vrij, 2000).

Fortunately, there are a number of Fact Checking (FC) agencies such as Snopes[1], Full Fact[2], Politifact[3], Truth or Fiction[4], etc. where journalists work on the hard tasks of: monitoring social media, identifying potential false claims and debunking or confirming them (Babakar and Moy, 2016), while providing a narrative that includes sources related to that claim. Those sources are mainly included in the text in the form of URLs and could be any type of web document that refers to the rumour being checked, debunking it or supporting. In this article, we use the term origin to refer to any supporting source. Despite the constant effort of the FC agencies, manual fact checking is an intellectually demanding and laborious process, and as Jonathan Swift once said in his classic essay "the Art of political lying": "Falsehood flies, and truth comes limping after it" (Arbuthnot and Swift, 1874).

In this scenario, the creation of a fast, reliable and automatic way of detecting fake news (Adair et al., 2017) being spread on the internet is of the

---

[1] `https://www.snopes.com`
[2] `https://fullfact.org`
[3] `https://www.politifact.com`
[4] `https://www.truthorfiction.com`

Proceedings of the Second Workshop on Fact Extraction and VERification (FEVER), pages 90–98
Hong Kong, November 3, 2019. ©2019 Association for Computational Linguistics

utmost need.

2 Motivation

Different types of modalities exist when it comes to automatic fake news detection in text (Azevedo, 2018; K et al., 2019). Here we will group them in accordance to the nature of data they take as input: social network based, where indicators as user statistics, propagation structure and behaviour of the network are considered as features; content based, where the content is what is analyzed, whether linguistic, psycho-linguistic, statistical, stylometric or a mix of those are taken into account. The Veritas (VERIfying Textual ASpects) Dataset initiative intends to improve classifiers that fall into this category; and temporal based, where a correlation between timestamps of users, events and/or articles and the genuineness of a web-document is created.

In order to improve the efficiency of content based classifiers, the retrieval of the entire origin text is essential for training a deep learning model, since the larger the text body retrieved the higher the likelihood of obtaining good measurements for the considered linguistic features. Focusing solely on microblogs, such as Twitter, has been avoided as not only their average text's length would not fit the linguistic approach but also most of them contain urls and/or images that do not convey semantic information or cannot be processed by our textual approach, respectively. The ultimate goal of our work is to develop such classifier, but in this article we will present the journey on the initial step: the dataset creation process. After having a sufficiently large dataset, that includes the origins of the checked claims, certain linguistic and stylometric features can be extracted from them and used to train the our goal model.

3 State of the Art

3.1 Available Corpora on Fake News

The lack of suitable corpora for the intended approach is the main influence behind the creation of the Veritas Dataset, and by consequence, the Veritas Annotator. Below we present a list of datasets commonly used in related tasks. Note that, although those are valuable resources for many related tasks, none of them include the three most important characteristics required for a content based supervised classifier: high volume of entries, gold standard labels and the fake news articles (i.e., the origin) on their whole.

Emergent is a data-set created using the homonymous website as source, a digital journalism project for rumour debunking containing 300 rumoured claims and 2,595 associated news articles - a counterpart to named 'source article' in Veritas Dataset. Each claim's veracity is estimated by journalists after they have judged that enough evidence has been collected (Ferreira and Vlachos, 2016). Besides the claim labeling, each associated article is summarized into a headline and also labelled regarding its stance towards the claim.

NECO 2017 is an ensemble of three different datasets (Horne and Adali, 2017), summing up 110 fake news articles, more than 4k real stories and 233 satire stories. While the datasets listed above can prove useful for certain purposes, their low number of fake news entries make them insufficient for properly training a classification model.

FakeNewsNet is a data repository containing a collection of around 22K real and fake news obtained from Politifact and GossipCop[5] FC websites. Each row contains an ID, URL, title, and a list of tweets that shared the URL. It also includes linguistic, visual, social, and spatiotemporal context regarding the articles. This repository could still be used for supervised learning models if it were not for the fact that it doesn't provide sufficiently long texts to be used by a classifier based on linguistic aspects. For the same reason, CREDBANK (Mitra and Gilbert, 2015) and PHEME (Derczynski and Bontcheva, 2014) are also unsuitable the authors' use case. Those three datasets focus on the network indicators (e.g. number of retweets, sharing patterns, etc) of fake news, instead of its contents. CREDBANK is a crowd sourced corpus of "more than 60 million tweets grouped into 1049 real-world events, each annotated by 30 human annotators", while PHEME includes 4842 tweets, in the form of 330 threads, related to 9 events.

NELA2017 is a large news article collection consisting of 136k articles from 92 sources created for studying misinformation in news articles (Horne et al., 2018). Along with the news articles, the dataset includes a rich set of natural language features on each news article, and the corresponding Facebook engagement statistics. Unfortunately, the dataset does not include labels regarding the veracity of each article.

BuzzFeed-Webis 2016 includes posts and linked articles shared by nine hyperpartisan publishers in a week close to the 2016 US elections. All posts are fact-checked by journalists from BuzzFeed. The dataset contains more than 1.6K articles which are labeled using the scale: no factual content, mostly false, mixture of true and false, and mostly true. Regrettably, the author obtained poor results on detecting fake news with this data, while managing to discriminate between hyperpartisan and mainstream articles (Potthast et al., 2018).

LIAR is another corpus used for training models on fake news detection. It includes around 13K human-labeled short statements which are rated by the fact-checking website PolitiFact into labels for truthfulness using the scale: pants-fire, false, barely-true, half-true, mostly-true, and true (Wang, 2017). The domain-restricted data as well as the small amount of text that can be retrieved from this corpus makes it unsuitable for linguistic fake news detection for generic domains.

Another large volume fake news dataset was created by scraping text and metadata from 244 websites tagged as "bullshit" by the BS Detector Chrome Extension. However, it is not a gold standard dataset as the scraped data was not manually verified.

3.2 Related Work

Other work has been done to identify the origin of rumors/fake claims. In (Popat et al., 2018), Popat et al. have used the entities present on the article headline to find possible origins on search engines. Wang et al., from Google, have also presented a similar approach to the problem with the addition of click-graph queries (Wang et al., 2018), that re-

turn information about which link was clicked by the users after a query was made.

FANE (Rehm et al., 2018) would be the work considered the most similar to ours. It proposes a set of webpages annotations, automatic and manual, that could make the user aware of the veracity of that page's content. The article presents a somewhat abstract idea of implementation and makes clear that the approach would only be effective when the browsers and content vendors adopt the web annotation standards proposed by W3C. Nonetheless, we fully agree with the authors when they state that human input is imperative if we want to win the battle against misinformation.

In some applications, the origin identification task can be similar to stance classification, which was the target task for the FNC-1 challenge, where obtained the best results with a combination between a deep learning model and a boosted tree classifier. Althought there is no publication describing the classifier, this blogpost[6] explains their approach.

4 Creating our Dataset

With the requirements for a linguistic-based classifier described in the last section in mind, how could a dataset that would include not only a manually verified label over the veracity of a claim, but also the web article from where that claim could be extracted? It was decided to divide the process into two steps:

4.1 Crawling fact-checking articles

We have been able to collect about 11.5 thousand origin candidates from more than 6 thousand fact checking (FC) articles by using specific scripts for each fact-checking agency and with the aid of various third-party libraries as newspaper3k[7], beautifulsoup[8], scrappy[9], depending on the structure of the website. Each one of those articles include a claim that was checked by a journalist, i.e., the article's author and a verdict regarding the claim's veracity. Along with the claim there is a narrative where the author explains how the many sources were used to come to the final verdict. In most of the times, one (or more) of the sources is also an

---

origin of the checked claim. Here we define the origin of a claim as a source that directly supports the claim.

At this stage, each of the FC articles were represented by an entry in our database, with the following attributes:

Page The the FC Article URL.

Claim The main checked claim, often included in both the FC article's and the Claim Origin's headline.

Claim Label The verdict provided by the journalist over the main claim. This label regards how much of truth the journalist found in the claim. Different agencies have different label sets but they mainly vary from truth to false, including intermediate values and one or more labels to address claims that could not be checked neither debunked.

Tags The set of tags assigned to the claim by the fact-checking agency. They are similar to hashtags[10] on twitter and describe abstractly the topic of the claim and the entities cited by it.

Date The date the claim was checked. More precisely, the publishing date of the FC Article identified by `page`. To obtain this attribute, we make use of the public available service provided by (SalahEldeen and Nelson, 2013). This interface, makes use of search engines' indexing, as well as HTTP header and foot stamps in `archive.is` and twitter. If that approach doesn't work, newspaper3k is used.

Author The journalist that signs the FC article.

Source list A list of source URLs contained in the FC article, including the possible origin(s).

4.2 Identifying the origin amongst the sources.

Following the acquisition of the FC articles it was still needed to identify the claim's origin from amongst the list of URLs mentioned by the FC article, i.e., the sources. The actual complexity of this task surpassed our initial expectations. Many different approaches have been applied and evaluated, always following the same process of manually checking a representative sample of the selected origins. On each evaluation, the sample size was defined in order to have 95% confidence level with 5% confidence interval. Here we explain briefly the different approaches tried:

At first, it was assumed that the text contained in the first <blockquote> HTML tag would be the origin. That assumption was correct on 74% percent of the time but since only the content of the first <blockquote> tag was considered, there were many cases where that was only partially the origin's content. If, instead, every <blockquote> content was assumed to be from origins, there would be cases where snippets from multiple origins would be mixed, or in even worse scenarios, the inclusion of textual content from non-origin sources. Adding this level of noise to the data would make the training of a classifier unfeasible.

The approach was then changed to assuming that the first link on the FC article was generally the origin. This was correct only on 53% of the samples analyzed.

Having failed on the first two attempts to correctly identify the origin of the claim checked, we were determined to try another heuristic, this time making use of a stance classification ensemble model[11], that would consider all the sources from a given FA, obtain their contents, and calculate the agreement score between the FA article's claim and the sources' contents by a linear combination of a convolutional network and a gradient boosted tree classifier. For each FC article, the source with the highest score would be then considered the origin. This worked really well in the cases where there is an origin amongst the sources, but since those do not represent the totality of the samples, the overall accuracy of the approach was lower than expected.

We then had to resort to manual annotation, detailed in the section below. In summary, by the above mentioned experiences on the origin identification task, we could define some simple filtering rules that restrict the list of origin candidates for each FC article, the remaining OCs are then presented to the user annotating, who is asked to vote on whether the current OC is indeed an origin or not.

---

[10] https://en.wikipedia.org/wiki/Hashtag

[11] https://github.com/Cisco-Talos/fnc-1

Ver.	#Entries	Attributes	#Samples	Correct Origin	Agencies
1.0	4663	FC Article, Claim, Origin Text, Label	355	74%(partial)	`Snopes.com`
2.0	5107	FC Article, Claim, Label, Article Date, Author, Tags, Origin Text, Origin Domain, Origin URL	357	53%(whole)	`Snopes.com` `Politifact.com` `Emergent.info`
2.1	6671	FC Article, Claim, Label, Article Date, Author, Tags, Origin Text, Origin Domain, Origin URL	363	47%(whole)	`Snopes.com` `Politifact.com` `FactCheck.org` `Emergent.info`

Table 1: Versions of Veritas

By having human indicating what are the origins of each claim, not only the suitable data collection for our Automatic Fake News Classifier is generated, but the very task of origin identification can be, at this point, automated by training another classification model that would also incorporate the simple filtering rules we have defined and, in a circular manner, learn to identify more origins, or at least, better origin candidates.

Table **??** shows the number of entries of the Veritas Dataset[12] on each stage, since the FC article crawling step is executed periodically, the total number of entries changes as new pages were introduced. On the other hand, more refined filtering rules were implemented and some entries included in past versions were removed in the subsequent ones.

It is important to note that since each FC article can contain any number of sources, the first attribute of the dataset (FC article URL) is not unique on each entry, at this stage.

By the end of the origin identification process, instead of having a source list for each entry of our dataset, only the identified origin URL will remain, along with some of it's attributes:

Origin URL The URL referring to the web-page that originated the claim.

Origin Domain The Origin URL's domain. This can have great impacts in results of a neural network classifier accuracy, or even in the weighting of a simpler classifier method. Examples of using source rank based on the URL domain as a cue for its veracity are

not new (Popat et al., 2017; Nakashole and Mitchell, 2014).

Origin Text The whole text extracted from the Origin URL, from where the linguistic aspects could be measured and used as features by a classifier.

Origin Date Similar to the above described FC article date.

If a FC page did not have any of it's sources identified as an origin, it will not be included in the filtered version of the dataset.

5 The Annotation Process

5.1 Task and terms definitions

Given a claim (a statement) checked by a FC Agency article (e.g. snopes, politifact, truthorfiction, etc.) and a source contained in that article, i.e., an origin candidate (OC), the task consists in deciding whether or not the source could be considered the origin of the Claim. As defined earlier, an origin is a source that directly supports the claim. More specifically, in order to be considered an origin:

- It should support what is being stated in the claim, not necessarily with the exact same words.

- It has to be more than just related.

- Directly here means it should not simply repeat or proxy other articles supporting or denying the claim.

- It doesn't has to be the first document to publicize that claim.

---

[12]`https://github.com/lucas0/`
`VeritasCorpus`

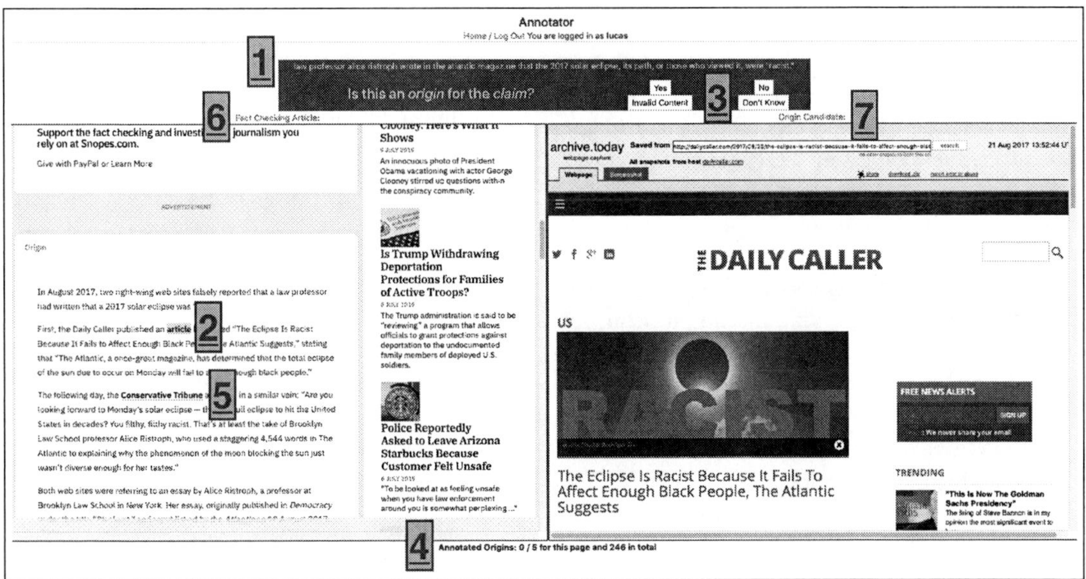

Figure 1: Annotator Interface

Figure 1 shows the Veritas Annotator as it is rendered by a web browser. Most of the screen space is used to display the FC article, on the left frame, and the origin candidate article, on the right. It also delivers information that may be important in order to ask the task question:

1. This section on the top of the annotator displays the Claim checked by the FC article. It is always visible, so there is no need for the user to search for it in the left frame.

2. The highlighted hyperlink in the FC article indicates which Source Page is being considered as the origin candidate at the current moment, this hyperlink's content is what is displayed on the right frame.

3. On the right-upper part of the screen, the user can find the four possible options for annotation, described separately on subsection below.

4. The counter of Annotations for the current user.

5. Other origin candidates hyperlinks for that same FC article. If clicked, the content of that link will be displayed on the right and from that point, the annotation will be regarding the newly selected origin candidate.

6. A hyperlink to the FC article.

7. A hyperlink to the origin candidate.

5.2 The Annotator Interface

On the first access of the Annotator[13], users have to register with a unique username and password. Returning users should login with the same credentials they have registered before. This ensure no user will annotate the same OC more than once while also providing ways of evaluating the efficacy of the method by analyzing user's label allocation distributions and inter-user agreement.

Once logged in, and after every annotation is done, the user interface automatically requests from the Veritas Annotator a new origin candidate to be displayed and annotated, the selection of which entry should be assigned to each user has a randomness factor to it - to avoid any possible bias of storing order - but also follows a priority list: Initially, the Annotator ignores the OCs already annotated by that user, then it prioritizes the ones that were annotated twice, and amongst those, the ones that were given a "YES" by the other users. If there are no entries with two annotations, the priority goes to the ones with one annotation, and then to the ones with no annotations. After all the origin candidates were annotated three or more times, the annotator then retrieves the entry with the least number of annotations and displays it to the user.

<hr>

[13]http://veritas.annotator.
insight-centre.org/

The priority rules are defined this way so that a third annotator can break the tie for any OCs with two opposing annotations, to avoid having a single annotation of some OC (not a good idea as it means the validity of the annotation relies entirely on a single annotator), and to have as many annotated OC as possible (in that order). OCs that were annotated "yes" by other annotators also have a higher priority since that is our target class, in other words, identifying the origin means selecting the origin candidates that were labeled as "YES" by the majority of users that annotated it.

The original intention was for the web pages (both FC article and OC) to be retrieved upon request during the annotation process. It became evident that this approach would introduce a lot of idle time for the tool, which could make the task extremely tedious for annotators.

Initially, after selecting which OC should be displayed, the Annotator would then request and display the content of both the OC and the FC page URLs. That approach was generating many request and exhibition errors and more importantly, was increasing the time between annotations enormously, given that some OC pages are not hosted on their original addresses anymore but instead loaded from web archives. Since the list of FC and OC URLs that needed to be examined was know beforehand, a better approach would be to retrieve the webpages' HyperText Markup Language (HTML) code in advance and store them on the server, so that when requested by the user interface of the annotator they could be readily available. By performing this change, an overall decrease in the loading time was noticeable while also avoiding the need for the same site to be retrieved more than once, which accelerated the development, testing and evaluation.

On the upper part of the Annotator main screen there a table where the Claim analysed in the FC article is always visible and by the right side of this box, the four possible answers for the task question "Is this and origin for the claim?" are presented in the form of buttons. The instructions for when each button should be selected were extracted from the annotator guidelines[14] and are presented below. Because of a space limitation, only one example is displayed in this article, although a variety can be found also within the an-

notator guidelines.

YES If the origin candidate article presented in the right suits the definition of origin, the a "YES" should be selected.

Invalid Content The user should select this option in the unusual case in which the presented content is not readable, either due to a failure of the Annotator to make a request, encoding or language related problems.

NO When the origin candidate page is displayed correctly but the content of it does not fall into the definition of origin.

I Don't Know For the cases where the user is not sufficiently assured about what is being stated in either the claim or the OC page.

Right below the box containing the claim and the buttons, the bigger part of the screen is vertically split into two frames displaying the FC page and the OC side-by-side. Above each frame there is a hyperlink not only indicating which frame displays which article but also allowing the user to access the content of that page directly. On the very bottom of the page, a count informs the user of how many OCs they have annotated in relation of the total of OCs of the current FC page and in total.

The development of the annotator had it's own issues. As some FC Agencies have been operating for more than a decade, it was only natural to expect different website layouts and variance in many aspects, such as the type of encoding used in the sites, usage of HTML tags, classes used for verdict, structure, etc. Also, since we have no previous information about the origin candidate websites, they can be from any domain. Consequently, the retrieval, storage, and then display of HTML code in the Annotator lead to various issues as invalid references to resources and overlay cookies acceptances messages, request redirection, etc. The code[15] used to develop the tool is publicly available.

6 Results

Shortly after the end of the Annotator's development stage, a gathering was organized with volunteers from different backgrounds to collect annotations. In total, 10 people participated and 2222

---

annotations were made, in regards to 459 unique FC articles and 943 unique origin candidates. The quality of the verification task is controlled by majority voting, when considering only origin candidates there were annotated at least 3 times, we restrict the number of entries to 546, from where only 108 had "yes" as the majority votes. This is the initial number of documents of the final version of our gold standard dataset. As more annotations are done, this number will increase. There were also 56 other origin candidates that received more "yes" votes than "no", "invalid content" or "I don't know", but did not reach the minimum number of votes of 3, recommended by crowdsourcing studies(Hsueh et al., 2009).

The inter-user agreement score, computed using Fleiss' Kappa[16] (a multi-user version of Cohen's Kappa[17]) yielded approximately 0.16 as result, demonstrating a slight agreement between annotators.

This is not a sufficiently large number so other annotation sessions and events will still be organized in order to obtain more gold standard entries, although improvements in the linguistic-based fake news classifier could be seen and initial development of the mentioned automatic origin identification model was made possible.

7 Conclusion and Future Work

In general, this article describes the struggles of creating the first-of-its-kind Veritas dataset, intended for the task of automatic Fake News detection, which was our initial point. It also describes how that dataset creation process led us to the creation of an Annotator Interface, with its particular difficulties.

By performing this work, we expect to contribute not only with a new valuable language resource, but also with the ongoing work of other researchers also creating their own datasets, by describing the variety of different approaches implemented and evaluated.

Besides the inclusion of pages from agencies other than Snopes, we can see little to none improvement to be done in the Annotator itself. A higher inter-user agreement is desired but hard to obtain, given the high subjectivity of the annotation task, although perhaps a reformulation of

the guidelines providing more defined instructions could lead to an improvement on the Fleiss' Kappa score.

The results achieved so far are considerable, and the ramifications of them into future work, exciting. To start with a bootstrap process, in which a binary classifier is being trained on the manually labeled OCs from the Veritas Annotator in order to perform the origin identification task automatically. Depending on the "certainty" - how close the predictions are to 1 - of this classifier, an OC could be automatically labeled as the origin, or sent to the group of entries to be manually annotated, from where more training input is generated, increasing it's accuracy. This is a closed loop where the time spent by the human annotator is minimized while the results are enhanced both in quantity and quality.

Another application of this dataset is the already mentioned fake news classifier based on linguistic features (Azevedo, 2018) those two works are already being implemented and the initial results are promising, but out of the scope of this publication.

Additional data enrichment can be done by mapping Veritas Attributes to the schema:ClaimReview[18] tags as they are being used by other authors (X Wang and C Yu and S Baumgartner and F Korn, 2018) and solidifying as a convention.

References

Bill Adair, Chengkai Li, Yang Jun, and Cong Yu. 2017. Progress Toward the Holy Grail: The Continued Quest to Automate Fact-Checking. *Computation + Journalism Symposium*, (September).

John Arbuthnot and Jonathan Swift. 1874. *The Art of Political Lying*. K. Tompkins.

Lucas Azevedo. 2018. Truth or lie: Automatically fact checking news. pages 807–811.

Mevan Babakar and Will Moy. 2016. The state of automated factchecking. *Full Fact*.

Charles F Bond Jr and Bella M DePaulo. 2006. Accuracy of deception judgments. *Personality and social psychology Review*, 10(3):214–234.

Leon Derczynski and Kalina Bontcheva. 2014. Pheme: Veracity in digital social networks. In *UMAP workshops*.

William Ferreira and Andreas Vlachos. 2016. Emergent: a novel data-set for stance classification. In

---

[16]https://en.wikipedia.org/wiki/Fleiss%27_kappa
[17]https://en.wikipedia.org/wiki/Cohen%27s_kappa

[18]https://schema.org/ClaimReview

Proceedings of the 2016 conference of the North American chapter of the association for computational linguistics: Human language technologies, pages 1163–1168.

JF George and BT Keane. 2006. Deception detection by third party observers. In *deception detection symposium, 39th annual Hawaii international conference on system sciences*.

Jeffrey T Hancock, Jennifer Thom-Santelli, and Thompson Ritchie. 2004. Deception and design: The impact of communication technology on lying behavior. In *Proceedings of the SIGCHI*, pages 129–134. ACM.

Benjamin D Horne and Sibel Adali. 2017. This just in: Fake news packs a lot in title, uses simpler, repetitive content in text body, more similar to satire than real news. In *Eleventh International AAAI Conference on Web and Social Media*.

Benjamin D Horne, Sara Khedr, and Sibel Adali. 2018. Sampling the news producers: A large news and feature data set for the study of the complex media landscape. In *Twelfth International AAAI Conference on Web and Social Media*.

Pei-Yun Hsueh, Prem Melville, and Vikas Sindhwani. 2009. Data quality from crowdsourcing: a study of annotation selection criteria. In *Proceedings of the NAACL HLT 2009 workshop on active learning for natural language processing*, pages 27–35. Association for Computational Linguistics.

Anoop K, Manjary Gangan, Deepak P, and Lajish V L. 2019. *Leveraging Heterogeneous Data for Fake News Detection*, pages 229–264.

Tanushree Mitra and Eric Gilbert. 2015. Credbank: A large-scale social media corpus with associated credibility annotations. In *Ninth International AAAI Conference on Web and Social Media*.

Ndapandula Nakashole and Tom M Mitchell. 2014. Language-aware truth assessment of fact candidates. In *ACL (1)*, pages 1009–1019.

Kashyap Popat, Subhabrata Mukherjee, Jannik Strötgen, and Gerhard Weikum. 2017. Where the truth lies: Explaining the credibility of emerging claims on the web and social media. In *Proceedings of the 26th International Conference on World Wide Web Companion*, pages 1003–1012. International World Wide Web Conferences Steering Committee.

Kashyap Popat, Subhabrata Mukherjee, Andrew Yates, and Gerhard Weikum. 2018. Declare: Debunking fake news and false claims using evidence-aware deep learning. *arXiv preprint arXiv:1809.06416*.

Martin Potthast, Johannes Kiesel, Kevin Reinartz, Janek Bevendorff, and Benno Stein. 2018. A stylometric inquiry into hyperpartisan and fake news. In *Proceedings of the 56th Annual Meeting of the Association for Computational Linguistics (Volume 1: Long Papers)*, pages 231–240, Melbourne, Australia. Association for Computational Linguistics.

Georg Rehm, Julian Moreno-Schneider, and Peter Bourgonje. 2018. Automatic and manual web annotations in an infrastructure to handle fake news and other online media phenomena. In *Proceedings of the Eleventh International Conference on Language Resources and Evaluation (LREC-2018)*.

Hany M SalahEldeen and Michael L Nelson. 2013. Carbon dating the web: estimating the age of web resources. In *Proceedings of the 22nd International Conference on World Wide Web*, pages 1075–1082. ACM.

Kai Shu, Amy Sliva, Suhang Wang, Jiliang Tang, and Huan Liu. 2017. Fake news detection on social media: A data mining perspective. *SIGKDD Explorations*, 19:22–36.

Aldert Vrij. 2000. *Detecting lies and deceit: The psychology of lying and implications for professional practice*. Wiley.

M. Mitchell Waldrop. 2017. News feature: The genuine problem of fake news. *Proceedings of the National Academy of Sciences of the United States of America*, 114 48:12631–12634.

William Yang Wang. 2017. " liar, liar pants on fire": A new benchmark dataset for fake news detection. *arXiv preprint arXiv:1705.00648*.

Xuezhi Wang, Cong Yu, Simon Baumgartner, and Flip Korn. 2018. Relevant document discovery for fact-checking articles. In *Companion Proceedings of the The Web Conference 2018*, pages 525–533. International World Wide Web Conferences Steering Committee.

X Wang and C Yu and S Baumgartner and F Korn. 2018. Relevant document discovery for fact-checking articles. *Companion of the The Web Conference 2018 on The Web Conference 2018 - WWW 18*, page 525533.

FEVER Breaker's Run of Team NbAuzDrLqg

Youngwoo Kim and **James Allan**
Center for Intelligent Information Retrieval
University of Massachusetts Amherst
Amherst, MA 01003
{youngwookim, allan}@cs.umass.edu

Abstract

We describe our submission for the Breaker phase of the second Fact Extraction and VERification (FEVER) Shared Task. Our adversarial data can be explained by two perspectives. First, we aimed at testing model's ability to retrieve evidence, when appropriate query terms could not be easily generated from the claim. Second, we test model's ability to precisely understand the implications of the texts, which we expect to be rare in FEVER 1.0 dataset. Overall, we suggested six types of adversarial attacks. The evaluation on the submitted systems showed that the systems were only able get both the evidence and label correct in 20% of the data. We also demonstrate our adversarial run analysis in the data development process.

1 Introduction

The Fact Extraction and Verification (FEVER) workshop focuses on developing fact-check systems, which can resolve "fake-news" and misinformation problems. In the shared task of FEVER, the goal is to develop a system which can verify the given claim, by retrieving evidence from the documents from Wikipedia and classifying the claim into either *Supports*, *Refutes* or *NotEnoughInfo*. While the systems in the shared task of first FEVER workshop (FEVER 1.0) showed impressive performance, it was questionable if they are robust against adversarial claims that are different from the test data from the original dataset (Thorne and Vlachos, 2019).

The second workshop on Fact Extraction and VERification has a shared task that can investigate the robustness of the systems. The shared task is in a Build it Break it Fix it setting. In the first phase, participants (Builders) develop fact-check systems as what was done in last year's shared task. In the second phase, participants (Breakers) will have access to the systems and *attack* the systems to generate claims which are challenging for the builders. In the third phase, the Fixers would fix the systems to be robust toward the Breakers' claims.

We participated in the second phase (Breakers Run) in the competition. We submitted 203 instances over seven types of attacks. For 6 out of 7 attack types (except SubsetNum), the claims were manually written. The claims for SubsetNum were generated based on a template.

Our submission resulted in Raw Potency of 79.66% but resulted in bad Correct Rate of 64.71% and the Adjusted Potency of 51.54%.

Our data were annotated to have 25.7% as incorrect label and 22.8% as ungrammatical, which includes 8.9% overlap. While the ungrammatical cases evenly appeared among all the cases, incorrect label cases are concentrated in NotClear attack.

We consider there are two types of challenges for the Fact-Checking system. The first is retrieval challenge and the second is language understanding challenge.

The results of the Fever 1.0 showed that the most of the evidences can be found among the candidate sentences that are retrieved by taking the terms in the claim as a query (Yoneda et al., 2018; Hanselowski et al., 2018a).

Three of our attacks focuses on retrieval challenges. The claims from EntityLess attack have few entities that can be used to retrieve evidence documents. The claims from EntityLinking different name from that which is in the evidence sentence, so the system need to link other name from the other article that explains alternative names for an entity. The claims from SubsetNum require 3 sentences as the evidence, where two of the evidence document can be found from the terms of the claim, but the other evidence cannot.

Proceedings of the Second Workshop on Fact Extraction and VERification (FEVER), pages 99–104
Hong Kong, November 3, 2019. ©2019 Association for Computational Linguistics

Remaining three attacks focuses on precise understanding of the text. We considered the case that the relevant article mentions the claim, but another sentence from the article says the claim to be not true (Controversy) or to be not clear (NotClear). If the system blindly picks most relevant sentences, the system can miss such clarifying information. The claims from FiniteSet consider the cases that some expression can imply that no more event of the particular type can happen other than the mentioned events.

In section 2, we explain our motivations for the attack types. In section 3, we explain how we generate 6 types of attacks. In section 4 we discuss the shared task results. In addition to actual submission results, section 5 discuss about the analysis in adversarial attack development phase

2 Design motivations

The claims of original FEVER dataset are made from the randomly chosen sentences (Thorne et al., 2018). We expect that many sentences share similar semantic patterns, while there are only few sentences that have different pattern than the majority. Randomly sampling sentences would result in many claims that can be handled by similar fact checking strategies, which makes the dataset hard to contain challenging and exceptional claims that are less trivial to fact-check. Here is an example of exceptional claims. Given a sentence, if the claim is entailed by the sentence, it is okay to conclude *Supports* for most cases. However, there are a few cases that the following sentence denies what's written in the previous sentence. Our attack types Controversy and NotClear test such cases.

In relation extraction domain, it was considered as a serious challenge to have ability to disambiguate a polysemous entity mention or infer that two orthographically different mentions are the same entity (Rao et al., 2013). We refer this challenge as entity linking and suggest that entity linking should be more intensely tested for fact-checking task. In the FEVER 1.0, many system solely relied on the neural network to handle entity linking. For the names of entities that are mentioned often in the corpus, word embedding could be trained enough to handle it. We expect that neural network might fail when it comes to the rarely mentioned surface names. We expect that original FEVER dataset will not have many such cases.

	Supports	Refutes	NE	Total
EntityLess	1	7	2	10
EntityLinking	8	1	0	9
SubsetNum	50	50	0	100
Controversy	0	10	0	10
NotClear	0	0	34	34
FiniteSet	4	6	0	10
NE	0	0	30	30
Total	63	74	66	203

Table 1: Label statistics for our submission. NE stands for *NotEnoughInfo*.

3 Claim generation for each type of attacks.

Our submission includes six types of adversarial cases and one type that only contain *NotEnoughInfo* to make all of three labels to have similar number of claims. Examples for the six attacks are listed in Table 2 and Table 3.

3.1 EntityLess[1]

This attack contains case that the evidence articles cannot be easily searched by the words in the claim. The claims only contains more common terms such as 'university', 'alumni' and 'U.S.'. In the example in the Table 2, the evidence is in 'Harvard University' article, while the important term 'Harvard' is not given in the claim. We expect that the system would wrongly answer *NotEnoughInfo*.

3.2 EntityLinking

This case tests the ability to identify different surface names for the same entity. The collection has the sentences that introduce multiple names of an entity. We selected one of such sentences which we expect to be not too popular and it is used as a first evidence. As a second evidence, we searched the sentence that mentions the entity and replaced the name of the entity with another name. We expect that the system would wrongly answer *NotEnoughInfo*.

3.3 SubsetNum

This case is generated based on a simple logic: if region A is part of B and B is smaller than C, A is smaller than C. In the example is Table 2, the sec-

---

[1]This attack was originally named 'TwoHops' in our submission.

No	Type	Claim	Label
1	EntityLess	No university has more than 5 alumni who became U.S. presidents.	Refutes
2	EntityLinking	Kanha Tiger Reserve has a significant population of swamp deer.	Supports
3	SubsetNum	The area of Nerva, Spain is larger than the area of Madhya Pradesh.	Refutes
4	Controversy	September Dossier revealed the fact that Iraq had reconstituted its nuclear weapons programme.	Refutes
5	NotClear	In 1899 Arnold Droz-Farny proved Droz-Farny line theorem.	NotEnoughInfo
6	FiniteSet	Since 1960, no person was executed for his crime in Republic of Ireland.	Refutes

Table 2: Claims and the each cases of attack described in section 3.

No	Evidence
1	[Harvard University] Harvard's alumni include eight U.S. presidents,
2	[Kanha Tiger Reserve] The park has a significant population of Bengal tiger, Indian leopards, the sloth bear, **barasingha** and Indian wild dog. (...) The **barasingha**, also called **swamp deer**, (....)
3	[Province of <u>Huelva</u>] Its area is **10,148 km^2.** [Nerva, Spai] <u>Nerva</u> is a town and municipality located in the province of <u>Huelva</u>, southern Spain. [Madhya Pradesh] Its total area is **308,252 km^2.**
4	[September Dossier] The dossier even **alleged** that Iraq had reconstituted its nuclear weapons programme. Without exception, all of the allegations included within the September Dossier have been since proven to be **false**, as shown by the Iraq Survey Group.
5	[Droz-Farny line theorem] The theorem was stated by Arnold Droz-Farny in 1899, but it is **not clear** whether he had a proof.
6	[Michael Manning (murderer)] Michael Manning was an Irish murderer who became the twenty-ninth and **last** person to be executed in the Republic of Ireland. The execution by hanging was duly carried out on 20 April **1954** (...)

Table 3: Evidences for the claims of Table 2. The words in bracket are the title of the article. Evidence 5 is not actually an evidence because the label is NotEnoughInfo. The sentence was listed to show that it might be mistakenly considered as an evidence.

	OK	GR	UN	UN,GR	Total	Correct Rate
EntityLess	2	1	2	0	5	0.60
EntityLinking	3	1	1	0	5	0.57
SubsetNum	36	7	3	1	47	0.40
Controversy	4	2	1	0	7	0.20
NotClear	3	0	9	8	20	0.15
FiniteSet	1	3	1	0	5	0.77
NE	12	0	0	0	12	1.00

Table 4: Acceptability judgments.
- OK : The claim is grammatical and the label is supported by the evidence.
- GR : The claim is ungrammatical.
- UN : The claim is grammatical but the label is incorrect.

ond and third evidence could be directly retrieved from the claim, but not the first evidence.

The claims were automatically generated. We extracted the information using the predefined templates. We first extracted the list of the entities that refer to regions. Then we extracted subset relations. The area information of each entity was parsed. We expect that the system would wrongly answer *NotEnoughInfo*.

3.4 Controversy

This case tests if the system can distinguish the mentions that are not actually true. Two evidence sentences are required. A sentence suggests information and the following sentence says that the previous statement is not true. All the claims for these cases are *Refutes*. We expect that the system would wrongly answer *Supports*.

3.5 NotClear

Wikipedia has sentences that say "It is not clear ..." (Table 2). We wrote the claims that are mentioned to be not clear and we consider this implies *NotEnoughInfo*. Because the label is *NotEnoughInfo*, we did not include the evidences.

The annotators did not accepted most of the claims (85%) and annotated they are not *NotEnoughInfo*(including the one in the table). It is not clear if they accepted the sentences with 'not clear' as evidences or they found from other documents. We expect that the system would wrongly answer *Supports*or *Refutes*.

3.6 FiniteSet

A sentence "A is ninth and last to do B." implies that there are only nine possible events for B. Moreover, if another event is claimed to be happened at the time which is later than when A happened, it cannot be true. For many cases keyword 'last' is just enough to restrict the times. Both *Supports* and *Refutes* cases are generated. We expect that the system would wrongly answer *NotEnoughInfo*.

3.7 NE

Our adversarial claims are mostly *Supports* or *Refutes*. In order to make each label has same similar number of claims we add claims whose label is *NotEnoughInfo*. These claims are not particularly adversarial compared to others.

4 Task Evaluation

The breaker's runs were evaluated by the following metrics:

$$\text{Potency(b)} \overset{\text{def}}{=} \frac{1}{|S|} \sum_{s \in S} (1 - \text{FEVER}(\mathcal{Y}_{s,b}))$$

$$(1)$$

$$\text{Adjusted\_Potency}(b) \overset{\text{def}}{=} r_{accept} \times Potency(b)$$

$\text{FEVER}(\mathcal{Y}_{s,b})$ is the official evaluation metric, which is roughly the fraction of the instances that got both the evidences and label correct.

Our submission resulted in the raw potency of 79.66%. Accepted rate was 64.71%. Adjusted potency was 51.54%.

The raw potency of 79.66 implies that systems only got 20% got correct. Considering that 15% of the whole data was NE category which was not actually adversarial, the systems totally fail on our adversarial data.

During the shared task, we tested each type of attack on the running docker images of the shared task test server

For the final Fixer phase, the accepted instances from all breaker's run were collected. The collected data were provided to the fixers so that the systems can be revised or re-trained on the adversarial data. There was only one fixer system (CUNLP) and it showed FEVER score of 32.92% before they fixed the system. After they fixed the system it achieved the FEVER score of 68.80%. Note that these scores for the fixer system are results of all breaker's submissions not only our submission.

We were not provided the performance for the only our runs, but still we can make some speculation about the potency of adversarial instances in this shared task. We expect that the adversarial runs were rather limited in their diversity, the fixer was able to revise this challenges either manually or by machine learning models ability to adapt to new types of data.

5 Development Analysis

Here, we show a few adversarial instances that we generated during the development process. Note that some of these claims (2, 4) are of different categories from what was introduced in section 3, because they were not included in final submission. We evaluated these claims on the provided

No	Attack Type	Claim	Label
1	Time	Barack Obama is the first USA president to be born in America.	Refutes
2	SubsetSum	Idonesia does have the larger population than the town of Abu Al-Khaseeb	Supports
3	EntityLess	More than 10 people have walked on the moon.	Supports
4	Numeric	Borneo is larger than Crete Island	Supports
5	Controversy	Apollo astronauts did not actually walk on the Moon.	Refutes

Table 5: Claims tested in our development phase

No	Evidence
1	[Bill Clinton] William Jefferson Clinton (born William Jefferson Blythe III; August 19, 1946) is an American politician who served as the **42nd** president of the United States from 1993 to 2001. (...) Clinton was born and raised in **Arkansas** (...) [Barack Obama] **Barack** Hussein **Obama** II (born August 4, 1961) is an American attorney and politician who served as the **44th** president of the United States from 2009 to 2017. [Arkansas] Arkansas is a state in the southern region of the **United States**
2	[Indonesia] With over 261 million people, it is the world's 4th most populous country (...) [Abu Al-Khaseeb] Abu Al-Khaseeb (sometimes spelled Abu Al-Khasib) is a town in Abu Al-Khaseeb District, Basra Governorate, southern Iraq. [Iraq] Around 95% of the country's 37 million citizens are Muslims, with Christianity, Yarsan, Yezidism and Mandeanism also present
3	[List of Apollo astronauts] Twelve of these astronauts walked on the Moon 's surface or [Harrison Schmitt] (...) he also became the **twelfth** and second-youngest person to set foot on the Moon.
4	[Borneo] Borneo is the third-largest island in the world and the largest in Asia [Crete] Crete is the largest and most populous of the Greek islands, the 88th largest island in the world
5	[List of Apollo astronauts] Twelve of these astronauts walked on the Moon 's surface

Table 6: Evidences for the claims of Table 2.

sandbox interface, which runs the previously submitted systems. The systems are UCL (Yoneda et al., 2018), Athens (Hanselowski et al., 2018b), UCL-MR (Yoneda et al., 2018), Papelo (Malon, 2018), GPLSI, Columbia and the baseline system (Thorne et al., 2018).

The claims and evidences are listed in Table 5 and 6. Claim 1 in the Table 5 requires fact-check system to collect and combine many evidences. The system has to check if there are presidents who were born in America and precede Barack Obama's term. Claim 2 is an example of the previously explained SubsetSum attack. Claim 3 could be challenging because it does not contain any good keyword in it. It also requires systems to be able to compare numbers. Claim 4 requires to compare numbers. We expected systems could make mistake as evidence sentences have numerous "largest" in them. Claim 5 has related documents that could be mistakenly taken as evidence to support the claim. There is an article "Moon landing conspiracy theories", which contains sentence saying "12 Apollo astronauts did not actually walk on the Moon". Because this evidence sentence is very similar to the claim in terms of term matching, this might be retrieved as an evidence and might confuse the system.

Table 7 shows the results of each systems, mainly focusing on if the systems get the classification labels correct. The systems rarely select the evidences that we submitted. However, as there are many alternative evidences for these claims, we could conclude this as total failure.

	UNC	Athene	UCL MR	Papelo	GPLSI	Columbia	baseline
<u>1</u>	X	O	O	X	X	X	O
2	O	X	X	X	O	X	O
<u>3</u>	X	O	X	X	O	X	O
<u>4</u>	**O**	X	X	X	O	X	X
<u>5</u>	X	O	O	X	X	X	O

Table 7: Results of each system on the claims of Table 5. O and X denote if the system correctly get the classification label. Only one case had both the label and evidences correct: UNC on the 4th claim. Claim 1, 3, 4 and 5 are underlined to denote that they may have many possible evidences.

6 Conclusion

This year's FEVER shared task showed that currently systems for fact checking are sensitive to these adversarial attacks. To develop robust systems for fact check, we need to build better evaluation dataset which contains challenging and diverse test instances.

Acknowledgement

The authors wish to thank anonymous reviewers for their helpful advice and the FEVER Organizers for their efforts in managing the insightful workshop.

References

Andreas Hanselowski, Hao Zhang, Zile Li, Daniil Sorokin, Benjamin Schiller, Claudia Schulz, and Iryna Gurevych. 2018a. Ukp-athene: Multisentence textual entailment for claim verification. In *Proceedings of the First Workshop on Fact Extraction and VERification (FEVER)*, pages 103–108.

Andreas Hanselowski, Hao Zhang, Zile Li, Daniil Sorokin, Benjamin Schiller, Claudia Schulz, and Iryna Gurevych. 2018b. Ukp-athene: Multisentence textual entailment for claim verification. In *Proceedings of the First Workshop on Fact Extraction and VERification (FEVER)*, pages 103–108.

Christopher Malon. 2018. Team papelo: Transformer networks at fever. In *Proceedings of the First Workshop on Fact Extraction and VERification (FEVER)*, pages 109–113.

Delip Rao, Paul McNamee, and Mark Dredze. 2013. Entity linking: Finding extracted entities in a knowledge base. In *Multi-source, multilingual information extraction and summarization*, pages 93–115. Springer.

James Thorne and Andreas Vlachos. 2019. Adversarial attacks against fact extraction and verification. *arXiv preprint arXiv:1903.05543*.

James Thorne, Andreas Vlachos, Christos Christodoulopoulos, and Arpit Mittal. 2018. FEVER: a large-scale dataset for fact extraction and verification. In *NAACL-HLT*.

Takuma Yoneda, Jeff Mitchell, Johannes Welbl, Pontus Stenetorp, and Sebastian Riedel. 2018. Ucl machine reading group: Four factor framework for fact finding (hexaf). In *Proceedings of the First Workshop on Fact Extraction and VERification (FEVER)*, pages 97–102.

Team DOMLIN: Exploiting Evidence Enhancement for the FEVER Shared Task

Dominik Stammbach
DFKI, Saarbrücken, Germany
`dominik.stammbach@dfki.de`

Günter Neumann
DFKI, Saarbrücken, Germany
`neumann@dfki.de`

Abstract

This paper contains our system description for the second Fact Extraction and VERification (FEVER) challenge. We propose a two-staged sentence selection strategy to account for examples in the dataset where evidence is not only conditioned on the claim, but also on previously retrieved evidence. We use a publicly available document retrieval module and have fine-tuned BERT checkpoints for sentence selection and as the entailment classifier. We report a FEVER score of 68.46% on the blind test set.

1 Introduction

The nowadays vast amounts of textual information, its ease of sharing and its error pronesses call for automatic means of fact checking (Thorne et al., 2018a). Automated Fact checking is the assignment of a truth value to a given (factual) statement, also referred to as a claim. Such an assignment by itself lacks interpretability, thus it is desirable to have access to the evidence used to reach an assignment (Vlachos and Riedel, 2014). This has led to the Fact Extraction and VERification (FEVER) challenge, i.e. the task is to classify a claim into 'SUPPORTS', 'REFUTES' or 'NOT ENOUGH INFORMATION' and to also retrieve the relevant evidence sentences from Wikipedia (Thorne et al., 2018a). An example claim is *'Cary Elwes was born in 1982.'* and we have to retrieve the evidence sentence *'Cary Elwes, born 26 October 1962, is an English actor and writer.'* from the Wikipedia page about Cary Elwes. Because the evidence contradicts the claim, the claim is refuted. In this paper, we present our system descriptionfor the *builder* phase of the second Version of this challenge (FEVER 2.0).

The *builder* phase in FEVER 2.0 is equivalent to the first FEVER shared task and participants try to beat the top performing systems of the first FEVER challenge which act as a baseline, i.e. beat 64.21% FEVER score (Thorne et al., 2018c). Some of the systems from the first FEVER challenge are publicly available and can be used by participants in FEVER 2.0[1].

In a preliminary experiment, we have fine-tuned a BERT checkpoint (Devlin et al., 2018) as the textual entailment classifier and have achieved 92.8% label accuracy on the supported/refuted examples of the development set using oracle evidence. Thus, we have focused on the evidence retrieval part of the challenge.

In our hand-in, we have used the document retrieval module developed by UKP-ATHENE in the first fever challenge (Hanselowski et al., 2018). We have built on the 'two-hop' evidence enhancement strategy proposed in (Nie et al., 2018) and propose a two-staged sentence selection strategy. We used BERT for sentence selection and for recognizing textual entailment[2] (RTE) between a claim and retrieved evidence for that claim.

2 Related Work

Most work on the FEVER dataset is based on the baseline system proposed in the dataset description (Thorne et al., 2018a), using a pipeline consisting of document retrieval, sentence selection and RTE. We implemented such a pipeline as well and have built on several ideas found in the first FEVER challenge.

We have used the document retrieval module developed by (Hanselowski et al., 2018) which achieved the highest evidence recall in the first fever challenge (Thorne et al., 2018c). They use the MediaWiki API[3] which queries the Wikipedia

---

[1] http://fever.ai/resources.html
[2] https://en.wikipedia.org/wiki/Textual_entailment
[3] https://www.mediawiki.org/wiki/API:Main_page

Proceedings of the Second Workshop on Fact Extraction and VERification (FEVER), pages 105–109
Hong Kong, November 3, 2019. ©2019 Association for Computational Linguistics

search engine. Every *noun phrase* is considered to be a possible entity mention and is fed into the MediWiki API, yielding up to seven Wikipedia pages per claim.

Nie et al. (2018) propose a 'two-hop' evidence enhancement process, that is they gather all hyperlinks in their already retrieved evidence sentences and apply their sentence selection module on all sentences found in these documents retrieved by following the hyperlinks. A 0.8% increase in FEVER score (using oracle lables) is reported by using this strategy.

Malon (2018) use the open-GPT model (Radford et al., 2018) for sentence selection and entailment classification. We have trained similar models, but used BERT instead. BERT is a noisy auto-encoder pre-trained on masked language modeling tasks and was the state of the art on a number of natural language understanding (NLU) tasks (Devlin et al., 2018) during the *builder* phase of FEVER 2.0, e.g. the NLU benchmark GLUE (Wang et al., 2018) and on SQuAD (Rajpurkar et al., 2016), a question answering dataset. Classification in BERT is achieved by training a special '[CLS]' token which is prepended to every sequence (or sequence pair), gather the '[CLS]' token's hidden representation and perform classification on top of that. We used the cased English version of BERT$_{\text{BASE}}$ for all our experiments.

Hanselowski et al. (2018) use the hinge loss function[4] to maximize the margin between positive and (sampled) negative evidence sentences. Thus, we adapted BERT for sentence selection to be trained with the hinge loss as well.

3 Our Model

We have submitted a pipeline appraoch consisting of document retrieval, a two-staged sentence selection strategy followed by an RTE module. In this section, we describe the different modules of our pipeline in more detail.

3.1 Document Retrieval

We have re-used the document retrieval developed by (Hanselowski et al., 2018). We have experimented with using the union of the retrieved documents of the three best performing systems in the first fever challenge, but found that document recall of using such an ensemble only slightly increases while precision drops massively (Table 1).

---

[4]https://en.wikipedia.org/wiki/Hinge_loss

In Table 1, we report precision, recall and F1 for the relevant documents retrieved by the union of different retrieval modules in the development set.

System	Pr (%)	Rc (%)	F1 (%)
Athene UKP TU Darmstadt	28.3	78.6	41.6
Athene + UCL Machine Reading Group	7.8	80.1	14.0
Athene + UCL + UNC-NLP	6.2	80.2	11.0

Table 1: Results for different Document Retrieval strategies

Because of the only slight increase in recall, but the big drop in precision and the increase in computation, we restricted ourselves to only use the document retrieval system developed by (Hanselowski et al., 2018).

3.2 Sentence Selection

In 16.82% of cases in the FEVER dataset, a claim requires the combination of more than one sentence to be able to support or refute that claim (Thorne et al., 2018c). While inspecting such cases, we have found that sometimes, evidence is not only conditioned on the claim, but also on already retrieved evidence. Two examples of such cases can be found in Table 2.

Claim	Evidence 1	Evidence 2
Ryan Gosling has been to a country in Africa.	He [...] has traveled to Chad , Uganda and eastern Congo [...].	Chad [...] is a landlocked country in Central Africa
Stanley Tucci performed in an television series.	He won two Emmy Awards for his performances in Winchell and Monk	Monk is an American comedy-drama detective mystery television series created by Andy Breckman and starring Tony Shalhoub as the eponymous character, Adrian Monk.

Table 2: Examples where evidence sentences are not only conditioned on the claim

Thus, we propose a two-staged sentence selection process building on top of the 'two-hop' evidence enhancement process in (Nie et al., 2018). We believe that the relevant document for the second evidence (in Table 2) can only be retrieved by gathering the hyperlinks in *Evidence 1*, and adopt that 'two-hop' strategy. Because *Evidence 2* is not only conditioned on the claim, but also the first evidence sentence, we find it impossible (as humans) to correctly classify the second evidence without having information about the first evidence. Thus, we want to model this fact accordingly and describe our sentence selection strategy in the following.

We fine-tune two different BERT checkpoints with different training examples. For the first model, we select only the first sentence in every evidence set as a positive example. This covers the 83.18% of cases where the example only requires one evidence sentence. If an evidence set consists of more than one sentence, we only use the first one and ignore the other evidence sentences. Negative examples are sampled from the same document a positive example appears in (as long as it is not contained in the evidence set of an example) and from non-relevant documents returned by the document retrieval module. Following (Malon, 2018), we add the page title for co-reference resolution to the evidence sentence. An input example consists of *"[CLS]" + claim + "[SEP]" + page_title + ":" + evidence_sentence + "[SEP]"*. We assign BERT segment embeddings A to the claim and segment embeddings B to the page title and the evidence sentence. Following (Hanselowski et al., 2018), we use the hinge loss function for sentence selection to maximize the margin between positive and negative examples.

We fine-tune a second BERT checkpoint (using hinge loss as well) to account for the examples in Table 2. We consider as positive examples all instances in the training set where the evidence set consists of exactly two sentences. Negative examples are sampled from hyperlinked documents in the first evidence sentence and from the same document as the second evidence, as long as a sampled sentence does not appear in any evidence set of the claim. Input to the model consists of *"[CLS]" + claim + page_title_1 + evidence_1" + [SEP]" + page_title_2 + ":" + evidence + "[SEP]"*. BERT segment embeddings A are assigned to the claim and the first evidence sentence, segment embeddings B are assigned to the second sentence.

During test time, we let the first model classify all sentences in all retrieved documents for a given claim. If a sentence receives a score bigger than 0, we apply the 'two-hop' strategy, i.e. we retrieve all hyperlinks in the document this sentence occurs in. We then collect all sentences in the documents found via hyperlinks and let the second model predict all these additionally retrieved sentences conditioned on the claim and the previously retrieved first evidence sentence. Finally, we rank all sentences with respect to their score and return the five highest scoring sentences as evidence for a claim.

We report results for the two-staged sentence selection process on the development set in Table 3 (assuming oracle labels for the FEVER score).

Model	Pr (%)	Rc (%)	F1 (%)	FEVER score (%)
First sentence selection module	24.9	87.4	38.7	91.6
Both retrieval modules	25.1	89.8	39.3	**93.2**

Table 3: Results for the two-staged Sentence Selection Module

We observe an increase of 1.6% in FEVER score (assuming oracle labels) by using the proposed two-staged sentence selection approach, twice as high as the 0.8% increase for evidence enhancement reported in (Nie et al., 2018), supporting the assumption that cases shown in Table 2 should be modelled accordingly. More importantly, we believe this strategy enables us, in theory, to retrieve most of the relevant evidence in the FEVER dataset. We think this was not possible before with the different sentence selection modules used in the first FEVER challenges.

3.3 Claim Verification

The last part of our pipeline is the claim verification (RTE) module. We adopt two strategies used in the FEVER baseline (Thorne et al., 2018b), namely how we retrieve evidence for the 'NOT ENOUGH INFORMATION' (NEI) examples and how we handle multiple evidence sentences for a claim.

For 'NEI' examples, we let the document retrieval module predict relevant pages and use our two-staged sentence selection module to select relevant evidence for these examples.

If we have multiple evidence sentences for a claim, we prepend the Wikipedia page title to each of them (for co-reference resolution) and concatenate all the evidence sentences. We only consider sentences receiving a score > 0 by the sentence selection module, but return the five highest scoring sentences for an increased FEVER score.

In Table 4, we report results for an RTE experiment using the five best scored evidence sentences (trained with five best scored evidence sentences for 'NEI' examples) and for an experiment using only evidence sentences with a score greater than 0 (trained 'NEI' examples accordingly).

It follows from Table 4 that if we use noisy evidence in the RTE module, we get low precision/high recall for the 'NEI' class but low recall for the other two classes. In case we only use trustworthy evidence, we get high recall for the supports/refutes classes and low recall for the

Class	Noisy Evidence			Trustworthy Evidence		
	Pr (%)	Rc (%)	F1 (%)	Pr (%)	Rc (%)	F1 (%)
Supports	75.78	46.34	57.52	75.06	92.90	83.64
Refutes	74.76	41.48	53.35	78.27	77.42	77.84
'NEI'	43.73	80.20	56.60	70.75	51.77	59.79
Overall Acc.	56.0%			75.7% (72.1%)		

Table 4: Experiments using noisy and only trustworthy evidence

'NEI' class. We think that in the noisy experiment, BERT has learned that if it is confronted with a long sequence (a claim and five evidence sentences), it most likely is a 'NEI' example, because 83.18% of the supportable/refutable examples only require one evidence sentence. During decoding, it would receive only long sequences and predicts most of them as the 'NEI' class. We report an overall label accuracy of 56% for that experiment.

However, if we only use trustworthy evidence, we get great scores for the supports/refutes classes but predict most of the 'NEI' examples as being verifiable. If we ignore the 'NEI' examples in evaluation, we achieve 85.3% label accuracy, getting close to the results in our preliminary experiment using oracle evidence for verifiable claims. We achieve an overall label accuracy of 75.7% for examples for which we find trustworthy evidence (17k examples). Otherwise, we classify a claim heuristically to belong to the 'NEI' class. Because this is not always correct, the overall label accuracy on the development set drops to 72.1%. This still clearly outperforms the 56% from the noisy experiment, hence we used this strategy in our submission.

The 'NEI' class seems to be the most problematic one to predict correctly. We tried to augment training examples for that class leveraging information found in the SQuAD 2.0 dataset (Rajpurkar et al., 2016). In SQuAD 2.0, a number of questions remain unanswerable given the information in the corresponding Wikipedia paragraph. We included these examples in the training set and have treated the question to be the claim and the corresponding paragraph to be the evidence. We hoped that this would give the model cues about when there is not enough information to answer a question and thus, the model would improve at handling examples from the 'NEI' class in a better way. However, this did not help and we report an overal label accuracy on the development set of 74.7% for examples we find evidence for and an overall label accuracy of 71.1% using our heuristic

for claims for which we do not find any evidence.

Finally, We have not managed to find a suitable solution to handle the 'NEI' class convincingly in the *builder* phase of the shared task and leave this problem to future research.

4 Conclusion

In this paper, we described our system for the *builder* phase of FEVER 2.0. We use a publicly available document retrieval system and propose a new, two-staged sentence selection strategy. In a first stage, we classify all sentences in all retrieved documents. In a second stage, we follow all hyper-links in evidence retrieved in the first stage and use a second classifier to classify all sentences in these newly retrieved documents. We propose this strategy, because sometimes, further evidence for a claim is not only conditioned on the claim, but also on previously retrieved evidence. We think that this strategy enables us, in theory, to retrieve a large amount of the evidence in the FEVER dataset which has not been the case before.

Lastly, we use BERT as our RTE classifier and report 85.3% label accuracy for the supports/refutes classes and an overall label accuracy of 72.1% on the development set. On the blind test set, we achieve 71.5% label accuracy and an overall FEVER score of 68.46%. The most problematic class in the dataset remains the 'NOT ENOUGH INFORMATION' class. We tried to improve performance for that class by augmenting the training set with SQuAD data, but could not report positive results. We leave the problem of the 'NEI' class to future research.

5 Acknowledgements

This work was partially supported by the German Federal Ministry of Education and Research (BMBF) through the project DEEPLEE (01IW17001) and the project Precise4Q (777107).

References

Jacob Devlin, Ming-Wei Chang, Kenton Lee, and Kristina Toutanova. 2018. Bert: Pre-training of deep bidirectional transformers for language understanding. *arXiv preprint arXiv:1810.04805*.

Andreas Hanselowski, Hao Zhang, Zile Li, Daniil Sorokin, Benjamin Schiller, Claudia Schulz, and Iryna Gurevych. 2018. Ukp-athene: Multi-sentence textual entailment for claim verification. In *EMNLP 2018*, EMNLP 2018, FEVER Workshop.

Christopher Malon. 2018. Team papelo: Transformer networks at FEVER. In *Proceedings of the First Workshop on Fact Extraction and VERification (FEVER)*, pages 109–113, Brussels, Belgium. Association for Computational Linguistics.

Yixin Nie, Haonan Chen, and Mohit Bansal. 2018. Combining fact extraction and verification with neural semantic matching networks. *CoRR*, abs/1811.07039.

Alec Radford, Karthik Narasimhan, Tim Salimans, and Ilya Sutskever. 2018. Improving language understanding by generative pre-training.

Pranav Rajpurkar, Jian Zhang, Konstantin Lopyrev, and Percy Liang. 2016. SQuAD: 100,000+ questions for machine comprehension of text. In *Proceedings of the 2016 Conference on Empirical Methods in Natural Language Processing*, pages 2383–2392, Austin, Texas. Association for Computational Linguistics.

James Thorne, Andreas Vlachos, Christos Christodoulopoulos, and Arpit Mittal. 2018a. FEVER: a large-scale dataset for fact extraction and VERification. In *Proceedings of the 2018 Conference of the North American Chapter of the Association for Computational Linguistics: Human Language Technologies, Volume 1 (Long Papers)*, pages 809–819, New Orleans, Louisiana. Association for Computational Linguistics.

James Thorne, Andreas Vlachos, Christos Christodoulopoulos, and Arpit Mittal. 2018b. FEVER: a large-scale dataset for fact extraction and verification. *CoRR*, abs/1803.05355.

James Thorne, Andreas Vlachos, Oana Cocarascu, Christos Christodoulopoulos, and Arpit Mittal. 2018c. The fact extraction and VERification (FEVER) shared task. In *Proceedings of the First Workshop on Fact Extraction and VERification (FEVER)*, pages 1–9, Brussels, Belgium. Association for Computational Linguistics.

Andreas Vlachos and Sebastian Riedel. 2014. Fact checking: Task definition and dataset construction. In *Proceedings of the ACL 2014 Workshop on Language Technologies and Computational Social Science*, pages 18–22. Association for Computational Linguistics.

Alex Wang, Amanpreet Singh, Julian Michael, Felix Hill, Omer Levy, and Samuel Bowman. 2018. GLUE: A multi-task benchmark and analysis platform for natural language understanding. In *Proceedings of the 2018 EMNLP Workshop BlackboxNLP: Analyzing and Interpreting Neural Networks for NLP*, pages 353–355, Brussels, Belgium. Association for Computational Linguistics.

Team GPLSI. Approach for automated fact checking

Aimée Alonso-Reina, Robiert Sepúlveda-Torres, Estela Saquete[*], Manuel Palomar[*]
University of Havana
I.U for Computer Research, Univesity of Alicant
[*] Department of Software and Computing systems, Univesity of Alicant
aimeear1993@gmail.com, rsepulveda911112@gmail.com, {stela, mpalomar}@dlsi.ua.es

Abstract

Fever Shared 2.0 Task is a challenge meant for developing automated fact checking systems. Our approach for the Fever 2.0 is based on a previous proposal developed by Team Athene UKP TU Darmstadt. Our proposal modifies the sentence retrieval phase, using statement extraction and representation in the form of triplets (subject, object, action). Triplets are extracted from the claim and compare to triplets extracted from Wikipedia articles using semantic similarity. Our results are satisfactory but there is room for improvement.

1 Introduction

The proliferation of user-generated content and Computer Mediated Communication (CMC) technologies, such as blogs, Twitter, and other social media enable mass scale news delivery mechanisms (Conroy, Rubin, & Chen, 2015; Rubin & Lukoianova, 2015). The emergence of social networks and their use for the dissemination of news are a double-edged sword. On the one hand, its low cost, easy access and rapid distribution of information encourages people to search and consume news from social networks. On the other hand, it allows the proliferation of "fake news", i.e., low quality news with intentionally false information (Shu, Sliva, Wang, Tang, & Liu, 2017).

Automated fact checking for proving news veracity by reliable sources is a vital task related to the processes of fake news detection (Bondielli & Marcelloni, 2019). It consists of classifying the veracity of each news item by assigning a veracity value. Artificial Intelligence (AI) techniques are applied in order to automate this process. Computational fact checking may significantly enhance our ability to evaluate the veracity of dubious information (Ciampaglia et al., 2015). The work of (Thorne, Vlachos, Christodoulopoulos, & Mittal, 2018) has resulted in the development of a dataset containing facts with their corresponding classification, and evidences. This was applied in Fever 1.0 Shared Task.

The dataset was obtained by generating claims and recovering their corresponding evidence from Wikipedia. This crowd-sourced online encyclopedia has been shown to be nearly as reliable as traditional encyclopedias, despite covering many more topics (Ciampaglia et al., 2015).

Fever Shared Task is a challenge meant for developing automated fact checking systems. The central component is a trained dataset for creating new models, applying AI techniques to recognize patterns contained in the dataset. An example of a claim, evidence and classification tuple is shown in figure 1.

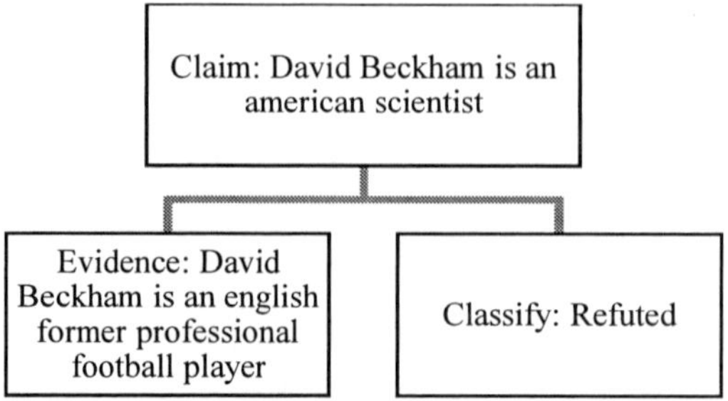

Figure 1: Fever dataset. Tuple example.

Proceedings of the Second Workshop on Fact Extraction and VERification (FEVER), pages 110–114
Hong Kong, November 3, 2019. ©2019 Association for Computational Linguistics

Finally, there is a testing strategy that automatically classifies claims and generates evidences.

We are proposing a modified approach to the Fever 2.0 Shared Task by adapting a previous proposal developed by Team Athene UKP TU Darmstadt (Hanselowski et al., 2018).

We agreed with the Fever baseline and the Team Athene and divided the process into three tasks: document retrieval; sentence retrieval; and, recognizing textual entailment.

A non-formal diagram illustrates the relations among the tasks that are applied in our proposal. The shadowed frame shows the task that we have modified (see figure 2).

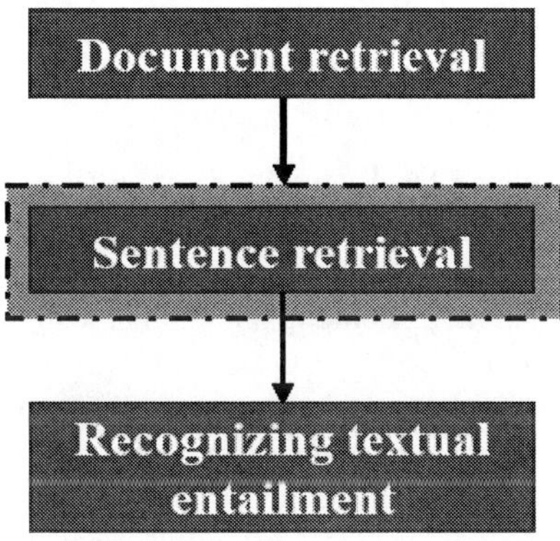

Figure 2: System internal structure.

2 Document retrieval

The main goal of the document retrieval task is to obtain relevant pages, using Wikipedia as a data source. This task retrieves those pages containing elements related to the claim under evaluation.

For each claim, a set of noun phrases is extracted and used for indexing the pages containing these terms.

The library AllenNLP (Gardner et al., 2018) is applied for extracting the noun phrases for each claim and a Wikipedia proprietary library is used for indexing.

Three alternatives for document retrieval were considered. First, the baseline proposal (Thorne et al., 2018), a basic approach that might present information loss. Second, Apache Lucene, although is a robust tool, its integration with our approach was very complex and inefficient. Third, the Team Athene proposal, was considered by our team as the best option for this task because it combines accuracy with simplicity.

3 Sentence retrieval

To select the sentences best related to the claim under analysis, a sentence retrieval task is defined. In this step, the Team Athene approach was selecting candidate sentences as a potential evidence set for a claim. These sentences were extracted from the Wikipedia articles retrieved during the document retrieval phase (Hanselowski et al., 2018).

Our approach uses statement extraction and representation in the form of triplets (subject, object, action) to represent the information transmitted by a sentence. These triplets are extracted from the claim using the statement detector defined in the paper (Estevez-Velarde et al., 2018).

Through triplet comparison, we aim to determine whether the facts from the claim are supported by the information source. To compare triplets, we used *Spacy*'s model *en_core_web_lg* (Honnibal & Montani, 2017), which is one of the new neuronal models of SpaCy v2.0 for labeling, analysis and entity recognition.

The semantic similarity between two texts can be defined as $S: S \in \mathbb{R}; \; S \in [0,1]$. When two triplets are compared, three semantic similarities are extracted: similarity between subjects (s_s), similarity between objects (s_o), and similarity between actions (s_A). To decide which triplets are more similar, we use the average $A= avg\,(s_s, s_o, s_A)$ and the minimum of these three similarities $M= min(s_s, s_o, s_A)$. Two triplets are more similar, the bigger their minimum similarity is, and as a tie-breaker for minimum similarities, the average is used.

To select the facts that best match the claim, a score was defined, combining the Team Athene score with our similarity measures. At testing time, Team Athene calculated a score between a claim and each sentence from the retrieved documents. With that purpose, an ensemble of ten models with different random seeds was deployed (Hanselowski et al., 2018). They calculated the mean score of a claim-sentence pair over all ten models of the ensemble and established a ranking for all pairs. Finally, the sentences with the highest-ranked pairs were provided as an output of the model.

Defining n as the number of sentences to be extracted, the first step of our ranking algorithm is to select the $n * 3$ sentences best ranked by the

Team Athene score. The next step is to extract (subject, object, action) triplets for each sentence and compare these triplets to the ones extracted from the claim. Finally, we sort the sentences according to their similarity with the claim triplets, obtaining as evidence n sentences, (those considered more similar to the claim).

When extracting statements from a sentence, it is important to note whether the sentence can be considered a negation. This is implemented by checking for keywords such as *"never", "not"*, among others. Initially, when comparing two triplets, if only one of them was negated, they were considered not similar (based on a semantic perspective). Hence, the action similarity (s_A) was set to 0 and these triplets would not be taken to account by the ranking algorithm. However, after receiving feedback on the testing results, we realized that this approach was affecting the retrieval of evidence that refutes the claim. In order to provide a solution for this issue, we removed the restriction that was keeping these negated sentences of being taken to account by the ranking algorithm, creating an opportunity for them to be highly scored in the sentence retrieval phase and used as evidence.

In comparison with the Team Athene proposal, this phase contains a significant change that might vary the final results for the next phase.

4   Recognizing textual entailment

This task classifies the claims versus the supposed evidences that are obtained from previous tasks. It is well known as an active research area in Natural Language Processing in the last decade. That is corroborated by the number of related papers (Korman, Mack, Jett, & Renear, 2018; Padó, Noh, Stern, Wang, & Zanoli, 2015; Paria, Annervaz, Dukkipati, Chatterjee, & Podder, 2016).

A description for Stanford Natural Language Inference (SNLI) dataset is reported in (Bowman, Angeli, Potts, & Manning, 2015) and the development of multi-Genre Natural Language Inference (MultiNLI) may be consulted at (Williams, Nangia, & Bowman, 2017). Both of them were applied for training complex NLI models.

The Enhanced Sequential Inference Model (ESIM) (Chen et al., 2016) is one of the most commonly applied for accomplishing the recognizing textual entailment task . This model has been trained over different proposals by applying minimal changes into neural network parameters.

The ESIM model extended by (Hanselowski et al., 2018) is the one used in our proposal. The input is a set of ordered pairs, composed of the same claim and five sentences selected from the previous tasks.

Each word from these pairs is represented as a vector by concatenating two word embeddings. In this case, FastText (Bojanowski, Grave, Joulin, & Mikolov, 2017) and Glove (Pennington, Socher, & Manning, 2014) are applied. These word embeddings are selected because they have been previously trained with Wikipedia information. The vectors are passed to the model for the training and testing phases.

5   Results

Our results differ discretely from the Team Athene proposal. A more extensive experimentation is recommended in order to improve the final claim classification in comparison to that obtained by Athene.

The results obtained from the document retrieval task are coincident with the original proposal (Hanselowski et al., 2018), because the model applied for obtaining Wikipedia pages is the same.

To accomplish the sentence retrieval task, five sentences were selected, ranked according to the best score.

To show the differences between the sentence retrieval task of our approach and that of the Team Athene, all the evidences sets are collected and compared in this task. We used the "Shared Task Development Dataset (Labelled)". This dataset contains 19,998 tuples equal to that of the "Shared Task Blind Test Dataset (Unlabelled)" which was used to submit our predictions. Table 1 shows the comparative result.

Variation in the evidence sets	Count	%
Nil	7988	39.94
One variation	10582	52.91
Two variations	1265	6.32
Three variations	119	0.59
Four variations	30	0.15
Five variations	14	0.07

Table 1. Result of evidence sets comparison.

As can be seen in Table 1, an intuitive analysis was carried out that allows us to believe that the results of the retrieval sentence task are different between the teams. This implies changes in the result classification for the textual entailment task.

Moreover, we calculate the accuracy of the collected evidence sets for the "Shared Task Development Dataset (Labelled)". These results are shown in table 2 for Team Athene and table 3 for our team.

Evidence sets	Team Athene	%
At least one evidence in common	12594	62.97
All evidences are different	7404	37.02

Table 2. The Team Athene accuracy in terms of finding one evidence in common.

Evidence sets	Team GPLSI	%
At least one evidence in common	12547	62.74
All evidence different	7451	37.25

Table 3. The Team GPLSI accuracy in terms of finding one evidence in common.

The accuracy of sentence retrieval for two teams is similar. This low score affects negatively on the calculation of the Fever score.

The final task of our proposal aims to classify the claim as one of three classes: "SUPPORTS", "REFUTES", "NOT ENOUGH INFO". This task does not differ from the Team Athene approach. However, expected differences among the results are obtained, albeit with low percentage between teams. The changes proposed for the sentence retrieval task and the differences among sentences justify these results.

Table 4 shows the results from participant teams on Fever 2.0 Shared Task, the three best teams from last year (2018), and Fever Baseline. The results are ordered considering the Fever Score for each team.

Team	Resilience (%)	Fever Score (%)
Dominiks	35.82	68.46
CUNLP	32.92	67.08
UNC	30.47	64.21
UCL MR	35.82	62.52
Athene	25.35	61.58
GPLSI	19.63	58.07
CalcWorks	DNQ	33.56
Baseline	11.06	27.45

Table 4. Main results of the challenge.

The updated code of our approach may be accessed at URL:

```
https://github.com/rsepulveda911112/f
ever-2019-team-gplsi
```

6 Conclusions

The GPLSI team has developed an automated system that modifies the sentence retrieval task drastically and get similar results. The relevance of the applied model for obtaining triplets and similarity metrics are confirmed.

We consider that to improve the fever score we must improve the accuracy of the sentence retrieval task.

For the task of recognizing textual entailment in the future, we think that the classification can be improved by incorporating features into the ESIM model. These characteristics should improve both the detection of contradictions that would deliver the classification "REFUTES" and, the accuracy of the "NOT ENGOUGH INFO" classification when there is a lack of relevant data that can refute or support a claim.

Acknowledgments

This research work has been partially funded by the University of Alicante (Spain), Generalitat Valenciana and the Spanish Government through the projects Tecnologías del Lenguaje Humano para una Sociedad Inclusiva Igualitaria y Accesible (PROMETEU/2018/089), Modelado del Comportamiento de Entidades Digitales mediante Tecnologías del Lenguaje Humano (RTI2018-094653-B-C22) and Integer: Intelligent Text Generation, Generación Inteligente de Textos (RTI2018-094649-B-I00).

References

Bojanowski, P., Grave, E., Joulin, A., & Mikolov, T. (2017). Enriching Word Vectors with Subword Information. *Transactions of the Association for Computational Linguistics*, *5*, 135–146. https://doi.org/10.1162/tacl_a_00051

Bondielli, A., & Marcelloni, F. (2019). A survey on fake news and rumour detection techniques. *Information Sciences*, *497*, 38–55. https://doi.org/10.1016/j.ins.2019.05.035

Bowman, S. R., Angeli, G., Potts, C., & Manning, C. D. (2015). A large annotated corpus for learning natural language inference. Retrieved from http://arxiv.org/abs/1508.05326

Chen, Q., Zhu, X., Ling, Z., Wei, S., Jiang, H., &

Inkpen, D. (2016). Enhanced LSTM for Natural Language Inference. Retrieved from http://arxiv.org/abs/1609.06038

Ciampaglia, G. L., Shiralkar, P., Rocha, L. M., Bollen, J., Menczer, F., & Flammini, A. (2015). Computational Fact Checking from Knowledge Networks. *PLOS ONE, 10*(6), e0128193. https://doi.org/10.1371/journal.pone.0128193

Conroy, N. J., Rubin, V. L., & Chen, Y. (2015). Automatic deception detection: Methods for finding fake news. In *Proceedings of the 78th ASIS&T Annual Meeting: Information Science with Impact: Research in and for the Community* (p. 82). American Society for Information Science.

Estevez-Velarde, S., Gutierrez, Y., Montoyo, A., Piad-Morffis, A., Munoz, R., & Almeida-Cruz, Y. (2018). Gathering object interactions as semantic knowledge. In *Proceedings on the International Conference on Artificial Intelligence (ICAI)* (pp. 363–369). The Steering Committee of The World Congress in Computer Science, Computer ....

Gardner, M., Grus, J., Neumann, M., Tafjord, O., Dasigi, P., Liu, N., ... Zettlemoyer, L. (2018). AllenNLP: A Deep Semantic Natural Language Processing Platform. Retrieved from http://arxiv.org/abs/1803.07640

Hanselowski, A., Zhang, H., Li, Z., Sorokin, D., Schiller, B., Schulz, C., & Gurevych, I. (2018). *UKP-Athene: Multi-Sentence Textual Entailment for Claim Verification*. Retrieved from https://www.ukp.tu-darmstadt.de/

Honnibal, M., & Montani, I. (2017). spacy 2: Natural language understanding with bloom embeddings, convolutional neural networks and incremental parsing. *To Appear, 7*.

Korman, D. Z., Mack, E., Jett, J., & Renear, A. H. (2018). Defining textual entailment. *Journal of the Association for Information Science and Technology, 69*(6), 763–772. https://doi.org/10.1002/asi.24007

Padó, S., Noh, T.-G., Stern, A., Wang, R., & Zanoli, R. (2015). Design and realization of a modular architecture for textual entailment. *Natural Language Engineering, 21*(2), 167–200. https://doi.org/10.1017/s1351324913000351

Paria, B., Annervaz, K. M., Dukkipati, A., Chatterjee, A., & Podder, S. (2016). A Neural Architecture Mimicking Humans End-to-End for Natural Language Inference. Retrieved from http://arxiv.org/abs/1611.04741

Pennington, J., Socher, R., & Manning, C. D. (2014). *GloVe: Global Vectors for Word Representation*. Retrieved from http://nlp.

Rubin, V. L., & Lukoianova, T. (2015). Truth and deception at the rhetorical structure level. *Journal of the Association for Information Science and Technology, 66*(5), 905–917.

Shu, K., Sliva, A., Wang, S., Tang, J., & Liu, H. (2017). Fake News Detection on Social Media. *ACM SIGKDD Explorations Newsletter, 19*(1), 22–36. https://doi.org/10.1145/3137597.3137600

Thorne, J., Vlachos, A., Christodoulopoulos, C., & Mittal, A. (2018). FEVER: a large-scale dataset for fact extraction and verification. *ArXiv Preprint ArXiv:1803.05355*.

Williams, A., Nangia, N., & Bowman, S. R. (2017). A Broad-Coverage Challenge Corpus for Sentence Understanding through Inference. Retrieved from http://arxiv.org/abs/1704.05426

Author Index